Olympic Facts and Fables

The best stories from the first
century of the modern Olympics

Tom Ecker

TAFNEWS PRESS
Book Division of Track & Field News

First published in 1996 by Tafnews Press,
Book Division of Track & Field News,
2570 El Camino Real, Suite 606,
Mountain View, CA 94040 USA.

Standard Book Number 0-911521-45-3

Printed in the United States of America

Cover design and production: Teresa Tam

Cover photograph: ALLSPORT/Nathan Bilow

CONTENTS

It has been a long road, covering 31 years and countless miles. But it has not been a lonely road. I have been privileged to meet so many wonderful "fellow travelers" along the way, people who have been willing to share their Olympic memories with me. Some of them, so alive with enthusiasm when we chatted about Olympic events of the past, are gone now. They are all greatly missed. To them, and to all the others who have traveled the road, this book is humbly dedicated.

FOREWORD

When I received a draft of Tom Ecker's *Olympic Facts and Fables,* it took only a few pages of reading to convince me that this wasn't just another Olympic book. Instead it's a compilation of the most interesting stories about Olympic personalities and their accomplishments. As such, it's terrific reading from beginning to end. Whether you are an Olympic buff or know nothing about the Games, you'll be drawn in to the wonderful world of the Olympics—the pageantry, the drama, and the competitive spirit, as well as the tribulations and problems that have so often threatened the survival of the Olympic movement.

While Tom was conducting his research, he was bothered by the inconsistencies and conflicting stories from the various Olympic histories, and through indefatigable research (including interviews with prominent Olympic figures), he has managed to clear up much of the confusion. He has even uncovered some fascinating stories that are told here for the first time.

As a participant in two Olympic Games, I have some feeling for the sacrifice and hard work, the emotions, and the satisfactions that come with Olympic success. Tom Ecker captures all this brilliantly and I found true delight in revisiting some of the Olympic heroes and heroines of the past, such as Jim Thorpe, Paavo Nurmi, Fanny Blankers-Koen, Muhammad Ali, Mark Spitz, Olga Korbut and Carl Lewis. Their stories and many, many others help bring the Olympic Games to life in these pages.

Bob Mathias
Olympic decathlon champion,
1948 and 1952

INTRODUCTION

December 31, 1995, and January 1, 1996, were dates of transition in Olympic history. December 31 marked the end of the XXVth Olympiad and the end of the first century of the modern Olympic Games.* January 1 marked the dawning of a new century of Olympic history. For me it was a time to reflect on the events of those first 100 years.

For nearly half of the past century, I have been carrying on an open love affair with the Olympic Games. In 1948, after the London Olympics came to a close, I posted clippings and photographs of young Bob Mathias, the Olympic decathlon champion, on the wall of my room. I was 13, only four years younger than Mathias, and was awed and inspired by his athletic talent, his courage, his versatility, and his humility.

I decided to model my own sports career after Mathias, but over the next few years I found myself noticeably short on athletic talent, courage, and versatility, but necessarily long on humility.

I continued to follow the Olympics with great enthusiasm, and beginning in the 1960s I became involved in international sports as an Olympic coach, technical committee member, lecturer, tour escort, and even a torchbearer. Fortunately, these experiences have permitted me to meet, to know, and to collect information from many of the key players in the Olympics—athletes, coaches, doctors, managers, officials, researchers, authors, journalists, TV commentators, and spectators.

Over the years, I have compiled a large personal library of Olympic books, articles, newspaper clippings, interview notes, and memorabilia collected throughout the world. My search for information has taken me to the museum and archives at the International Olympic Committee headquarters in Lausanne, Switzerland, as well as the Olympic sites, museums, and libraries at ancient Olympia and the Olympic Academy in Greece, and at all but two of the cities that have hosted the modern Olympics.

Although I never intended to become an Olympic historian, I soon discovered that the historian title is automatically associated with those who have a passion for events of the past and who are determined to sort out the truth. In my case, the process began in 1965 when I was given the opportunity to interview Olympic legend Jesse Owens, winner of four gold medals in the 1936 Olympics in Berlin. This book is built on more than 30 years of research beginning with that interview.

One thing I have learned in three decades of trying to distinguish Olympic fact from myth is that the truth can be extremely elusive. After poring through more than 300 Olympic books, it has become clear to me that Olympic history is generously sprinkled with historical contradictions and inaccuracies. Over the years many Olympic stories have been embellished, facts have been altered, and incidents have been fabricated. Olympic historian Bill Henry, struggling to determine the truth about the early Olympic Games, wrote of "a web of tangled fact and fable that cries for clarification."

Attempting to separate fact from fable has produced some interesting revelations for me. One is that inaccuracies, embellishments, distortions, and fabrications, when they are written with authority, tend to be accepted as absolute truths once they are in print. It is easy to accept what you are reading as the truth when you have no reason to doubt it. Because of this, many Olympic fables can be traced back through several books in which the authors have created a chain of historical inaccuracies.

I believe the most consistently reliable sources have been the first-hand written accounts, some of them collected in diaries, but most of them in the newspapers of the day. Equally important, when they are available, are the photographs taken at the Olympics that support or disprove statements made in Olympic history books.

Somewhat less reliable (or at least lacking in completeness) have been the official Olympic reports produced by each Games' organizers (except 1920, when the organizers didn't bother). The official reports generally have emphasized the positive, played down the negative, and of-

---

*An Olympiad is a four-year period beginning with the year that is divisible by four; the Olympic Games are celebrated during the first year of each Olympiad. Thus, the first century of the modern Olympics began in 1896 and ended in 1995.

ten have left out many of the non-statistical facts.

Accounts that have sometimes proved to be very unreliable are those related long after the fact by the athletes themselves who have tended to alter and enhance their stories, even when they might not have intended to do so.

And finally, the least reliable of all the sources have been the many motion picture dramatizations of Olympic events in which accuracy is usually sacrificed to create what the moviemakers consider more satisfying drama. Unfortunately, there are no Academy Awards for historical accuracy.

My attempts to untangle the "web of Olympic fact and fable" has led to the creation of this book. Unlike most Olympic books which empha-size the "heroes" of the Games, this is a collection of Olympic anecdotes which spotlight many of the Olympic heroes, but also many of the lesser-known players.

Some of the stories included here are amazing, some are amusing, some bizarre, some tragic. Many of them relate little-known facts about the modern Olympic Games, while a few quash popular Olympic fables. Each of these stories has, in its own unique way, contributed to the drama that continues to capture the imagination of the world every Olympiad. So, let the Games begin!

—Tom Ecker
June, 1996

Olympiad I
ATHENS, 1896

THE OLYMPIC FOUNDER

Although he was given little credit for his role in the revival of the Olympics at the time, the man who fought tirelessly to reinstate the Games was a French nobleman named Baron Pierre de Coubertin. De Coubertin's plan, which he first announced at a meeting in Paris in 1892, called for a worldwide festival for the brotherhood of man, with no nations excluded and no nations claiming a victory.

The idealistic Baron made it clear that he was opposed to any sort of discrimination in his plans for the revival of the Olympics. The Games would be a series of competitions in which all differences of status, politics, religion, and race would be forgotten. However, there was one notable exception, which didn't seem to bother anyone at the time: women would be forbidden to take part in the Olympics, either as participants or officials.

THE BIRTH OF THE INTERNATIONAL OLYMPIC COMMITTEE

Serious plans for reviving the Olympics were not discussed officially until 1894, when de Coubertin was attending an international conference on amateurism in Paris. De Coubertin added an item to the agenda: "Regarding the possibility of the revival of the Olympic Games. Under what conditions could they be reestablished?"

De Coubertin's idea was met with enthusiasm. It was decided at the conference to conduct the Olympics every four years in the leading cities of the world. The Games would be held during the first year of each Olympiad (the Greek word for four years), and would be awarded only to cities, not to countries. Each Olympiad would begin with the year that is divisible by four, just as in ancient Greece.

Representatives from nine nations attended the Paris conference, which developed into the founding meeting of the International Olympic Committee (IOC). Germany, a country with great interest in international sports competition, had not been invited. Apparently disregarding de Coubertin's call for international brotherhood, the French delegates said they would boycott the conference if the Germans were included.

A SHAKY BEGINNING

De Coubertin's original plan was to award the first of the modern Olympic Games to his home city, Paris, in 1900. But the Greek delegates at the Paris meeting, citing history and tradition, asked that Athens be awarded the first Olympic Games in 1896. Even though the Greeks would have only two years in which to prepare, the committee granted their request.

Unfortunately, the enthusiasm of the Greek delegates was not shared by the Greek government, which did not have the money to finance the Olympics. When de Coubertin arrived in Athens late in 1894 to begin planning for the Games, he was met with indifference and rejection.

The IOC decided then to move the site from Athens to Budapest, Hungary, where the Hungarians would be celebrating their 1,000th birthday as a nation in 1896. But Hungary was in no better financial condition than Greece, and they, too, had to refuse to host the Games.

THE FIRST OLYMPIC SPONSOR

Desperate to find a host city for the first Olympics, de Coubertin traveled back to Greece to try to stimulate interest in his Olympic project. There he met with Greece's Prince Constantine, who told him he would try to get a financial contribution from a wealthy Greek philanthropist, Georgios Averoff.

Responding to the Prince's request, Averoff offered to finance the restoration of the 2,000-year-old Panathenean Stadium in central Athens. The cost was almost one million drachmas, equal to about 110,000 dollars then and more than 2 million dollars today. With ad-

**One of the early International Olympic Committee meetings.
De Coubertin is seated at left, pen in hand.**

ditional contributions from Greek citizens and from Greeks living abroad—plus the sale of Olympic coins and stamps—enough money was raised to finance the Games.

On the day before the opening ceremonies, a marble statue of Averoff was unveiled in the square in front of the stadium. The statue, which has since been moved off to the side of the square, well out of the way of passing pedestrians, is not on the list of Athens tourist attractions. Local Greeks, and even a local tour escort, were not able to identify him recently when asked who Averoff was and what he had done.

THE OLYMPIC PROGRAM

Nine sports were to be contested in the first Olympics: track and field, cycling, fencing, gymnastics, lawn tennis, shooting, swimming, weight lifting, and wrestling. It was announced that a new event would be on the track and field program—a long distance race that would be called the marathon.

It was decided that the marathon, which would start on the bridge near the village of Marathon and finish in the Olympic stadium, would be the final event on the track and field program.

SELECTING THE U.S. TEAM

In the United States, as in most of the other countries, there was no national effort to select an Olympic team. Athletes who wanted to participate could do so, provided they had the time to spare and were willing to pay the costs of the trip. Talent was not a consideration.

A Princeton University history professor, William Sloane, was anxious to have the United States represented in the Olympics. Sloane had met de

Coubertin during one of the Baron's trips to America and was impressed by his devotion to the Olympic movement.

Sloane asked Robert Garrett, captain of the Princeton track team and the son of a wealthy Baltimore banker, if he would be willing to participate in the Olympics. Garrett liked the idea so much he talked three of his Princeton teammates into joining him. It is now generally accepted, although he refused to comment on it at the time, that Garrett financed the trip to Athens for his three teammates, since they could not afford the journey themselves.

With some persuasion, Sloane managed to convince the Boston Athletic Association to send five of its track and field athletes to the Games. Another Bostonian, Harvard student James Connolly, applied for a leave from school so he could participate in the Olympics. When the leave was not granted, he quit school and joined the others for the trip to Athens, where he was to become the first Olympic champion of the modern era.

Joining the four track and field athletes from Princeton and the six from Boston were a swimmer and two pistol shooters, forming America's entire 13-man Olympic team.

THE LONG JOURNEY TO GREECE

One of the persistent fables associated with the 1896 Olympics is that the American team thought they would be arriving in Athens almost two weeks prior to the opening ceremonies, but, because of a calendar mixup, they arrived the night before instead. This story has been included in several Olympic history books.

According to the legend, the Americans did not realize the Greeks were using the Julian calendar, which differed from the Gregorian calendar by 12 days. This mixup was supposed to have caused the American team to arrive in Athens late, out of condition, and exhausted. The truth is that the team would have arrived 12 days *earlier* than expected, not 12 days later, if they had not known about the calendar difference.

De Coubertin, who had traveled to Greece on several occasions during the two years of Olympic preparations, was well aware that the Greeks used the Julian calendar, but he set the official Olympic schedule according to the Gregorian calendar, which was observed by most of the rest of the world.

The Americans set sail for Europe aboard the German steamship *Fulda* on March 9, and after enduring a 17-day boat and rail journey, they arrived in Athens on March 26. In a letter dated March 26, 1896, de Coubertin wrote: "Today the Germans have come, and the Swedes and the Americans." The letter was written 11 days before the opening day of the Olympics.

The Americans did arrive in Athens a few days later than they had planned, but if they were exhausted on opening day, it was probably because they were invited to a banquet the night before and stayed up much of the night drinking retsina wine with their Greek hosts.

THE AMERICANS DOMINATE ON THE TRACK

The U.S. athletes, most of whom were not of championship caliber at home, began their domination of the track and field events by finishing first in all three 100-meter preliminary heats. Only one of the victorious sprinters had ever won a U.S. championship, and that was in the quarter-mile.

The Greeks were fascinated by the starting technique used by the American sprinters. While everyone else used a standing start, the Americans crouched behind the starting line with their hands on the track, giving them an immediate advantage in each sprint race. Albin Lermusiaux, a dapper Frenchman who was entered in the 100 meters, 800 meters, 1500 meters, and the marathon, wore white kid gloves to the starting line in the 100. When American sprinter Thomas Curtis asked him why, Lermusiaux replied, "Zat is because I run before ze keeng."

THE FIRST OLYMPIC CHAMPION OF THE MODERN ERA

The first final event of the opening day was the hop, step and jump (now known as the triple jump), an event that was hardly performed outside Greece and the British Isles. James Connolly, who had dropped out of Harvard to make the trip to Athens, won easily in what the Greeks considered to be a major upset. Connolly, therefore, became the first Olympic champion since Prince Varastates of Armenia won in boxing, the last event of the final ancient Games.

5

Connolly stood on a small wooden stand as the band played *The Star Spangled Banner* and the 44-star U.S. flag was raised to the top of the stadium flagpole. A noisy cheering section, made up of American sailors on shore leave from the *U.S.S. San Francisco*, led the cheers for Connolly's victory. Many Greek spectators tried to join in, but they were not very successful in understanding and repeating the words of the cheers. A British newspaper account said: "American rooters in the stands raised that curious college shout, ending in 'Rah-Rah-Rah' which they appear to have learnt from the Red Indians."

Connolly went on to become a distinguished newspaper reporter, war correspondent, and writer of sea sagas, authoring 25 novels and more than 200 short stories.

THE U.S. "PROFESSIONALS"

The Americans continued their winning ways in the track and field events, finishing first in the 100-meter final, high hurdles, high jump, long jump, pole vault, shot put, discus throw, and 400-meter run. At one point, the impatient Greek crowd, realizing the successes of the U.S. athletes must have been due to superior training methods, began referring to the Americans as "professionals."

The 1500-meter run was won by an Australian, Edwin Flack, but the Greeks announced that the winner was an American. When it was pointed out to them that Flack was an Australian, a Greek official remarked, "Oh, well, that is about the same thing."

A SURPRISE WINNER

Robert Garrett, whose specialty on the Princeton track team was the shot put, was walking through the stadium on the opening day of competition and picked up a discus that was lying on the ground. He had never seen a real discus before. At Princeton, he had located a drawing of an ancient Greek discus and had one made of steel, but his facsimile was so difficult to throw, he gave up on the idea. Now, on the day of the discus competition, he found that the official discus was much smaller and lighter than his homemade version. So he decided to enter the event, which was about to begin.

The two Greek favorites, who had been practicing the event for months, were in first and second

place throughout the competition. But on his final throw, Garrett outthrew the leader by 7$\frac{1}{2}$ inches to win the Olympic title, much to the disappointment of the partisan Greek crowd. A Greek journalist pointed out later that the two Greeks had thrown "with much better form."

SWIMMING HAZARDS

Although the first of the modern Olympic Games was considered a great success, many of the events bordered on the ludicrous. The swimming events were held in the "ice-cold" waters of the Bay of Zea, with waves as high as 12 feet and the water temperature at 55 degrees.

A bugle sounded, signaling a small steamboat to transport the swimmers out to the starting point, which was marked by a string of floating gourds. As soon as the swimmers were all in the water, a gun was fired and they raced toward shore where they were to touch a red flag, as officials watched from a nearby barge.

Alfred Hajos, the 100-meter and 1200-meter winner, said, "My will to live completely overcame my desire to win." The American swimmer, Gardner Williams, jumped into the water, screamed out a profanity, followed by "I'm freezing!" and scrambled back aboard the boat. Only three of the 29 entries in the 500-meter swimming event bothered to compete; only two finished.

A VERSATILE COMPETITOR

An unusual combination of Olympic championships was accomplished by Karl Schumann of Germany. On the third day of the competition he won three gymnastics events. Two days later he won the heavyweight Greco-Roman wrestling championship.

AN UNKNOWING WINNER

An Oxford student from Ireland, John P. Boland, who was in Greece visiting a friend, came upon a lawn tennis competition and asked if he could enter. He won the singles competition over a Greek in three straight sets.

The final of the tennis doubles competition matched Germany against Greece. When one of the Germans fell ill at the last moment, Boland, who was observing, was asked if he would be a substitute. The Greek team was defeated for the championship, but no one seemed to be concerned that they had lost to a German team made up of a German and an Irishman.

When his visit was completed, Boland returned to Oxford, but did not learn until several years later that he was an Olympic champion.

A PERSISTENT CYCLING CHAMPION

The marathon route was also used for the cycling road race. The six competitors—four Greeks, one Englishman, and one German—rode their bicycles from Athens to Marathon, signed their names in a book, and then rode back to Athens.

The winner, Aristidis Konstantinidis of Greece, who jokingly complained that it took him longer than the other competitors to sign his name, was involved in two accidents on the route back to Athens. He smashed his original bicycle beyond repair, borrowed a second from one of his helpers, and promptly swerved to avoid a spectator and crashed into a wall. He borrowed a third bicycle and still completed the race 20 minutes ahead of the second place finisher.

THE FIRST-EVER MARATHON RACE

Although there are many references in the literature to a revival of the marathon race in the modern Olympic Games, there was no such race in competition prior to 1896. The marathon race was the brainchild of Michel Bréal, a French linguist and historian. Bréal suggested in 1894 that a 40-kilometer distance race commemorating the run of Pheidippides become a part of the 1896 Olympic program.

According to legend, Pheidippides, a greek soldier and a champion runner in the ancient Olympics, had been the courier chosen to bear the news of a surprise Greek victory over the invading Persians on the plains of Marathon in 490 B.C. Exhausted from the battle and the 25-mile run, he arrived in Athens and blurted out the message, "Rejoice, we conquer," before he collapsed and died.

Largely because of national pride, and also because the Greeks had not won any of the other events held in the Olympic stadium, the public demanded that the first Olympic marathon champion be a Greek. Georgios Averoff, the philanthropist who had financed the rebuilding of the Olympic stadium, offered his daughter's hand in marriage and a dowry of one million drachmas to the marathon winner—if he were a Greek. A doctor offered a barrel of vintage wine. A tailor offered clothing for life. Other donated prizes included 2,000 pounds of candy, free shaves and haircuts for life, groceries for life, plus cattle, sheep, and jewelry.

Of the 25 marathon entries, 21 were Greeks. There was one entry each from France, Australia, Hungary, and the United States. In recent years there have been persistent stories about a Greek woman named Melpomene who is supposed to have run in the Olympic marathon in 1896, but this definitely could not have happened. Women were strictly forbidden to participate in any Olympic event in 1896.

The long endurance race was begun at Marathon at 2 p.m. after the runners had already had to endure a long speech by the starter. The weather conditions were perfect; it was cloudy and cool.

Through much of the race, the three leaders were non-Greeks. But as the runners neared Athens, first the American, then the Frenchman (the sprinter who had worn white kid gloves in the 100 meters), and finally the Australian (Edwin Flack, who had already won the 800- and 1500-meter runs), collapsed from the fast pace.

The steady pace of a Greek runner, Spiridon Louis, prevailed. He staggered into the stadium, covered with perspiration and dust, seven minutes ahead of the second place finisher. Spiridon was greeted joyously by Prince George and Prince Constantine, who ran around the track with him to the finish line. Then they carried him on their shoulders to the royal box so he could be congratulated by the king.

The crowd in and around the stadium was delirious with joy. People were cheering and sobbing. Many women removed their jewelry and threw it at Louis' feet as he rounded the track.

A MARATHON PROTEST

The first three marathon finishers were all Greeks, but the fourth place finisher, Gyula Kellner of Hungary, immediately lodged a protest, saying that only two runners were ahead of him until near the end of the race, and no one had passed him. An inquiry was held and it was found that the third place finisher, a Greek named

Spiridon Belokas, had covered a portion of the route hidden in a carriage. Belokas was disqualified for "having violated the rules."

THE SPIRIDON LOUIS LEGENDS

One of the legends has it that Spiridon Louis was a poor shepherd who trained for his Olympic marathon victory by praying in front of holy icons and fasting for two days and two nights before the race. Other sources say he was a mailman, a soldier, a farmer, or a messenger.

It is known that Louis was earning his living at that time selling water to the Athenians, who did not have good sources of water in the city.

Twice a day Louis would load two barrels of water on his mule and run beside the animal the 14 kilometers (8½ miles) from the water supply in the village of Amarousi to Athens.

His routine of running shorter-than-racing distances with periods of rest in between was not unlike modern endurance training methods. As has been pointed out by the former Greek coach and Olympic historian, Otto Szymiczek, this "training" background obviously provided Louis an advantage over the other marathon participants, although no one knew it at the time.

The legends are mixed as to the gifts that Louis accepted after the Games. Some sources say he accepted nothing. Others say he became a wealthy man. One source says the Greek government gave him a farm.

Szymiczek, who offered Louis a coaching job shortly before his death, said that Louis was poor and depressed at that time. Louis told Szymiczek that the only gift he accepted in 1896 was a horse and cart for transporting water more easily, a gift from King George himself.

THE OLYMPIC PRIZES

On the final day of the Games, Greece's King George presented awards to all the Olympic champions. Each winner received a diploma, a silver medal stamped with the head of Zeus, and a crown of olive branches from the sacred groves of Olympia. Second place finishers received a diploma, a bronze medal, and a crown of laurel branches. There were no prizes for third.

The medals and diplomas were designed personally by Pierre de Coubertin, who selected silver and bronze for the medals because he believed gold looked too commercial. Several Olympic history books have mentioned how many gold medals were won by various athletes and teams in the 1896 Olympics, but there would be no gold medals in the Olympics until 1908, when de Coubertin reluctantly agreed to accept the idea of awarding gold medals for first place.

DE COUBERTIN IS SHUNTED ASIDE

Throughout the Athens Olympics the Greek newspapers ignored Pierre de Coubertin's role in the revival of the Olympic Games. In fact, de Coubertin's name did not appear in any of the Greek newspaper accounts, either immediately before or during the time of the Games.

Burton Holmes, an American travel writer whose firsthand account of the Athens Olympics is included in his book, *The Olympian Games in Athens, 1896*, wrote: "But to the Greeks themselves is due the credit of the revival of the Olympian Games." Nowhere in the Holmes book is there any mention of de Coubertin.

A PERMANENT SITE IN GREECE?

On the day of the closing ceremonies, articles appeared in the Athens newspapers urging the Greek parliament to pass laws making Athens

Spiridon Louis wins the marathon.

the permanent site of the Olympic Games. That night, at a post-Olympic banquet for participants and officials, King George announced that Athens could be the "stable and permanent" site of the Olympic Games.

The American athletes who were attending the banquet, celebrating their victories and ignorant of any political consequences, circulated a petition for Athens to be selected as the permanent site of the Olympics. The king, now enthusiastic about the idea, told de Coubertin he should either accept the decision or resign from the IOC.

De Coubertin was not deterred. The next day he went to the Crown Prince, who agreed with him that holding the Olympics in large cities throughout the world would be more beneficial than confining the Games to Athens. He also acknowledged that hosting the Olympic Games every four years would create an ongoing financial burden for the Greek people.

But the Greek public did not agree. An Athens newspaper, finally acknowledging de Coubertin's existence, described him as "a thief, seeking to rob Greece of her inheritance of joyful history."

The Baron, desperate to save the Olympics, returned to Paris and called a meeting of the IOC. He announced that the Games of the second Olympiad would be held in Paris in 1900. Greek outrage at the decision soon turned to indifference. War had broken out in Greece and the Greek people quickly lost interest in the Olympic Games.

Olympiad II
PARIS, 1900

A DREAM TURNS TO DISAPPOINTMENT

Baron de Coubertin's plans for the Paris Olympics were grandiose, with the Olympic events to be staged in replicas of Greek gymnasiums and stadiums, complete with statues and temples. Displayed there would be works of art and literature documenting the history of sport. His plans for the Olympic program and its organization were further assurance that the 1900 Olympics would be a great success.

Receiving no cooperation from the Union of French Athletic Associations (UFAA), whose members were openly hostile to the idea of hosting the Olympics, de Coubertin decided to bypass the UFAA and run the Olympic Games in conjunction with the 1900 Paris World's Fair.

DISASTER STRIKES

In November of 1898, a political move that turned the 1900 Olympic Games into a lengthy, disorganized embarrassment was dropped on de Coubertin.

The UFAA announced its exclusive right to any and all sporting events to be organized in Paris in 1900. De Coubertin was ordered to resign from the Olympics to show the world that France was unified in its Olympic effort.

Although de Coubertin and the IOC were shocked and surprised by this development, the greatest surprise emerging from the 1900 Olympic Games was that they did not completely destroy the fledgling Olympic movement. Continual political infighting and many unwise decisions turned de Coubertin's dream for the most comprehensive and best organized international sports event in history into a mere sideshow for the World's Fair.

New Olympic committees were named by the UFAA, most of them made up of members who knew little about the Olympic movement. Almost immediately, confusing and conflicting announcements were sent to participating nations.

The fair's chief organizer, Alfred Picart, who was openly contemptuous of sports, proceeded to establish a program of events and a time schedule that resulted in near chaos for the Olympics.

The Olympic events—many of them bizarre in nature—were scheduled from May 14 through October 28, and were spread out all over Paris. Often, because of poor organization and a lack of advertising, the public, press, and even the athletes themselves, could not find the venues.

To make matters worse, the organizers decided to drop the use of the words "Olympic Games" and substitute the words *Championnats Internationaux* (International Championships). The word Olympic did not appear at any of the venues or in any of the official programs associated with the World's Fair.

UNUSUAL EVENTS

In 1898 it was announced that the Olympic program at Paris would be the same as in Athens in 1896, except that boxing, polo, archery, and soccer would be added. But after de Coubertin resigned from the Olympics, Daniel Merillon, president of the French Shooting Federation, was named director of the fair's sports events, and immediate changes were announced. Of course Merillon expanded the shooting program, and he also began to add additional "sports."

There were events called the underwater swim for distance and the 200-meter hurdles-swimming event, with the competitors struggling through three floating barrels in the River Seine.

There were also competitions in croquet, tug of war, badminton, cricket, billiards, checkers, wild boar shooting, cannon shooting, leap frog, three-legged races, fire fighting, life saving, hot air ballooning, and fishing in the Seine. (Presumably the person who caught either the most fish or the largest fish was the Olympic champion.)

To sort out which of these sports events were

truly "Olympic" and which were not remains a challenge to this day. Some references include the winner of even the most bizarre of the events as Olympic champions and others do not.

A PROFUSION OF SHOOTING EVENTS

Included in the Olympic program were 23 different shooting events, using many different kinds of firearms. The only time animals have been intentionally killed in the Olympics was the 1900 live pigeon shooting event, won by Leon de Lunden of Belgium with a score of 21 birds killed.

In the 200-meter shooting event, there were 2,700 prizes awarded.

A WELL-KEPT SECRET

There are many accounts of participants—even winners—in the Paris Olympics who did not know they were participating in the Olympic Games. It was not uncommon for passers-by to enter events in the "International Championships," just for fun, and then leave.

Many of the athletes who traveled to Paris, however, went there specifically to participate in the Olympics. James Connolly, who had won the Olympic triple jump title in Athens, said later that he knew about the Paris Olympics and others should have known, too.

But the events were spread out, over both time and distance, and communication between venues was almost nonexistent, explaining why word did not get to everyone who participated.

MAKESHIFT VENUES

The track and field events were held in the largest park in Paris, the Bois de Boulogne, where a 500-meter track was laid out on the thick, heavily-watered grass, described as "bumpy." There were no landing pits for the jumpers, the sprint course ran downhill, and the timekeepers for some of the oval events were unable to see the starting line because of a grove of trees inside the track. One competitor wrote later: "The track was the worst I have ever seen used for a championship event."

In the discus and hammer throws, the competitors had to aim carefully in order to miss the trees, including a large one in the center of the throwing sector. Robert Garrett, who had won the Olympic discus title in Athens four years earlier, had difficulty missing the trees and finished seventh. Describing Martin Sheridan's discus throwing, a newspaper wrote: "He made long throws, but they were badly directed, hitting a tree or a fence." Sheridan did not place.

The swimming events were held in the River Seine, where the wakes of passing boats and the occasional encounters with floating garbage made swimming difficult, yet the swift current helped produce some spectacular times. In the 200-meter freestyle, Australia's Freddy Lane broke the world record by 13 seconds.

A WINNING PICKUP TEAM

The French tug of war team was defeated by a combined team from Denmark and Sweden, each country claiming a half-championship. A pickup team of American athletes decided to challenge the Swedish-Danish team to an additional tug of war competition, which the Scandinavians graciously accepted. The American team won, some historians say with the help of exuberant American fans who ran onto the field to help. Even though several books list the Denmark-Sweden team as the Olympic champion, the United States team is listed as the champion in the U.S. Olympic Committee's official records.

THE MARATHON

The running of the marathon typified the organization of the entire Olympic program. As soon as the runners left the stadium and entered the streets of Paris, they were engulfed in a crowd of people, bicycles, and automobiles. Only seven of the 19 runners managed to finish the race.

Arthur Newton, a transplanted South African representing the U.S., who was considered one of the finest long distance runners in the world, was the favorite to win the marathon. Newton claimed after the race that he had taken the lead halfway through the race. However, he was shocked to cross the finish line and learn he had actually finished fifth.

There are differing opinions as to what happened. Some say Newton never was in the lead. Others say he got lost and followed the wrong route. But most of the sources say he finished fifth because he didn't know any shortcuts. The winner, Michel Théato of France, who was a delivery boy and had knowledge of the back streets of Paris, had finished the race more than an hour ahead of Newton.

OLYMPIC AWARDS

Before resigning from the Olympics, de Coubertin had commissioned three French artists to design a statue, a medal, and a diploma to be presented to the Olympic winners, but the new organizers decided that umbrellas and books would be the official awards.*

In 1912, the IOC reconstructed the results of the 1900 Olympics and ordered official medals be struck and presented to the champions, some of which had to be awarded posthumously. Many of those who received the new Olympic medals, including marathon winner Michel Théato, did not know until then that they had participated in the Olympics.

THE FIRST PROFESSIONAL OLYMPIANS

Prior to the running of the marathon, the Paris organizers announced they would award cash prizes to the top ten finishers. It was an announcement that must have made de Coubertin

Alvin Kraenzlein

Many Olympic history books list Alvin Kraenzlein of the University of Pennsylvania as the first winner of four individual gold medals in the Olympic Games. He was actually the first winner of four individual umbrellas.

and the other IOC members cringe, since pure amateurism was one of the basic Olympic tenets at that time.

When the IOC later began trying to sort out which of the 1900 events they would consider as official Olympic events, the marathon was included. They seem to have overlooked the fact that the seven marathon runners who managed to finish the race all received prize money and thus were ineligible for the Olympics.

THE FIRST FEMALE OLYMPIANS

For the first time, there were events for women at the Olympic Games. Many sources say there were 11 women who participated in the Paris Olympics, but the records list at least 12 by name—four in lawn tennis and eight in golf.

Great Britain's Charlotte Cooper defeated Hélène Prévost of France in lawn tennis to become the first female Olympic champion. On the same day, Cooper teamed with Reginald Doherty to win the mixed doubles, collecting her second Olympic title.

The first female American champion was Margaret "Peggy" Abbott, who won the women's golf competition by two strokes. It was the only time women's golf was contested in the Olympics. Abbott died 55 years later, presumably unaware that she was an Olympic champion.

SUNDAY CONFLICTS

The scheduling of track and field events on a Sunday, which the French officials had said they would not do, caused eleven athletes from the United States—some of them favorites—to withdraw from the competition. Three 400-meter runners, two 1500-meter runners, two high jumpers, one long jumper, and three pole vaulters refused to participate on Sunday.

The long jump favorite, Meyer Prinstein of Syracuse University, jumped 23 feet, 6½ inches in Saturday's preliminary competition to lead the field into the finals. When it was announced the final would be held the next day—on Sunday—Prinstein was told by Syracuse officials that he could not participate on the Christian sabbath, even though he was Jewish.

Prinstein's chief long jump rival, Alvin Kraenzlein of the University of Pennsylvania, competed in the finals on Sunday, jumping 23 feet 6⅞ inches, which beat Prinstein out of an Olympic championship by ⅜ of an inch. Prinstein responded by challenging Kraenzlein to a Monday jump-off. When Kraenzlein refused, Prinstein hit him with his fist.

A POLE VAULT REVERSAL

Decisions regarding the pole vault competition caused considerable consternation for three Americans—Daniel Horton, Bascom Johnson, and Charley Dvorak—who were told the pole vault would be rescheduled from Sunday to Monday. After the three had left the pole vault area, the officials changed their minds and decided to hold the competition on Sunday after all, with American Irving Baxter winning the Olympic title.

When the three protested the decision, the officials decided to stage an unofficial pole vault competition to help appease them. Horton and Dvorak both vaulted higher than the winning height in the official competition, and Horton was declared the winner.

There is disagreement in the literature as to what happened next. Most accounts say the officials declared Horton the new Olympic champion, but when he began celebrating, the officials reversed their decision and announced that Sunday's results would stand after all. Other accounts say that the pole vaulters knew they were participating in an exhibition event, not in an official competition. One reference says that Horton was awarded an umbrella as a consolation prize.

MISTAKEN IDENTITY

There were no national flags or team uniforms, so at times it was difficult to distinguish between competitors. In the 400-meter run, the French fans cheered heartily for the winner, Maxie Long of the United States, thinking his blue Columbia University uniform was that of a French track club.

A MAJOR UPSET

The 400-meter hurdle race drew only five competitors, since it was an event that was hardly known outside France. The ten "hurdles" were 30-foot telephone poles, plus there was an added water jump just before the finish line. The French crowd was bitterly disappointed when the French favorite, Henri Tauzin, who had never lost a hurdle race, was defeated by American John Tewksbury, who had never run the race before.

THE WRONG ANTHEM

One of the more embarrassing moments came when Rudolf Bauer of Hungary took the victory stand as the winner in the discus throw. The band played *The Star Spangled Banner* as the U.S. flag was raised.

The Hungarian naturally objected and the ceremony was halted until a Hungarian flag could be located. As the Hungarian flag was finally raised, the band played the Austrian national anthem.

THE OFFICIAL QUESTIONNAIRE

During the time of the 1900 Olympics, the organizers distributed an official questionnaire to all of the participants, presumably to try to determine what factors might contribute to athletic ability. On the questionnaire were such provocative questions as: "What was the state of health and the physical strength of your grandfather?," "What is the color of your hair, beard, and eyes?," and "Were you reared as an infant naturally or artificially?"

A CRITIQUE OF THE 1900 GAMES

An Australian runner, Stan Rowley, who had placed in three races for his own country, joined three British runners to win the 500-meter team race for Great Britain. Rowley, Australia's lone entrant in the 1900 Games, wrote home from Paris: "To treat the Olympic Games as world championships would be an insult to the important events they are supposed to be. They are treated by most of the competitors as a joke."

Describing the starting techniques used in the track events, Rowley wrote: "The starter was a Frenchman and all the foreigners would persist in dancing on their marks like jumping jacks, with the result that they invariably beat the gun by some yards. A number of us, including the Americans, made up our minds to do likewise, with the result in every race you could see a man about five yards ahead with a flying start."

THE BARON RETURNS

With disaster looming at every venue, French officials turned to Baron de Coubertin for technical advice. He agreed to help, but only if the sports competitions would be considered "Olympic." The officials finally agreed and de Coubertin became involved again, but it was too late to save the foundering Paris Olympics.

In late October, after five-and-a-half months of continued disorganization and confusion, the 1900 Olympic Games came to a quiet close. De Coubertin was rightfully disappointed. Blaming himself for allowing the Games to degenerate to such a low level, he wrote: "There was much good will, but the interesting results had nothing Olympic about them. We have made a hash of our work."

Olympiad III
ST. LOUIS, 1904

A CHANGE OF PLANS

In the spring of 1901, the IOC awarded the 1904 Games to Chicago, where they were to be contested over a 16-day period in September. But after St. Louis threatened to stage competing sports events during the 1904 World's Fair and a great deal of political pressure was applied, much of it by President Theodore Roosevelt, the Games were switched to St. Louis. The Olympic Games would be attached to the World's Fair, as they had been in Paris four years earlier.

A SECONDARY ATTRACTION

The 1904 World's Fair may be remembered more for the invention of two new food items, the hot dog and the ice cream cone, than for the Olympic Games. The St. Louis Olympics were completely overshadowed by the fair, and were, for the most part, an American championship with a few token entries from overseas nations. In many events, the only entrants were from the United States. Great Britain, and Sweden, strong contenders in the Paris Games, sent no one to St. Louis. The fair organizers promised to send a ship to Europe to bring more foreign competitors to the Games, but this plan never materialized.

THE BARON STAYS AWAY

As impossible as it might seem, the St. Louis organizers turned out to be even less competent than their Paris counterparts. The organizers, with no knowledge of the Olympics, arranged a program that was described in one account as "circus events on the periphery of the fair." So disappointed in the arrangements was Baron de Coubertin that he didn't even bother to attend.

EVERY EVENT WAS "OLYMPIC"

According to the Official Guide to the World's Fair, published by the fair organizers in March of 1904: "By a decision of the International Olympic Committee, all sports and competitions during the World's Fair are designated as Olympic events."

This meant that all of the 85 different sports that were to be contested as part of the fair would be Olympic events, including handicap races, YMCA championships, professional events, and even elementary school and high school competitions open only to students from Missouri.

Besides the more traditional sports, there were competitions in curling, golf, women's boxing, and such unusual sports as roque (a form of croquet), and a diving "plunge for distance," which was included in the swimming events.

Along with the traditional track and field events, there was a sack race and an obstacle race, where competitors had to dive headfirst through raised barrels. There was even a bow and arrow competition open only to Sioux Indians, but no prizes were awarded because no one was able to hit the target.

THE SCOPE OF THE OLYMPICS

Although the fair, and thus the Olympics, ran for seven months (April 30 to December 1), the Official Guide to the World's Fair included this note: "August 29 to September 3 has been set aside for the Third Olympiad, when the Olympic Games proper are to be held." However, only three sports—track and field, weight lifting, and tug of war—were contested during the six days of the Olympic Games "proper."

There is much disagreement in the literature regarding the number of Olympic sports that were contested. If all the fair's sports and competitions were Olympic events, as the IOC announced in 1904, then there were 85 Olympic sports. If only those contested during the Olympic Games "proper" were counted, then there were only three Olympic sports. The IOC later decided to select 38 separate sports as having been held "under the Olympic banner."

The official report filed by the St. Louis organizers after the Games closed claimed there were over 9,000 individual participants in the St. Louis Olympics, but official IOC figures put the number at 496.

THE "CLASSIC" MARATHON

The fair's Official Guide, which listed all of the events that would be contested in the "Olympic Games proper," included this note: "The classic marathon will be the great event of the week." The marathon was already being touted as the highlight of the Olympics, even though the event was only eight years old and had been run in Olympic competition only twice before.

OLYMPIAN WAY

The primary sites of the Olympic Games in 1904 were the Washington University track and the adjacent gymnastics hall, which were tucked into a far corner of the huge exhibition grounds at the fair. On all the plans for the layout of the grounds, the street leading from the exhibition midway to Washington University was to be changed from Forsythe Avenue to Olympian Way, presumably to help promote the Olympics as more than just another exhibit at the fair. However, the change was never made and the street remains Forsythe Avenue to this day.

AMERICAN DOMINATION ON THE TRACK

The biggest crowds, just over 2,000 at the most, were for the track and field events, where in the 23 IOC-recognized events, the United States won 22 firsts, 22 seconds, and 20 thirds. The only first place that was not won by an American was in the 56-lb. weight throw, won by Canadian Étienne Desmarteau. Finishing second was perennial hammer throw champion John Flanagan, who said he had lost because he was suffering from "the effects of Missouri water."

"ANTHROPOLOGY DAYS"

One of the low points of the St. Louis Olympics was a two-day competition called Anthropology Days, in which "exotic ethnic groups" competed in a variety of sports events. The competitions were said to be conducted under the pretense of scientific research. However, it is more likely the organizers were trying to make the Olympics more international by recruiting contestants from among the overseas guests who were working in the exhibits and the sideshows of the fair.

The competitions were hailed as "the first athletic meeting in which savages were the exclusive participants," including Moros from the Philippines, the Ainu tribe from Japan, the Cocopa tribe from Mexico, Sioux Indians from the U.S., plus Patagonians, Pygmies, Igorottes, and Turks. After suffering through miserable performances in several track and field events, the "savages" were allowed to compete in some of their specialties—dart throwing, mud fighting, pole climbing, dancing, and archery. Unfortunately, these Anthropology Games attracted more spectators than the actual Olympic Games.

Pierre de Coubertin commented later, "Such an event, so contrary to the Olympic ideal, could hardly have been held anywhere else in the world other than on this frontier of the southern states."

THE PENALTY FOR A FALSE START

One of the triple winners in track and field was Archie Hahn, "the Milwaukee Meteor." Hahn won the 60-, 100-, and 200-meter sprint races. In the 200, Hahn's three opponents in the final were all charged with a false start. To penalize the three, the clerk of the course had them move their starting line one yard behind the official starting line. When it was pointed out that the rules called for a two-yard penalty, the clerk said there was not room enough to move the contestants back that far.

NOT SO EXHAUSTING

Many accounts of the St. Louis Olympics tell of the plight of a German 800-meter runner, Johannes Runge, who, so the accounts say, mistakenly entered the wrong race. Besides the Olympic 800-meter run, there were also high school, novice, and handicap 800-meter runs. According to the story, Runge entered the handicap 800-meter run by mistake, which he won.

Then he realized what he had done, and with barely enough time to catch his breath, he ran the Olympic 800-meter race, finishing fifth and collapsing from exhaustion.

This fable has been repeated many times. It is true that there were high school, novice, handicap, and Olympic 800-meter runs, but they were all on separate days. Runge won the handicap race (after starting with a 10-yard handicap) on Monday, July 29. The Olympic 800-meter race, in which he finished fifth, was run three days later, on Thursday, September 1.

AN AMAZING MARATHON RACE

The 1904 marathon was more than an endurance event—it was torture. The race was run at midday, over a very hilly 24-mile course, with both the temperature and the humidity in the 90s. Only one water stop was allowed.

The official Olympic report says 10,000 people were on hand to see the start of the race in the stadium. However, a photograph of the start shows very few people around the runners and no one in the stands.

Although the marathon field included many outstanding long distance runners, including three former Boston Marathon champions, only 14 of the 31 competitors managed to finish the race. Much of the route was over dusty roads, making breathing extremely difficult for the runners, many of whom had to run behind the automobiles carrying officials, journalists, and doctors.

One American runner, Bill Garcia, collapsed during the race when his lungs and stomach became so filled with dust that he could not continue. Garcia was taken to a hospital where it was discovered that the lining of his stomach had hemorrhaged.

Even though the two previous Olympic marathons had been run in less than three hours, there was no sign of a finisher after three hours and ten minutes. Finally, at three hours and 13 minutes, Fred Lorz of the United States entered the stadium and was cheered heartily as he crossed the finish line.

Lorz was photographed with Alice Roosevelt, the President's daughter, as she was about to place a wreath of laurel on his head. Then it was learned that Lorz had dropped out of the race at the third mile and had been given a ride in an automobile. When the automobile broke down on the way back to the stadium, Lorz decided to get back in the race "as a

joke." He was disqualified and was supposedly "suspended from sports for life." He did win the Boston Marathon the next year, however.

THE FIRST ADMISSION OF
DRUG ABUSE IN THE OLYMPICS

The real marathon winner, Thomas Hicks of the United States, entered the stadium 15 minutes later (one account says two-and-a-half hours later), exhausted, covered with dust, staggering, and appearing delirious. It was no secret that Hicks' two handlers had given him concoctions of brandy, raw egg whites, and strychnine several times during the final ten miles—perhaps the first documented case of drug use in the modern Olympic Games.

One of the handlers, Charles Lucas, who accompanied Hicks during the race, wrote later: "The marathon race, from a medical standpoint, demonstrated that drugs are of much benefit along the road."

Hicks was given brandy and strychnine with eight miles to go, and after collapsing and beg-

Marathon winner Thomas Hicks, with his supporters.

ging to be allowed to quit, he was given more brandy and strychnine at the entrance of the stadium. He reached the finish line six minutes ahead of the second place finisher and collapsed on the track. After a four-day recovery, Hicks announced his retirement from running.

After the Olympics were over, Lucas wrote an emotional, angry, and revealing condemnation of Fred Lorz, the runner who had hitched a ride during the marathon: "The greatest honor ever brought to American shores by an American athlete was robbed of its luster when Fred Lorz, after riding a number of miles in an automobile, ran the last five miles of the marathon race, and was hailed like a conquering hero by the American people.

The honor of winning the race was heaped upon this man, who had robbed a man who, four miles out on the road, was running the last ounces of strength out of body, kept in mechanical action by the use of drugs, that he might bring to America the marathon honors."

THE COLORFUL RUNNER FROM CUBA

The most popular runner in the marathon was Felix Carvajal, the five-foot Cuban mail carrier who became better known for his antics than for his marathon running. Carvajal had raised funds to travel to St. Louis with a daily routine of running laps around the public square in Havana, each time drawing a sizable crowd of curiosity seekers. Then he would climb up on a box and ask for contributions to send him to the Olympics.

When he had raised sufficient funds, Carvajal took a boat to New Orleans, where he immediately lost all his money in a dice game. Without any funds and desperate to get to the Olympics, he alternated running and hitching rides on farmers' wagons until he finally reached St. Louis.

The amiable Carvajal charmed the American weight throwers, who shared their quarters and food with him. When Carvajal showed up at the start of the marathon wearing long pants, a long-sleeve baggy shirt, and street shoes, American team captain Martin Sheridan, who had taken a particular liking to the personable Cuban, located a knife and cut Carvajal's pants off at the knees.

During the race, Carvajal stopped along the way several times to chat with spectators about the race and to practice his English. At one point he stopped at an orchard to pick and eat some green

apples. At that point and until the 18th mile, Carvajal had a commanding lead in the race, even though he had stopped several times along the way. But then a case of cramps, obviously the result of eating the green apples, slowed his pace and he had to settle for fourth place.

THE FIRST AFRICAN COMPETITORS

Two Zulu tribesmen from South Africa, Lentauw and Yamasani, who were at the World's Fair as part of the Boer War exhibit, decided to enter the marathon. They were the first African athletes to participate in the Olympics. Lentauw finished ninth in the marathon, even though a large, vicious dog chased him more than a mile off the course. Yamasani finished twelfth.

GREEK RECRUITS

A Greek marathon runner, Demeter Velouis, finished fifth, even though he was not one of Greece's official Olympic entries. Greece had sent only two competitors to St. Louis—a discus thrower and a weight lifter. Yet ten Greeks showed up for the start of the marathon, all of them Greek immigrants who were living in America.

The 1904 Official Report says: "Probably no race ever run in the history of athletics ever presented a more international character." (The international character consisted of three South Africans, one Cuban, one Irishman, one Canadian, the ten Greeks who were living in America, and 23 Americans.) Albert Corey, the second place finisher, was born in France and may still have been a French citizen at the time, but he represented the Chicago Athletic Association at these Games.

BASKETBALL AN OLYMPIC SPORT

Although official records show that basketball was not added to the Olympic program until 1936, there was an Olympic basketball tournament at the St. Louis Games. Played on an outdoor court on the infield of the Washington University track, 44 teams competed for Olympic medals. The IOC decided later that basketball would not be one of the sports recognized as official.

A SWIMMING EVENT BECOMES A BOXING MATCH

The swimming events, which were held in one of the fair's artificial lakes, with the swimmers starting from a raft, produced one of the biggest controversies of the games. In the 50-yard freestyle event, a bitter dispute between two judges over the close finish erupted into a stand-up fight among the judges and spectators. Zoltán Halmay of Hungary was declared the winner, but one of the judges said J. Scott Leary of the United States had won. After the fight was broken up, the two swimmers had to settle the matter by competing in a swim-off, which the Hungarian won with ease.

AN UNSTABLE STARTING PLATFORM

Some of the swimming events had to be delayed because the raft, which kept sinking, had to be raised and repaired several times during the competitions. Even when it was at its best, the raft could not support the weight of six swimmers at the start of a race. The swimmers would be ankle deep in water by the time the gun sounded, and then the raft would shift backwards in reaction to the forward movement of the swimmers, causing them to fall flat into the water.

SOME AFTERTHOUGHTS

When the World's Fair finally closed in December, the Olympic Games also came to a close—seven months after they had opened. The attitude of the athletes toward the St. Louis Olympics was summed up best by one of the American competitors, who wrote: "Our prime interest had been in seeing the World's Fair."

THE "INTERIM" OLYMPICS

After the 1904 Games came to a close, the IOC selected Rome to host the 1908 Olympic Games, a decision that angered the representatives from Greece. In response, the Greeks, still insistent that Greece be established as the permanent Olympic site, announced they would be hosting competing Olympic Games in Athens in 1908.

De Coubertin, fearing that competing Olympic Games

would bring about a total collapse of the Olympic movement after the near-disastrous Paris and St. Louis Games, reluctantly agreed to an alternative plan. The IOC would allow the Greeks to host "interim Olympic Games" every four years, beginning in 1906.

Generally referred to as the "Intercalcated Games," or by some the "Panathenaic," the "Panhellenic," or the "Athenian" Games, the 1906 celebration in Athens was so successful it probably saved the badly-damaged Olympic movement. But as successful as the 1906 Games were, they were unofficial and are not even mentioned in books produced or authorized by the IOC.

Twenty nations competed before enthusiastic sellout crowds for the 11 days of competitions in Athens. However, one person who was noticeably absent was de Coubertin, who showed his aversion for the event by attending the Paris Conference on Arts and Letters instead. He said, "I would be able to use this as an excuse for not going to Athens, a journey I particularly wished to avoid."

The 1906 interim Olympics were the first and the last interim Games held. By 1910 the Greeks were on the verge of war with Turkey again and plans to host additional Olympic Games were forgotten.

The unstable swim start platform in St. Louis.

Olympiad IV
LONDON, 1908

FROM ROME TO LONDON

The 1908 Olympic Games were originally scheduled for Rome, but the violent eruption of Mt. Vesuvius in 1906, which destroyed several villages and created an unexpected financial burden for the Italians, forced the Rome organizers to give up the project. Pressed for time, the IOC asked Great Britain to take over the organization of the 1908 Games. Seven months later, in November of 1906, after much deliberation and with only a year and eight months to prepare, the British agreed to host the Games in London.

GOLD REPLACES BRONZE

At the IOC meetings in The Hague in 1907, final plans were made regarding the London Olympic Games. For the first time, gold medals would be awarded to the Olympic winners, with silver medals for second and bronze for third.

ENDLESS PROTESTING

Over the years there have been many rivalries between nations at the Olympics, usually based on political differences, but there has never been a collection of controversies and protests to compare with the acrimonious conflicts between the United States and Great Britain during the 1908 Olympic Games. When the Games were awarded to London, the IOC made a fateful decision which seemed harmless at the time, but it completely changed the complexion of the 1908 Games. The judges of all events would be British, since the British were regarded the fairest, most impartial judges in sport. As it turned out, the Americans couldn't have disagreed more.

Although there were complaints from other countries, the American officials were the undisputed champions in the number of protests filed because of decisions made by the British officials and judges. At one point, the Americans even filed a protest against the British attitude toward American protests.

The trouble began when the American team arrived at the stadium for the opening ceremonies. They noticed immediately that there were no American flags among the flags of all the participating nations that were displayed prominently around the stadium. When the U.S. officials demanded to know why their flag was not included, a British official said they couldn't find any. The Americans were incensed by the snub and the flimsy excuse.

Throughout the Games, the Americans filed protest after protest. They complained that the drawings for heats were done in secret and that some preliminary races were being rigged to favor the British. They complained that Canadian Tom Longboat, who had been ruled a professional in the United States, should not be allowed to enter the marathon. And they complained that British officials were openly coaching and encouraging British athletes during the competitions.

NO DIPPING ALLOWED

The first real controversy of the 1908 Olympics was caused by the failure of the American flagbearer, shot putter Ralph Rose, to lower the Stars and Stripes as he passed before the royal box during the opening ceremonies. The British fans, who were not fond of the Americans anyway, were outraged. It was expected that each nation's flagbearer would dip the flag as a gesture of respect when passing before the King. Later, Rose said he had not dipped the flag because he didn't know he was supposed to.

But it was the response of Irish-American Martin Sheridan that has lived on. Sheridan, who was no friend of the British because of his Irish heritage and who was still fuming because of the absence of American flags in the stadium, said later during an interview: "This flag dips to no earthly king."

No one is certain today if Sheridan was speaking for himself or if he was an official spokesman for the American team, but the tradition has continued ever since. In 1942, the tradition of not dipping the flag became law when the U.S. Congress passed legislation making it illegal for the flag to "be dipped to any person or thing." To this day, the American flag has not been dipped before a head of state during any Olympic opening ceremony.

THE THROWING "WHALES"

The U.S. flagbearer, shot putter Ralph Rose, and the outspoken discus thrower Martin Sheridan, were ripe to be in the center of any kind of controversy, particularly one involving the British. They were members of a unique group of rotund, fun-loving, Irish-American practical jokers dubbed "the whales" by New York sports writer George Underwood. The whales dominated the Olympic track and field weight events—shot put, discus throw and hammer throw—during the early part of the twentieth century.

"They were so big they just looked like whales," said the AAU's Dan Ferris, when someone asked him about the nickname. "They all had paunches on them, unlike our athletes of today."

The leader among the whales was John J. Flanagan, Olympic hammer throwing champion in 1900, 1904, and 1908. Other whales were Pat McGrath, Pat McDonald (who was known as "the Prince of Whales"), Simon Gillis, Ralph Rose, and Martin Sheridan. Sheridan's trim body build, however, made him a whale in name only.

The whales were all of Irish descent (some of them were even born in Ireland), most of them were New York policemen, and all of them had huge appetites. A typical breakfast for the whales was six lamb chops, each topped with an egg. Sheridan once ate 32 eggs at one sitting. Rose consumed two pounds of steak and six eggs for breakfast every morning. Gillis once spread mustard on six boiled eggs and gulped them down, shells and all.

NO FLAG FOR THE FINNS

Finland, which was a Russian province at that time, was given permission by the Czarist government to participate in the Olympics, but they would have to carry the Russian flag—or none. The Finns chose none, and theirs was the only nation to enter the stadium without a flag.

Paunchless Martin Sheridan

AN OLYMPIC EVENT WITH ONLY ONE PARTICIPANT

The most bitter dispute of the games followed the controversial finish of the 400 meters. There were only four runners in the final race—the favorite, Wyndham Halswelle of Great Britain, and three Americans. To insure that the Englishman would get a fair race from the Americans, there were judges stationed every 20 yards around the track. As the runners came off the final curve, the Englishman was forced to run wide. A British official immediately ordered the finish tape be broken and declared "no race."

Following a long series of accusations and denials, and an examination of the runners' footprints on the cinder track, one of the Americans was disqualified for impeding Halswelle. The race was ordered to be rerun two days later, but the two remaining Americans refused to appear and Halswelle reran the final by himself to win the gold medal.

21

A CONTROVERSY OVER FOOTWEAR

Another squabble erupted when the American tug of war team lost to a British team made up of Liverpool policemen. The Americans complained that the policemen's heavy boots gave them an illegal advantage. The protest was not upheld since the boots, which were rimmed with steel, were the policemen's "everyday footwear."

GROWING INTEREST

Interest in the Olympics was not great at first, but as the Games progressed, crowds grew in size. It was becoming clear to the nationalistic British public that the Olympics had become contests between nations, not just individuals. On the final day of track and field, which included the marathon, there was an overflow crowd in the stadium, with the British fans appearing to enjoy the problems of the Americans more than the victories of the British.

A BIBLE-TOTING HURDLER

A fable that continues to surface in the Olympic literature is the story about Forrest Smithson, the ultra-religious hurdler from Portland, Oregon, who supposedly carried a Bible in his hand when he won the hurdle race in the 1908 Olympics. It is said he carried the Bible to protest having to run the race on a Sunday.

Careful examination of the photo that often accompanies the story shows that Smithson, carrying a Bible as he is clearing a hurdle, was not running in competition when the picture was taken. It was posed. And as far as the Sunday competition goes, Smithson's preliminary race was held on a Thursday, the semifinal was on Friday, and the final was on Saturday.

LUCK IN THE HIGH DIVE

In the platform diving event, a British diver, D.F. Cane, suffered a serious injury during one of his dives and spent several days recuperating in a hospital. Some accounts say he turned over too far during a double somersault dive, landing flat on his back. Other reports say he "dived with his mouth open and ruptured a small blood vessel in his chest."

Sweden's Hjalmar Johansson, who won the event, rescued the unconscious diver, dragging him out of the water and applying artificial respiration. Johansson was later awarded King Edward's cup for lifesaving by the Amateur Swimming Association.

Concern about the danger of attempting such "complicated" dives prompted the following entry in the Official 1908 Olympic Report: "No doubt the International Swimming Federation will seriously consider the matter, recognizing that though a diver should know where he is at the end of one somersault, the finish of the second must be largely a matter of luck."

THE OLYMPIC CREED:
CONFUSION AND MYSTERY

Of all the contradictions in the Olympic history books, there are none that compare with those surrounding the Olympic creed, which made its first appearance at the 1908 Olympics. The creed, according to a recent publication of the United States Olympic Committee, is: "The most important thing in the Olympic Games is not to win but to take part, just as the most important thing in life is not the triumph but the struggle. The essential thing is not to have conquered but to have fought well."

According to most of the history books, these words (or others with a similar message) were those of the founder of the modern Olympic Games, Baron Pierre de Coubertin. However, many history books also point out that the Baron gave credit to the Bishop of Pennsylvania for first coming up with the words. The Bishop had included them in a sermon he delivered at St. Paul's Cathedral in London during the 1908 Olympics. De Coubertin was in the audience.

The following Friday, speaking at a banquet at the Holborn Restaurant, de Coubertin is reported to have said, "Last Sunday during the services organized at St. Paul's in honor of the athletes, the Bishop of Pennsylvania made the point that the important thing in these Olympics is not so much winning as taking part. The important thing in life is not the victory but the battle. The essential thing is not to have conquered but to have been a good loser."

Some historians credit de Coubertin with the creed, while others are quick to point out that it is the Bishop of Pennsylvania who deserves the credit. Finally, after years of debate, the matter was settled by two devoted Olympic historians, Ture Widlund of Sweden and John Lucas of the United States.

The identity of the Bishop remained a mystery for nearly 75 years until Widlund discovered he was Ethelbert Talbot, an American Episcopalian bishop living in Harrisburg, Pennsylvania. It is small wonder it was so difficult to identify Talbot, since the Olympic literature credits the sermon to the Bishop of Pennsylvania, who in 1908 was Ozi W. Whitaker of Philadelphia. Talbot was the Bishop of *Central* Pennsylvania in 1908, a completely different diocese. De Coubertin had simply left out the word "central" when he referred to the sermon.

Lucas, in an equally tireless search for the truth, finally located a copy of Talbot's sermon, and to his surprise found the Bishop's actual words were not very close to those de Coubertin had quoted. The nearest passage was: "The only safety, after all, lies in the lesson of the real Olympia—that the Games themselves are better than the race and the prize. . . and though only one may wear the laurel wreath, all may share the equal joy of the contest."

The creed that so many have credited to "the Bishop of Pennsylvania" was obviously created by de Coubertin himself, who generously credited the Bishop.

The biggest surprise concerning the Olympic creed, which now appears on the electronic messageboards during all Olympic opening ceremonies and is included in most Olympic history books, is that is has dozens of different versions, ranging in length from 15 to 62 words.

ADDING 385 YARDS TO THE MARATHON

The event that received by far the most attention at the 1908 games was again the marathon. Not only did the race attract worldwide attention, it also established the present official marathon distance.

Realizing the Olympic marathon distance should be standardized, the IOC decided the official distance would be 26 miles—no more and no less. Yet the distance became 26 miles, 385 yards, because of a last-minute decision to provide a better view of the finish for spectators, and especially for the royal family.

The marathon starting line was on a road in front of Windsor Castle, so the grandchildren of King Edward and Queen Alexandra could get a good view of the start. The course was measured accurately from Windsor Castle through the streets of London to the stadium.

The finish line was on a curve of the 586-yard track in the stadium, across the field from the box where the royal family would be sitting.

When Queen Alexandra arrived at the stadium, she insisted that the marathon finish line be in front of the royal box, not across the field. The finish line was changed immediately and the additional 385 yards became a permanent part of the marathon.

THE FALL OF DORANDO

As it turned out, the marathon's extra 385 yards was too much for an Italian candymaker named Dorando Pietri, who was the first runner to reach the stadium. Pietri, who had mistakenly been listed as P. Dorando before the race and is still referred to as Pietri Dorando in some history books, was suffering from total exhaustion and also from a shot of strychnine his well-meaning trainer had given him along the route.

The spectators were shocked to see Pietri stagger into the stadium, look around, obviously in a daze, and turn the wrong way. Immediately he was surrounded by sympathetic officials (including Arthur Conan Doyle, the creator of Sherlock Holmes), urging him to turn around.

Here is the eloquent and moving eyewitness description of Pietri's marathon finish, as written by a British journalist: "With 75,000 people in the seats and nearly 25,000 more packed into every inch of standing room all round the enormous amphitheatre of the Olympic Stadium, with the Queen of England in the Royal box, surrounded by many members of her own and other Royal families, a miserable little figure tottered in at the northeastern entrance of the Stadium. For a moment, as the news of his approach drew nearer, there had been a muffled roar of anticipation that rolled from tier to tier of iron and concrete, and reechoed across the vast expanse of turf in sullen waves of sound.

"But there was a sudden hush, almost a strangled sob of overwrought suspense, in all those hundred thousand throats, when that small, withered man fell forward onto the first visible

Dorando Pietri in the lead

yard of cinder track, dizzy with excitement, devastated by the utmost atrocities of fatigue, but indomitable, still. It was the Italian, Pietri. What followed was the most poignant scene that has ever been witnessed.

"It might have been beneath the skies of the South that we were all watching the struggles of some wounded toreador.

"The wretched man fell down, incapable of going on for the two hundred yards that alone separated him from the winning post in front of the royal box. He was lifted up, and fell again. He struggled pitifully along to within fifty yards of the finish and collapsed. "At that moment another competitor was seen coming through the entrance, and after a terrible effort the Italian rose up and hurled himself with the last fragment of expiring willpower past the post."

To the horror of the anti-American crowd, the competitor who was trotting around the track to the finish line was American Johnny Hayes.

At that point, British-American relations were so bad that the Italian flag was raised in the stadium, even though everyone knew Pietri would have to be disqualified and Hayes declared the winner.

In the meantime, Dorando Pietri was believed to be near death and was carried away on a stretcher. A newspaper account said: "Dorando lay at death's door. His heart was half an inch out of place."

The next day, Pietri, appearing completely recovered from his ordeal, was presented a special gold cup for courage by Queen Alexandra, which he accepted graciously.

However, he spent the rest of the day complaining that he would have won the race if the officials hadn't interfered.

PIETRI TURNS PRO

Capitalizing on his fame, Dorando Pietri, who was known only as Dorando to his admiring fans, became a professional runner after the 1908 Olympics. He competed in several marathons in the United States, including two races against Johnny Hayes on Madison Square Garden's 160-yard board track. Dorando won the first of the 288-lap marathons in the Garden on November 24, 1908, beating Hayes by just 60 yards.

When a rematch was scheduled, Dorando

became the first sports hero to have a popular song composed for him.

The song, *Dorando**, was written by a struggling 21-year-old singing waiter and songwriter, Israel "Izzy" Baline, who had recently changed his name to Irving Berlin.

The song, which was released just three days before the big rematch in Madison Square Garden on March 15, 1909, was a "comedy dialect" tune about two Italian-Americans who sold their barber shop to bet everything on Dorando.

The song describes Pietri's race at "Ma-dees-a Square" as "He run-a, run like anything, one-a, two-a hundred times around da ring." But, alas, "Dorando, he's-a drop. Goodbye, poor old barber shop." In the second verse, Dorando explains he had been given "da Irish beef-a stew" instead of "da spa-gett," and "it make me very sick."

The song might have been more successful if Dorando had dropped out of the race. However, he not only finished, but he lapped Johnny Hayes five times to win easily.

TWO WINNERS IN THE POLE VAULT

Because of the dramatic marathon finish, the pole vault, which was being contested at the same time, also had an unusual finish. Two Americans, Alfred Gilbert and Edward Cooke, were in a tie for first place at 12 feet 2 inches, and were ready to compete in a jump-off for the gold medal.

But because the marathon finish had created so many delays and interruptions, the judges finally decided to award two gold medals and no silver medal.

Gilbert later gained fame and fortune as the inventor of the Erector Set and the founder of the A.C. Gilbert Toy Company.

NO END TO THE FEUDING

The London Olympic Games came to an end, but the bickering between the United States and Great Britain continued. The British produced a

---

The Olympic history books that mention this song say it was either entitled Dorando, He'sa Gooda for Not, *or* Dorando, Dorando, Dorando. *However, a check of the sheet music, which is on file at the Library of Congress in Washington, D.C., shows the title was simply* Dorando.

60-page book entitled, *Replies to Criticism of the Olympic Games,* in which they printed the many complaints and protests lodged by American athletes and officials, with British responses to each of them. As a result, the sports organizations of the two nations severed all relations.

A British author, Thomas Rugby Burlford, continued to stir the controversy with the publication of his book, *American Hatred and British Folly.* His subsequent books were *Gruesome America* and *Facts for Irish-American Liars.*

Olympiad V
STOCKHOLM, 1912

ANOTHER ROUGH BEGINNING

Preparation for the 1912 Olympics included the usual political squabbles. Rebellious sports groups in the United States announced their opposition to participating in any event sponsored by the IOC. Finnish athletes demanded the right to participate as a separate nation, which brought immediate protests from Russia. The athletes from Bohemia insisted that they, too, be allowed to compete under their own flag, not that of Austria-Hungary. The Greeks demanded that the site be changed from Stockholm to Athens, and that the Olympics be held in Greece every eight years.

De Coubertin and the unwavering Swedish organizers held firm. The Games would be held in Stockholm, each country's Olympic Committee would have to solve its own internal problems, and the Olympic program would be reduced in size and scope to allow for better management. There would be only 13 different sports. Boxing, which was an activity prohibited by Swedish law, would not be included.

The Swedes, determined to provide the world with the best Olympic Games possible, then set their well-organized committees into motion. A worldwide advertising campaign was begun, Games officials were instructed down to every last detail of their responsibilities, housing arrangements were made, and a magnificent brick stadium was constructed in a beautiful sylvan setting near downtown Stockholm. The swimming and diving events would be held in a pool-like structure built into a nearby inlet from the Baltic Sea.

Innovations at the 1912 games included electronic timing, photo-finish cameras, and a public address system. Also new to the games were the overflow crowds—estimated to total more than one million for all of the events.

UNIQUE HOUSING FOR THE U.S. TEAM

The chartered ocean liner, *S.S. Finland,* which transported the American team from New York to Stockholm, provided both transatlantic transportation and Olympic housing for the U.S. athletes. Most of the participating teams were quartered in hotels throughout Stockholm, but the Americans continued living aboard the steamship, which was docked next to the Royal Palace.

On the ship was a 100-yard cork track so the athletes could continue training during the voyage. Also, there was a small canvas swimming pool in which swimmers could practice their strokes while suspended in the water with ropes around their waists.

Some of the American athletes complained that they felt cramped in the ship's small cabins. However, Philip Noel-Baker, who was a member of the British team, wrote: "The teams lived in different quarters scattered around town. The Americans were in the transatlantic ocean liner which had brought them from New York; we thought the ship was marvelous when we went to visit them."

THE ABSENT SPRINTER

Howard Drew of the U.S. was a qualifier for the 100-meter sprint final, but when the final was run, Drew was not in the race. Rumors began to circulate that Drew had been locked in his dressing room by teammates who did not want a black athlete to win the race. The story made the newspapers and has been included in some Olympic history books.

Drew explained later that he had suffered a leg injury in the semifinal round and was not able to compete further. He became just a spectator for the 100-meter final, and even went to the starting line to wish his teammates good luck.

A SAD TOUCH TO A VICTORY CEREMONY

When the great Finnish distance runner, Hannes Kolehmainen, won the 10,000-meter run, his first of four Olympic gold medals, the Russian flag was raised because Finland was still a part of Czarist Russia. Kolehmainen shook his head and commented that he would almost rather have lost the race than have the Russian flag raised after his victory.

TESTS OF ENDURANCE

In wrestling, the light heavyweight final between a Swede, Anders Ahlgren, and a Finn, Ivar Bohling, lasted for nine hours. Since neither had gained an advantage over the other, no gold medal was awarded. Each received a silver medal.

There was one wrestling match that lasted even longer. After wrestling for more than 11 hours in the middleweight semifinal match, Martin Klein, an Estonian competing for Russia, finally pinned his opponent, Alfred Asikainen of Finland. Klein was so exhausted that he was unable to wrestle for the gold medal. He forfeited the match and Claes Johansson of Sweden became the Olympic champion without having to go to the mat.

A FEW SQUABBLES

Although the Stockholm Games were the best organized, least political, and most successful of Olympics to that time, they were not without their incidents.

In fencing, the French and Italians both made proposals for rule changes that were rejected by Olympic officials. In protest, the Italians withdrew from the épée events and the French, who had been a preeminent fencing force in previous Olympics, refused to participate in any fencing events.

FAVORITISM IN WRESTLING

Swedish judges were accused of showing favoritism in the wrestling matches, interpreting the rules to favor Swedish entrants. A 12-page complaint, submitted by officials from most of the visiting nations, was filed with the IOC. At the conclusion of the Stockholm Games, it was agreed that in future Olympics judges could not be from countries with a particular interest in the outcome of an event.

A SURPRISE FOR THE U. S. SWIMMERS

Another flap developed over a surprise decision in swimming. After three Americans qualified for the final in the 100-meter freestyle, they left the pool. When they returned the next day for the final race, they learned that the officials had decided to conduct a semifinal race the night before— without the Americans. By default, the Americans had been eliminated from the competition.

After a series of protests and counter-protests, the Americans were allowed to swim in a special qualifying race. They would be allowed to swim in the final race if they could turn in a faster time than the slowest qualifier from the semifinal race. Duke Kahanamoku, the Hawaiian who was to win three gold and two silver medals in four Olympics, set a world record to qualify for the final. Also qualifying was Kenneth Juszagh. In the final race, Kahanamoku won easily and Juszagh finished third.

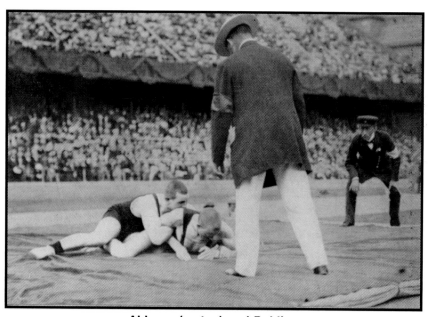

Ahlgren (on top) and Bohling

28

KAHANAMOKU'S UNUSUAL FIRST NAME

Duke Paoa Kahanamoku, handsome and charismatic, was of royal Hawaiian blood. He was born in the Palace of Princess Ruth in 1890 during a visit of the Duke of Edinburgh, the son of Queen Victoria and the younger brother of the future King Edward VII. In honor of the Duke's visit, Kahanamoku's father christened him Duke.

After Kahanamoku's Olympic swimming career ended in 1932, he appeared in several Hollywood movies, usually portraying Hawaiian kings. He was one of the pioneers of surfing and also endorsed a brand of ukuleles which can still be found in antique stores around the country.

WOMEN'S SWIMMING

For the first time, women's events were included in swimming, much to the dismay of the chauvinistic Baron de Coubertin. Exasperated by the decision to add three women's events to the Olympic program, de Coubertin never forgave the sport of swimming for what he described as "this impractical, uninteresting, unaesthetic, and indecorous feminine Olympiad."

Forty-two women participated.

A TUG OF WAR REVERSAL

There were only two entries in the tug of war competition—Great Britain and Sweden. The British again wore their steel-rimmed police boots that had caused a stir in London four years earlier. But the Swedes were ready for them. The tug of war was staged in sand, and the heavy police boots were of no help. The Swedes won easily.

A YOUNG OLYMPIAN NAMED PATTON

A new event, the modern pentathlon (not to be confused with the track and field pentathlon), was introduced in Stockholm. Developed by de Coubertin himself, the modern pentathlon's five events included horseback riding, fencing, pistol shooting, swimming, and cross country running. The first four places went to Swedes, while fifth went to a 26-year-old lieutenant from West Point, George Patton. Patton, of course, gained fame later as General "Blood and Guts" Patton, one of the best known (and most controversial) Allied commanders of World War II.

Patton finished ahead of the gold medal winner in three of the five events and might have been the Olympic champion had it not been for his poor performance in pistol shooting. Known for his shooting skill, Patton's low score may have been caused by his use of an army revolver, while the competitors who finished ahead of him all used target pistols.

If Patton had finished sixth or better in shooting, he would have been the Olympic champion.

A HOT MARATHON RACE

The marathon started at 1:48 P.M. on an unseasonably hot, muggy day. There were 68 starters. The course ran from inside the Olympic Stadium, which was filled to capacity, a little over 13 miles over country roads to the halfway point in the village of Rotebro, now a Stockholm suburb. There the runners ran around a pole and followed the same route back to the Stadium.

Later, to commemorate the event, a 13-foot marble column was constructed at the side of the road, near the turnaround point. Today, most people believe the marble column was the actual turnaround post.

Unfortunately, most of the runners did not stop at the first drinking station, which probably contributed to the large number of non-finishers.

Half of the starters failed to finish, many of them collapsing along the road. One of those who fell, Francisco Lazaro of Portugal, died the next day. It was the first fatality of the modern Olympic Games.

After 24 miles, two South Africans, Ken McArthur and Chris Gitshan, were well ahead of the field. McArthur agreed to wait for Gitsham when the latter stopped for a drink of water with two miles to go, but as Gitsham began drinking, McArthur took off for the stadium. Gitsham struggled to catch up, but McArthur beat him to the tape by less than one minute.

THE RUNNER WHO DISAPPEARED

One of the strangest stories to come out of the 1912 Olympic Games was the mysterious disappearance of Japanese marathon runner Siso Kanakuri. When the marathon was completed, Olympic officials began accounting for the 34 runners who had not finished because of the extreme heat. The officials were able to locate all of the runners but one—Kanakuri. The police were called in, but they too were unable to find him.

Kanakuri had disappeared.

As the years passed, there were occasional tongue-in-cheek reports of "Kanakuri sightings." Some said he was seen in the company of two Swedish girls and had no desire to return to Japan. Others said he was seen running around the streets of Rotebro, trying to find his way back to the Olympic stadium.

In 1962, on the 50th anniversary of the race, a Stockholm newspaper reporter was sent to Japan to try to find Kanakuri. Without much difficulty, the correspondent found the missing runner, who was teaching geography in a public school in the town of Tamana. Kanakuri explained that he had completed half the race when the heat overcame him. He stumbled into the yard of a Swedish family, who took him in, gave him drinks of raspberry juice, and provided a bed for a long nap.

When he awoke, the family gave him clothing and put him on a train back into Stockholm. Kanakuri was so embarrassed because he had not finished the marathon that he quietly left the country, taking a boat back to Japan. He had not realized that for 50 years he had been "the Japanese who disappeared" and had become a Swedish legend.

In 1967, when Siso Kanakuri was 76, he was flown back to Stockholm to participate in the opening of a new department store in Rotebro. Then he was taken to the Olympic Stadium, where he ran across the finish line, to the great delight of the Swedish people. Kanakuri's 55-year marathon race was finally over.

THE JIM THORPE DISQUALIFICATION

The most famous controversy associated with the 1912 Olympics concerned the great American Indian athlete, Jim Thorpe, who is considered by many to be the greatest all-around athlete of all time. Thorpe is described as a full-blooded Indian in some accounts and as half Indian and half Irish in others, but he was actually five-eighths Indian, one-fourth Irish, and one-eighth French. His father, Hiram Thorpe, gave him the Irish name, James Francis Thorpe. His mother, Charlotte View, gave him the Indian name Wa-Tho-Huck (Bright Path).

Thorpe won both the decathlon and pentathlon titles with ease in Stockholm, yet his name did not appear in the record books for a period of

70 years. Several months after the Olympics were over, Thorpe's medals, trophies, and records were stripped from him by the USA's Amateur Athletic Union (AAU) because they learned he had received money for playing baseball prior to participating in the 1912 Games. AAU officials pointed out that Thorpe had signed a statement, as did all of the American Olympians, certifying he had never broken the rules of amateurism.*

The London Express of January 28, 1913, reported: "James Thorpe, a full-blooded Red Indian who was America's principal contestant at the Olympic Games in Stockholm last July, has confessed that he was a professional athlete for three years previous to the Swedish international contests."

Apologizing to the IOC, the AAU asked that Thorpe's name be stricken from the record books. The gold medals were forwarded to the two second place finishers, Hugo Wieslander of Sweden and Ferdinand Bie of Norway.

Many have reported that Wieslander and Bie refused the medals when they arrived, but the truth is that they both accepted them. Some Olympic history books credit both Wieslander and Bie with saying, "We didn't win them. Thorpe did, no matter what your amateur rules are." It's a charitable quote, but it never happened.

THORPE'S CHALLENGE TROPHIES

The two trophies Thorpe won for his decathlon and pentathlon victories were challenge trophies, two of 20 such trophies that were presented to Olympic champions in Stockholm. Although many history books say Thorpe's tro-

---

Although the Olympic amateur rules of 1912 may seem absurd today, the Games were founded with a strict code of amateurism as one of its strongest foundations. From the first meeting of the International Olympic Committee in 1894 until the amateur rules began to be relaxed in 1976 and nearly eliminated in 1992, eligibility for the Olympics required competitors to be pure amateurs. An Olympic participant could not have received "any financial rewards or material benefit in connection with his or her sports participation," even working as a coach or physical education teacher. There were no exceptions.

Jim Thorpe

phies were taken away and should have been returned to him, challenge trophies always remained the property of the IOC and were never meant to be kept by the winners for more than four years.

At the conclusion of the 1912 Olympics, Thorpe and two witnesses were required to sign documents that the trophies would be returned to the IOC at the end of the Olympiad. Obviously they were returned some time after 1912, since they were presented to the decathlon and pentathlon winners at the next Olympics, held in 1920.

The trophy for the pentathlon was a bronze bust of the Swedish king, a gift from the Swedish royal family. The decathlon trophy—a gift from Czar Nicholas of Russia—was a 30-pound silver chalice in the shape of a viking ship, lined with gold and trimmed with rare jewels. After Thorpe was presented the 30-pound chalice on the victory stand, he turned to a teammate and remarked, "What the hell do I do with this?"

The priceless viking ship trophy, with six of its original jewels still intact, is now on display in the Olympic Museum in Lausanne, Switzerland. The bust of the Swedish king, which was last presented in 1924, has never been located.

THE THORPE LEGEND

The legend is that Thorpe had received a

small amount of money for playing semipro baseball in 1909 and 1910, the implication being that he had played for some obscure town team on Sundays. Most accounts say he received $25 a week. Some others say $15 a week. One says "a little expense money." One says "a pittance." *The Guinness Book of Records* says he received a *total* of $25. In the motion picture, *The Jim Thorpe Story,* on which Thorpe served as technical advisor, Burt Lancaster, playing Thorpe, said he played baseball one summer and received room, board, and expenses only.

A check of the Spalding baseball guides for 1909, 1910, and 1911 shows that Thorpe had been a full-salaried baseball player for those three years, playing for three different professional teams in the Eastern Carolina League—Wilmington, Rocky Mount, and Fayetteville. During the 1910 season, the only year for which complete records are available, Thorpe pitched for Rocky Mount, winning ten, losing ten, and batting .236.

The most reliable sources say Thorpe earned $25 a week, which would be the same as earning more than $400 a week in today's dollars. It was a very good summer salary for a college student at the time, especially since tax and social security deductions did not yet exist.

There is no doubt that Thorpe was in violation of the amateur rules of the time. He had either been too honest or too naive at the time to play professional baseball under an assumed name, which is what several other amateur athletes of that era had done. Thorpe pleaded in a letter to the AAU: "I will be partly excused by the fact that I was simply an Indian schoolboy and did not know all about such things. I did not play for the money. I played because I liked baseball."

For the next 70 years there were many requests—even petitions—to have Thorpe's Olympic accomplishments recognized by the IOC. One petition, which claimed 200,000 signatures, was circulated by the Ohio Jaycees. The petition stated in its opening sentence that Thorpe had received only $2 per game.

In 1973, President Richard Nixon was presented a petition with 400,000 signatures, asking his help to have Thorpe's medals and records restored. The petition said Thorpe "had once been paid a relatively small sum for playing exhibition baseball."

In 1975, President Gerald Ford wrote a personal letter to the IOC, and in 1979, the U.S. Congress passed a resolution asking the IOC to restore Thorpe's 1912 records and medals.

In 1982, nearly 30 years after Thorpe's death, the IOC voted to restore his name as the 1912 decathlon and pentathlon champion. Gold medals were presented to Thorpe's children at a special ceremony in 1983 and a special plaque in Thorpe's memory was placed on the outer wall of the Olympic stadium in Stockholm.

A RUSSIAN SLANT ON THE THORPE AFFAIR

A Russian Olympic history book, published at the height of the Cold War, suggests an underlying motive for the disqualification of Jim Thorpe. It states: "The advocates of racism and racial discrimination revolted against the homage paid by the American people to the hero of the Stockholm Olympiad. The fantastic success of the two-time Olympic champion undermined the racial theory of white superiority. The whole hullabaloo was started just because somebody in the USA did not like the growing popularity of the representatives of the native inhabitants of the country." Accompanying these dubious remarks is a photograph, not of Thorpe, but of Hawaiian swimmer Duke Kahanamoku.

"THE GREATEST ATHLETE IN THE WORLD"

Jim Thorpe's accomplishments in sports are legendary. Participating at tiny Carlisle College in Pennsylvania, he was an All-American football player in 1911 and 1912. When Carlisle upset Harvard 18-15 in 1911, Thorpe scored all of Carlisle's points. He was also an outstanding basketball and baseball player, and was a one-man track team, participating in enough different events to win many meets by himself.

The Olympic decathlon and pentathlon events were perfect for Thorpe's all-around ability. He won them so handily that Sweden's King Gustav V paid him a personal compliment during the awards ceremony. The king said, "Sir, you are the greatest athlete in the world." Most Olympic history books say that Thorpe replied "Thanks, King," but there

is no record from that time that he responded at all. In the movie, *The Jim Thorpe_Story*, the response was, "Thank you, Your Majesty."

It is now generally accepted that Thorpe added the "Thanks, King" response years later to make the story more entertaining. One Thorpe biographer says that in his later years Thorpe would sit outside his trailer home in Lomita, California, telling stories to anyone who would stop and listen. He told the "Thanks, King" story over and over.

FROM OLYMPIC ATHLETE TO IOC PRESIDENT

One participant in the decathlon and pentathlon who was to gain another form of Olympic fame was Avery Brundage. Brundage, who finished sixth in the pentathlon, became a member of the IOC in 1936 and served as IOC president from 1952 until 1972. During his tenure as IOC president, Brundage was a staunch advocate of the strict rules of amateurism, causing many of his critics to accuse him of refusing to reinstate Jim Thorpe's Olympic records because he had lost to Thorpe in 1912.

The young Avery Brundage

"AN ENCHANTMENT"

The splendid organization and efficient management of the Stockholm organizers, coupled with outstanding performances, established the Olympic Games, once and for all, as an important, permanent international event. There was a definite contrast between the acrimony of the London games four years earlier and the exceptionally pleasant atmosphere of Stockholm.

After 20 years of struggles, de Coubertin felt his long-anticipated goal had been met—these Games were truly an international festival of friendship and goodwill. He called the 1912 Olympics "an enchantment."

Philip Noel-Baker, a member of the 1912 and 1920 British teams and later a 36-year member of Parliament and winner of the Nobel Peace Prize, said later, "Sweden had done the Olympic movement proud."

The Stockholm Olympics were closed with a huge party in the stadium, complete with a ten-course meal, a 2,500-voice choir, and fireworks into the night. The Olympic movement had become permanently established and everyone was looking forward to the 1916 Olympic celebration in Berlin—a celebration which would never be held.

Olympiad VI
BERLIN, 1916
(Canceled because of World War I)

BERLIN IS SELECTED

Three cities were candidates for the 1916 Olympic Games—Berlin, Budapest, and Alexandria. As the storm clouds of war began to appear throughout Europe, de Coubertin believed that war might be averted if the Games were held in Germany. He decided to try to convince the other IOC members to award the Games to Berlin.

It was no secret that Germany's Kaiser Wilhelm craved power, but it was also true that he did not want to go to war to get it. And since the Stockholm Olympics had brought great prestige to Sweden, de Coubertin hoped the Kaiser might be able to muster support for a more peaceful solution to Europe's political differences by hosting the Olympics. At their next meeting, the IOC awarded the Games to Berlin.

A DIFFICULT DECISION

"The war to end all wars" began in the summer of 1914, with all of Europe believing it would be over shortly. As the war continued to expand, de Coubertin and the IOC were pressured to move the Games to either the United States or Scandinavia. But Berlin had not relinquished the right to be the host. Fearing further erosion of the Olympic movement, the IOC decided to cancel the 1916 Games.

HISTORY DOES NOT REPEAT ITSELF

At the time of the ancient Olympics, the Greeks always proclaimed a sacred truce during the time of the Olympic Games. If wars were in progress, all fighting would cease for the duration of the Games, and people would be allowed to travel to and from Olympia unhindered. Now, for the first time in the 1000-year history of the Olympic Games, instead of canceling wars because of the Olympics, the Olympics were being canceled because of war.

DE COUBERTIN MOVES
TO SWITZERLAND

In 1915, at the age of 51, Pierre de Coubertin decided to enlist in the French army. Since he thought it was not fitting for a mere soldier to be president of the IOC, de Coubertin asked a Swiss aristocrat, Baron Godefroy de Blonay, to take over the IOC presidency in his absence. However, the French army rejected de Coubertin because of his age.

With the war expanding in Europe, de Coubertin thought it would be best to move the IOC headquarters to Switzerland, a country which was not involved in the war. He left his French estate and established a new home for himself and the IOC in Lausanne, where the IOC headquarters is still located.

Olympiad VII
ANTWERP, 1920

A DIFFICULT REVIVAL

In April of 1919, just five months after World War I had come to a close, the IOC made the startling announcement that war-torn Antwerp would host the 1920 Olympics. The decision was a tribute to the gallant Belgians, who had been the victims of savage aggression and enemy occupation during the previous four years. Even as the IOC was meeting in Lausanne, Switzerland, soldiers in Belgium were identifying bodies and marking graves as they picked through the rubble.

There was little time for the Belgians, who were not really in the mood for games of any kind, to prepare for these "impromptu Olympics." However, there was great satisfaction in knowing that the Olympic spirit had only suffered an interruption and could continue to grow as it had so successfully prior to the war. The determined Belgians became united in their efforts to provide the world with the best Olympic Games possible.

For the first time in modern Olympic history, some countries were deliberately excluded from the games. The IOC decided not to invite World War I's "Central Powers"—Germany, Austria, Bulgaria, Hungary, and Turkey.

THE "DEATH SHIP"

The U.S. team was transported to Belgium aboard the *Princess Matoika*, a small freighter that had been converted to military use during the war. The *Matoika* was known as "America's death ship," since its most recent duty had been to transport 1,800 U.S. war dead from Europe back to the States. The caskets, reeking of formaldehyde, were still stacked on the pier as the U.S. team boarded the ship in Hoboken, New Jersey.

Almost immediately team members began to complain about the conditions aboard the ship, which they dubbed "the Princess Slowpoka." The lingering stench of formaldehyde, the cramped, rat-infested quarters, and the poor quality of food

during the 13-day crossing caused a near-mutiny. Occasional rough seas didn't help the mood of the athletes.

The American Olympic Committee's Official Report says: "The members of the team protested in a signed statement that the transport was dirty; that it was vermin-ridden, especially with rats; that the service both in the staterooms and troopship quarters and at the table was from poor to bad; and that sanitary arrangements were insufficient. Apparently they forgot the emergency of the situation and overlooked entirely the many little conveniences and luxuries installed for their comfort."

As unpleasant as the two-week crossing was, there were some happy moments. When the seas were calm, swimmer Duke Kahanamoku and his Hawaiian teammates sat on the deck, strumming ukuleles and singing Hawaiian songs. And there was the shipboard romance of diver Alice Lord and high jumper Dick Landon. They were married soon after the close of the Olympics.

THE U.S. ATHLETES REVOLT

Housing in Antwerp was at a premium for foreign spectators, and even for Olympic athletes, as was evidenced when the U.S. track and field men were assigned to a schoolhouse, with the athletes sleeping in classrooms on small cots with straw-filled pillows. The athletes were so upset about the conditions that the near-mutiny of the *Princess Matoika* became the revolution of Antwerp.

Because the cots were too small for them, three large weightmen, Pat McDonald, Matt McGrath, and Pat Ryan, were given permission to move to a hotel. McDonald and McGrath shared a room; Ryan had a single. Other members of the team asked permission to move, too, but the team leaders refused.

The revolution came to a head the first night in the schoolhouse when hop, step and jump world record holder Dan Ahearn missed the 10 o'clock curfew. In fact, he didn't get back to the schoolhouse at all that night; he had moved into the hotel with Ryan.

The team leaders removed Ahearn from the team for missing the curfew, and the revolution escalated. Ahearn's teammates circulated a petition with 200 signatures on it, to have Ahearn reinstated. Either Ahearn was back on the team or the petitioners would not compete in the Games.

Eventually the team leaders relented, Ahearn was reinstated, and an uneasy peace was restored. Newspaper accounts later attributed the relatively poor showing of the American Olympic team to the "mutineers" and the disruptions they had caused.

A SMOOTH OPENING

The opening ceremonies began at the Cathedral of Antwerp, where Cardinal Mercier, who had been an inspiration to the Belgians during the war, conducted a service in honor of the many athletes who had lost their lives. Following the services at the cathedral, the ceremonies continued at the stadium, where there was an overflow crowd in attendance.

Following tradition, the teams paraded, one by one, into the stadium and onto the infield. Most of the parading athletes had been in the military only months before, causing one journalist to remark, "The athletes have certainly learned how to march."

THE OLYMPIC FLAG

The Olympic flag, with its five interlocking rings representing the five continents linked together in friendship, made its Olympic debut in Antwerp. The five-ring symbol had been found inscribed on an altar at the ruins of Delphi in Greece. Delphi, which dates from the 6th century B.C., had been the site of the Pythian Games, which were held every four years to honor Apollo.

The linking rings were selected for the Olympic flag at an IOC meeting in 1913 and the flag was flown for the first time at an IOC meeting in 1914, before World War I began. It is generally accepted that the five rings represent the continents of Africa, the Americas, Asia, Australia, and Europe. However, de Coubertin himself said they should represent the great land masses of the world, not specific continents.

And although the literature always refers to the five colors of the Olympic flag, de Coubertin had said that at least one of the *six* colors of the flag—the white background and the blue, yellow, black, green, and red rings—appears on every national flag.

THE OATH

Also introduced at the 1920 Games was the Olympic oath, recited on behalf of all the athletes by a Belgian fencer, Victor Boin: "In the name of all competitors, I promise that we shall take part in these Olympic Games, respecting and abiding by the rules which govern them, in the true spirit of sportsmanship, for the glory of sport and the honor of our teams."

Since 1920, an athlete from each host nation has recited the oath during the opening ceremonies, but rarely has it been the same as the original version.

Words and phrases have been liberally rearranged. On two occasions, the athletes either relied too much on memory or forgot their notes, appearing for a moment to be at a loss for words. Gamely, both of them stumbled through the oath, changing its words but not its meaning.

CITIUS, ALTIUS, FORTIUS

There is confusion in the literature as to whether the Olympic motto, "Citius, Altius, Fortius," was also introduced at the 1920 Olympic Games. In a book that was co-edited by former International Olympic Committee president Lord Killanin, the claim is made that the motto was invented by Father Henri Didon, a Dominican monk, and had its first appearance at the 1920 Olympic Games.

However, at another point in the same book, it says the motto was coined at a 1921 meeting of the IOC for the 1924 Games by R.P. Didon, a French schoolmaster.

In other books, Father Didon is credited with introducing the motto at the 1900 Olympics after having used it "in building up the sporting spirit of his pupils in a football game." Some Olympic books attribute the phrase to Henri-Martin Didon, a French educator and sports enthusiast who found the words engraved on the lintel of his school's front door.

A few books say the motto was introduced at the first Olympic Games in 1896 by Reverend Father Didon of Paris. Yet others say "Citius, Fortius, Altius" was the motto of a college near LeHavre, and Father Didon merely reversed the final two words before suggesting it for the Olympics at an IOC meeting in 1897.

John A. Lucas, who is a tireless researcher and a reliable historian, credits Father Henri Didon (1840-1900), a French Dominican friar, who used the motto to inspire his students at Arcueil College in Normandy. Lucas also notes that de Coubertin made reference to Didon's "neat Latin phrase" in a speech in 1894, almost two years before the first of the modern Olympic Games.

Since de Coubertin made reference to the motto in 1894 and Didon died in 1900, it seems likely the motto made its first appearance well before 1920.

FINANCIAL TROUBLES

Tickets for the Antwerp Olympics were 20 cents—overpriced for those days—and the Games were not well-attended. The newly-erected 30,000 seat stadium was full for the opening ceremonies, but was seldom more than two-thirds full during the remainder of the games, even though officials opened the gates to school children, and eventually to the general public, free of charge. The end result was bankruptcy for the organizing committee, which did not even bother to produce an official report after the Games.

TINY FINLAND DOMINATES

In contrast to the unusually poor performance of the U.S. team, the athletes from tiny Finland made a spectacular showing in these Olympics.

Overall, Finland, in its first Olympics free from Russian rule, won 29 Olympic medals, 13 of them gold. Finland's Paavo Nurmi began a magnificent Olympic career in which he won nine gold and three silver medals in three Olympic Games. He set 24 world records during his running career. He likely would have won more medals had the 1916 Olympics been held and if he had not been ruled a professional in 1932.

NURMI'S UNPLEASANT EXPERIENCE

Nurmi often said that his "most unpleasant" gold medal was in the 10,000-meter run at the Antwerp games. He had lost the 5,000-meter run

to his French rival, Joseph Guillemot, in Nurmi's first Olympic appearance three days earlier, and the 10,000 was his opportunity for revenge.

The real cause of the unpleasantness for Nurmi and embarrassment for his opponent was caused by a time change. For some reason, Belgium's King Albert requested that the race be moved up from its original time of 5:00 p.m. to 1:45 p.m. Guillemot had just finished a large lunch when he got the word, and there was no time for the food to digest.

The race was close throughout, with Nurmi and Guillemot following pace-setter James Wilson of Great Britain during most of the race. On the last lap, Guillemot made his move, sprinting into the lead. Nurmi quickly regained the lead and pulled away from Guillemot, winning by 1.4 seconds. As soon as Guillemot crossed the finish line, Nurmi experienced the "unpleasantness." Guillemot could not control himself, vomiting all over Nurmi.

It was truly remarkable that Guillemot was even competing in the Olympics. He had been poisoned with mustard gas while fighting in the war, with his lungs so severely damaged that he was told he would never run again.

A POPULAR WALKER

The greatest crowd-pleaser in the Antwerp games was Ugo Frigerio of Italy, winner of two gold medals in the walking events. Frigerio would chat with spectators and lead cheers for himself as he was building up huge leads over his opponents. He even provided the band with sheet music to be played during the 3,000-meter walk, which he won handily. But he was not in step with the music, which he later complained had not been played at the correct tempo.

A MARATHON WITHOUT INCIDENT

For the first time in Olympic history, the marathon was uneventful, with the veteran Olympian, Hannes Kolehmainen of Finland, running away from the field. The only excitement was when third place finisher Valerio Arri of Italy turned three somersaults on the track as he crossed the finish line.

A CYCLING REVERSAL

The cycling road race crossed six sets of railroad tracks along the 110-mile course around Antwerp. At each crossing there was a judge to record any delays the cyclists might have had while waiting for trains. When Henry Kaltenbrun of South Africa was the first cyclist back into the stadium and across the finish line, he was heralded as the winner. Later it was learned that the fourth place finisher, Harry Stenqvist of Sweden, had been delayed four minutes at a railroad crossing. When the judges subtracted the four minutes from Stenqvist's time, he was declared the winner. No one took into account that Stenqvist also had a four-minute rest period during the race that the other cyclists had not enjoyed.

AN INTERRUPTION IN HUNGARY'S WIN STREAK

Hungary's domination of fencing's individual saber competition was broken at the 1920 Olympics. Hungarian fencers had won the event in 1908 and 1912, and were to go on to win in every Olympics after 1920 until 1968. But in 1920 Hungary had no opportunity to win, or even to compete, since they were one of the five nations not invited to the Olympics because of their participation in World War I.

THE KELLYS OF PHILADELPHIA

The star of the rowing competition was John B. "Jack" Kelly, a bricklayer from Philadelphia. Considered at the time to be the greatest oarsman ever, Kelly won gold medals in the single and double sculls.

Many years later, Kelly's daughter, Grace, also gained wide renown. Grace Kelly was an Academy Award-winning actress and became Princess Grace of Monaco when she married Prince Rainier.

Kelly's son, Jack, Jr., competed in rowing in four Olympics and later served as president of the Amateur Athletic Union (AAU).

DISPUTE AND DISQUALIFICATION IN SOCCER

The 1920 games were not without their difficult moments. In the soccer final between Belgium and the newly-formed nation of Czechoslovakia, it became obvious that the referee's decisions were being influenced by the 40,000 partisan Belgian spectators, decisions which were immediately disputed by the Czechs. When, late in the game, a Czech player was ordered to leave the field, the entire Czech team left the field in anger. The judges thereupon disqualified the Czechoslovakian team and award the gold medal to Belgium.

A COSTLY MISUNDERSTANDING

The controversial final of the 100-meter dash prompted several days of protests by the U.S. Olympic Committee, even though U.S. sprinters Charley Paddock, Morris Kirksey, and Jackson Scholz finished first, second, and fourth in the race. The other American, Loren Murchison, finished last because of an error on the part of the starter, according to U.S. officials.

As the runners took their marks, the clerk of the course, speaking French, warned Paddock to move his hands back, behind the starting line. Murchison and two other runners, thinking it was a command to stand up, were left at their marks when the gun was fired. Murchison was 10 yards behind the field at the finish line.

BORROWED SHOES

U.S. sprinter Allen Woodring went to Antwerp as an alternate, but he was allowed to compete in the 200 meters when fellow sprinter George Massengale became ill. Woodring practiced so hard in preparation for the event that he wore out his only pair of track shoes. In fact, one shoe split just before the 200-meter final.

Woodring rushed around, trying to borrow a pair of shoes that would fit him, but all he could find were shoes with spikes that were much longer than he was accustomed to. He wore the shoes anyway, fearing he would stumble during the race, but the long spikes were perfect for the rain-soaked track and he won the gold medal over favorite Charley Paddock.

AN AMAZING RECOVERY

As the competitors were beginning their warmups for the finals in the javelin throw, Finnish champion Jonni Myyrä was lying on the infield grass, relaxing. One of the American throwers made a short warmup throw which fell well short of where Myyrä was lying. But rather than sticking in the turf as the American had intended, the javelin landed flat, bounced, and hit Myyrä on the elbow of his throwing arm.

Myyrä was rushed to a nearby hospital, where doctors removed a bone chip from his elbow. In what has to be one of the most amazing and courageous recoveries in Olympic history, Myyrä returned to the stadium less than an hour later and won the javelin gold medal. Myyrä's teammates finished second and third—sweeping the event for Finland.

DUKE DOES DOUBLE DUTY

A foul claimed by the fifth place finisher against the fourth place finisher in the final of the 100-meter freestyle forced the entire field to repeat the event, even though everyone agreed neither of the swimmers involved in the controversy ever had a chance for a medal. The finish of the second race was exactly the same as the first, with America's Duke Kahanamoku winning the gold—for the second time.

A WATER POLO MELEE

The water polo final match between Belgium and Great Britain erupted into one of the worst scenes at the Antwerp Games. Angered by the rough play of the British team, the Belgian fans became outraged when the British won the match, 3-2. As the British team left the pool, anything that could be picked up was thrown at them by the angry Belgians, who screamed out that the British team "should be drowned." The Belgian officials refused to raise the British flag and the band would not participate in the victory ceremony. The British team had to be transported to their hotel in a military truck protected by armed guards.

A MISSING RUNNER

On the closing day of the Games, all medal winners—except one—participated in the presentation of medals by King Albert. The missing athlete, American sprinter Morris Kirksey, had

Duke Kahanamoku

been caught trying to get through a window into a locked dressing room to retrieve his running shoes. Since Kirksey could not speak French or Flemish, he was not able to explain his situation to the police, who promptly took him off to jail. He was released the day after the ceremonies—just in time to join his teammates for the steamer trip home.

ON TO PARIS

With the Antwerp games contributing to the world's psychological recovery from the horrors of war, the Olympics emerged stronger than ever.

De Coubertin was now ready to have the Games return to Paris, to celebrate the 30th anniversary of the revival of the Olympics, and more importantly to erase memories of the Paris Olympic fiasco of 1900.

Olympiad VIII
PARIS, 1924

ANOTHER SHAKY BEGINNING

The 1924 Olympic Games were originally scheduled for Amsterdam, but were finally awarded to Paris—the first city to host the Olympics for a second time. De Coubertin, who would be ending his term as president of the IOC after these Games, requested that Paris be selected over Amsterdam, since these would be his last Olympics.

But again the Olympic planning began on shaky footing. Faced with a slumping economy, the French had little money available to finance the Games. The IOC asked sports leaders in Los Angeles if they would be able to host the Olympics if Paris could not. Los Angeles agreed.

Then, when enough money had been raised in Paris and the preparations were proceeding on schedule, the organizers faced yet another crisis. In February 1924—just four months before the first Olympic events were to be contested—the River Seine overflowed its banks and much of the city of Paris was flooded. But the waters receded quickly, the venues were completed on time, and Paris was ready to stage the Olympic Games for the second time.

FIRST CLASS TREATMENT

U.S. sports officials, who learned much from dealing with the near-mutinous athletes four years earlier, decided to insure that transportation to the Olympics, lodging in Paris, and food en route and in Paris would be first class. A huge luxury ocean liner, the *S.S. America,* with "American Olympic Team" emblazoned on its sides, was chartered for the trip. On board the ship, for training purposes, were a 220-yard cork track, a small canvas swimming pool, boxing rings, and wrestling mats. Needless to say, there were no uprisings.

On arrival in Paris, the U.S. men's teams were transported by 70 automobiles to their accommodations at a scenic, historic estate at Rocquencourt, where 11 comfortable barracks had been built for the male athletes. The U.S. officials stayed in a chateau on the premises.

The U.S. women were housed in a hotel in the countryside, far from the center of Paris. They were so far out of the city that they spent up to six hours daily getting to and from their practice and competition venues.

The decision to house the women so far away was made by the U.S. Olympic Committee to "protect them from the temptations of Paris life."

THE STADIUM AND ITS "VILLAGE"

The opening ceremonies and the track and field events were staged in the impressive Colombes Stadium, which had a 500-meter running track and accommodated 60,000 spectators.

Next to the stadium there were small wooden cabins, designed to house many of the visiting athletes. Although the idea for the first complete Olympic village, with lodging for most of the athletes, dining halls and other ancillary buildings, must be credited to the organizers of the 1932 Olympics in Los Angeles, this collection of simple cabins definitely was a forerunner of the Olympic village. There was even a large sign at the entrance with the words "Village Olympique."

THE OPENING CEREMONIES

An overflow crowd jammed the stadium for the opening ceremonies on Saturday, June 5, with so much demand for tickets that scalpers made huge profits. Although there was some interest in seeing the athletes, the public was really interested in seeing the dignitaries who would oversee the ceremonies, including French president Gaston Doumergue, England's Prince of Wales (later King Edward VIII), the Crown Prince of Sweden, the Crown Prince of Romania, the Regent of Abyssinia, and Baron de Coubertin.

HEAT WAVE

Temperatures throughout the Olympics were

so high at times that journalists referred to the Olympic stadium as a "cauldron" or "furnace."

The intense heat persisted throughout most of the Games, only interrupted once by a cooling thunderstorm during the week-long track and field events.

AN UPSET IN THE 100 METERS

In the preliminary rounds of the 100 meters, held on Sunday, June 6, the crowd was anxious to see "the world's fastest human," Charley Paddock.

Paddock's eccentric maneuvers included a long, pre-start ritual designed to unnerve opponents and a characteristic leaping lunge for the tape at the race's finish.

Absent from the Sunday 100-meter preliminaries was Scottish divinity student, Eric Liddell, who had decided several months earlier, when the Olympic schedule was published, that he would not compete on "the Lord's day." Therefore, Liddell, who was Great Britain's top sprinter, would forego the 100 meters and enter the 200 and 400 meters.

When the final of the 100 meters was held the next day, all eyes were on the American favorites—Paddock, Jackson Scholz, Loren Murchison, and Chester Bowman. But it was a brash, cigar-smoking Englishman, Harold Abrahams, who came from behind to edge Jackson Scholz for the gold medal.

PADDOCK LEAPS TO A SECOND LOSS

In the 200 meters, Charley Paddock's characteristic leap at the finish, which turned him sideways in the air this time, left him well behind teammate Jackson Scholz, who won in 21.6, another Olympic record. In third place was the divinity student, Eric Liddell. Finishing well back in last place was Harold Abrahams, who had already won his gold medal in the 100 and seemed satisfied with that.

LIDDELL SURPRISES IN THE 400

Two days later, Eric Liddell surprised the experts by winning the 400 meters in 47.6—another Olympic record. Inexperienced in the 400, Liddell had run the first 200 in a blistering 22.2 seconds. He faded noticeably in the final stretch, but still had enough energy left to reach the finish three meters ahead of the field.

"CHARIOTS OF FIRE"

British gold medalists Harold Abrahams and Eric Liddell were the subjects of the entertaining, but often inaccurate 1981 Academy Award-winning motion picture, *Chariots of Fire*. After the Olympics, the two went their separate ways. The abrasive Abrahams became well known as the athletics correspondent for the *London Times* and as the longtime head of England's governing body for track and field, the Amateur Athletics Association. Soft-spoken Liddell became a missionary in China and died in a Japanese prisoner-of-war camp in 1945 at the age of 43.

AMERICA'S SUCCESSES

The Americans dominated these Olympics, winning more gold medals than any other country in track and field, swimming, target shooting, lawn tennis, wrestling, rowing, boxing, and rugby. It was the greatest showing ever by a U.S. Olympic team against true international compe-

Paavo Nurmi

tition, and it was predicted at the time that no future Olympic team would ever match that success.

NURMI RETURNS

The USA may have been the strongest team, but the individual star of the 1924 Games was Finland's barrel-chested running machine, Paavo Nurmi, who added five more gold medals to the two golds and one silver he had won four years earlier.

In Paris, he won the 1500-meter and 5000-meter races, the 3000-meter team race, and added two golds (individual and team) in the 10,000-meter cross country race, which was run as the temperature reached 113 degrees.

Because of the extreme heat during the cross country run, 23 runners were forced to drop out of the race, many of them ending up in the hospital, but Nurmi didn't seem to notice as he won with ease. Famed sportswriter Grantland Rice later wrote of Nurmi's accomplishments:

"Forty-four competing nations must pay tribute to the greatest track phenomenon that any age in sport has ever known."

There were no lap times called out to the runners in those days, so Nurmi carried his own stopwatch, referring to it often as he completed lap after lap. Nurmi knew that an even pace was more economical and therefore less tiring. The watch helped him maintain a steady pace, which gave him a physical advantage, and probably a psychological advantage, over his opponents.

A BATTLE FOR THE LONG JUMP RECORD

A world record was set by American Robert LeGendre in the long jump, but he won only a bronze medal. LeGendre set the record while competing in the pentathlon, the now-discontinued five-event track and field competition which included the long jump. LeGendre, who was reportedly upset that he had not also been selected for the long jump competition, jumped 25 feet 5 $^3/_4$ inches to break the world record by 2$^3/_4$ inches. However, his overall performance in the five events was only good enough for third place.

The next day, LeGendre's U.S. teammate, DeHart Hubbard, won the Olympic long jump title with a leap that appeared to match the world record set by LeGendre. However, Hubbard fell back after landing in the sand and lost valuable distance. The official measurement was 24 feet 5 $^1/_8$ inches, more than a foot short of LeGendre's new record, but it was still good enough for the gold medal. Hubbard thus became the first black athlete to win an individual gold medal at the Olympics.

UNSPORTSMANLIKE CONDUCT

In contrast to the peaceful proceedings in the stadium, there were shameful examples of poor sportsmanship at the Vélodrome d'Hiver, where the boxing matches were held. Throughout the boxing events, there were constant protests and counter-protests. Referees and judges had to endure catcalls and jeers from the unruly fans, and were even physically attacked in some cases. At one point, a group of angry Argentineans stormed the ring to protest a decision.

Some of the boxing problems came about because the referee was stationed outside the ring and did not always have a good view of the action. In a preliminary bout, French middleweight boxer Roger Brousse defeated the 1920 Olympic middleweight champion, Harry Mallin of Great Britain. But the referee had not seen that Brousse had bitten Mallin severely on the shoulder during a clinch. When Mallin showed the deep teeth marks to the referee after the match, Brousse was disqualified. Mallin went on to win his second middleweight gold medal.

FRIENDS TO THE END

The American featherweight boxing champion, Joe Sallas, was selected to represent the U.S. in the Olympics, but his best friend, Jackie

Fields, was not. Sallas began a campaign to have his friend added to the team, writing letters to the selectors and pleading with officials. The officials finally relented and added Fields to the team as an alternate.

After fighting their way through the early rounds, the two found themselves pitted against each other for the gold medal. The final was a fiercely-fought match between these best friends, who had hugged and cried in the dressing room before entering the ring. The decision went to Fields, who returned to the dressing room crying because his best friend had lost.

Because of this hard-fought match between boxers from the same country, Olympic rules were changed to limit each country to one boxer in each weight category.

"TARZAN" EMERGES

The French had constructed a magnificent swimming pool for the Games, the Tourelles Baths. The pool was outdoors, but it was built at a height of three stories above ground so that furnaces under it could keep the water temperature at a constant 75 degrees.

Starring in the pool was young Johnny Weissmuller—forever to be remembered as Tarzan for his later film roles—who won both the 100-meter and 400-meter races, setting world records in both. Finishing second to Weissmuller in the 100 was the man who had won the 100 in both the 1912 and 1920 Games—Duke Kahanamoku, whose time was also under the world record.

In the 400 meters, Weissmuller shaved a full 20 seconds off the Olympic record. Then he won his third gold medal when he anchored the Americans to victory in the 800-meter relay, and he added a bronze medal as a member of the water polo team.

A WARMUP FOR THE CHANNEL

Another gold medal-winning swimmer who was to achieve later fame was American Gertrude Ederle. She was a member of the world record-setting women's 400-meter relay team, and also finished third in the 100- and 400-meter freestyle events. Two years later, Ederle became the first woman to swim the English Channel, completing the swim in 14 hours, 31 minutes—almost two hours faster than any man had ever covered the distance.

BIASED JUDGING

In women's platform diving, there was another example of the biased judging that has plagued some Olympic events. The American judge awarded a three-way tie for first to the three American divers. The Swedish judge awarded first place to the Swedish diver. The Danish judge awarded first place to the Danish diver. When the British and French judges' scores were factored in, first and second went to Americans, third to the Swede, and fourth to the Dane.

CONFLICTS IN FENCING

In fencing, the matches were so closely and fiercely fought that open hostilities erupted among the judges and the competitors from France, Italy, Belgium, and Hungary. There were so many disturbances that IOC representatives finally had to step in to help restore order.

In the final match of the team foil between Italy and France, the Italians disputed a judge's decision. In protest, the entire Italian team withdrew from the competition and the remainder of their matches were forfeited.

A FUTURE PEDIATRICIAN

In rowing, the Yale crew won the eight-oar competition for the United States. Rowing in the number seven position for the gold medalists was Ben Spock, later to become Dr. Benjamin Spock, the widely-published authority on the care of infants.

THE END OF THE OLYMPICS?

The 1924 Olympic Games, which came to a quiet close on July 27, were lauded by most as the best Olympics yet. But this opinion was not shared by all. There were journalists in Great Britain, France, and the United States who called for an end to the Olympics, saying that the various controversies, particularly those in boxing and fencing, were disgraceful, and outweighed anything positive that had come out of the 1924 Olympics.

The Times of London, under the headline "Olympic Games Doomed," cited, in a rather dramatic way, the problems of "miscellaneous turbulence, shameful disorder, storms of abuse, free fights, and the drowning of national anthems."

The Times article concluded: "The death knell of the Olympic Games has, in fact, been sounded." This anti-Olympic movement was over as quickly as it started, and de Coubertin, unfazed by it all, began making plans for the next, all-important meeting of the IOC.

DE COUBERTIN RETIRES

Early in 1925, the IOC met in Prague to receive the resignation of Baron Pierre de Coubertin as president, and to select a successor. Although there were members who did not want to accept de Coubertin's resignation, after much discussion Count Henri de Baillet-Latour of Belgium was elected president. By acclamation, the IOC members then named de Coubertin as honorary president of the Olympic Games for life.

In de Coubertin's written farewell to his colleagues, he concluded:

"The world institution that we have built up is ready to face any eventualities."

As great a visionary as de Coubertin was, even he could not possibly have dreamed how complex and threatening some of those "eventualities" were going to be.

Johnny Weissmuller

Olympiad IX
AMSTERDAM, 1928

THE DUTCH GET THEIR CHANCE

The city of Amsterdam began bidding for the Olympics in 1912, but politely continued to withdraw its candidacy in favor of other cities.

When the IOC met in 1921 to award the 1924 Games, Amsterdam again stepped aside so that de Coubertin's request to have Paris host the Games could be granted. Because the Dutch delegates had been both persistent and cooperative over the years, the IOC awarded the 1928 Games to Amsterdam at the 1921 meeting, giving the Dutch organizers a full seven years to make their preparations.

FUNDRAISING ON A GRAND SCALE

Attempts to adapt Amsterdam's only stadium for Olympic use were unsuccessful, so it was decided that a new facility had to be constructed, even though there was no money available for the project. After a number of fundraising schemes failed, including the establishment of a national lottery, it was the Dutch citizenry who came to Amsterdam's rescue.

With a steady barrage of requests for funds appearing in Dutch newspapers, cash donations and guarantees poured in from communities throughout Holland and even from faraway Dutch possessions. Thus, the financial success of the Amsterdam Olympics was guaranteed.

A magnificent 40,000-seat stadium was constructed on 40 acres of land reclaimed from marshland. The ground was so unstable that 4,500 pilings had to be driven into the swampy land to support the stadium's foundation.

By the spring of 1928, Amsterdam was gearing up to host the world. As the Games approached, the Dutch workers put the finishing touches on the stadium, completing the track on the day before the events were to begin.

INNOVATIONS

There were a number of "firsts" in the Amsterdam Olympics. An Olympic flame burned throughout the Games, atop a 250-foot tower above the stadium's main grandstand. Pigeons (1,000 in number) were released during the opening ceremonies. A message board was installed in the stadium to help keep spectators better informed. And, for the first time, women were allowed to participate in track and field events.

GERMANY RETURNS

In the Olympic spirit of goodwill among all nations, Germany was welcomed back into Olympic competition for the first time since World War I. The other "Central Power" nations—Austria, Hungary, Bulgaria, and Turkey—were considered lesser offenders and had been invited to participate in Paris four years earlier.

WOMEN IN TRACK AND FIELD

The welcome for women track and field athletes was not so warm. Women had been accepted in some of the other Olympic sports, but many people, including Baron de Coubertin, were not prepared to accept the participation of women in track and field, particularly in the "more strenuous" events, such as the 800 meters.

De Coubertin, citing the prohibition of women at the ancient Olympics, voiced his disapproval of the decision to add women's events to the track and field program. He was joined by Pope Pius XI, who condemned the decision on behalf of the Vatican.

One journalist wrote that women should not be allowed to enter the Olympics at all because they could not control their emotions. A physician wrote that nature made women to bear children, not to participate in feats of extreme endurance. Another said that women competing in sports were doing themselves irreparable harm and would "become old too soon."

One historian says the women were allowed in the track and field events only if they would wear shorts that were long enough to come within 4½ inches of the knees. However, photographs taken during the competitions show that if there was such a rule, the women ignored it.

A BRIEF APPEARANCE FOR WOMEN'S GYMNASTICS

Women's gymnastics events, which had been allowed only as exhibitions previously, were added for these Olympics, too, but they did not survive for long. They were dropped from the program after the 1928 Olympics and would not appear again until 1952.

USOC PRESIDENT MACARTHUR

The president of the U.S. Olympic Committee in 1928 was an outspoken 48-year-old military officer, Major General Douglas MacArthur, who would later gain fame as the Allied Commander in the Pacific Theater during World War II. Before the Games, MacArthur boasted, "We have assembled the greatest team in our athletic history. Americans can rest serene and assured."

COMFORTABLE QUARTERS

The U.S. Olympic Committee spared no expense in providing for the American athletes. They chartered a luxury liner, the *S.S. President Roosevelt*, for the trip across the Atlantic, complete with a running track, cycling and rowing machines, a fully-equipped gymnasium, a swimming pool, and even a portable diving tower.

Aboard the ship were also eleven coaches, six trainers, four managers, and a wide selection of excellent food. Stories of the amounts of food consumed during the transatlantic crossing are legendary. Sprinter Frank Wykoff, for example, reportedly gained more than ten pounds during the voyage.

The *Roosevelt* was large and comfortable enough for the U.S. team to continue living aboard it throughout the Olympic Games. The shipboard location was convenient for the Americans, in contrast to the housing arrangements for many of the other teams. Some complained

of being assigned to hotels as far as 38 miles out of Amsterdam, and had to suffer through daily bus rides over rough cobblestone roads.

THE FRENCH REFUSE TO MARCH

On Sunday, July 29, the stadium was overflowing with spectators for the opening ceremonies, which included the parade of all of the entered nations—except the French, who refused to march because of a disagreement with an anti-French stadium gatekeeper.

The gatekeeper had refused entry to the French team the day before, and the argument that followed ended when the president of the French Olympic Committee was punched in the face. The Dutch Olympic Committee apologized, but when the French learned the gatekeeper had not lost his job, they refused to march.

STUCK IN TRAFFIC

Most of the Finnish athletes were not included in the opening ceremonies parade either. They were caught in the huge crowd outside the stadium and could not get in the gates. A few Finns climbed a wall and managed to march in the parade, but most remained outside.

THE GAMES ARE OPENED

Because the Dutch government did not approve of Sunday activities, Queen Wilhelmina

The U.S. soccer team keeps in condition aboard the S.S. President Roosevelt.

was not able to participate at the opening. However, she was able to send her consort, Prince Hendrik, to represent her. His Royal Highness, the prince consort, officially opened the Games, followed by anthems sung by a vast chorus of 1,200 voices.

De Coubertin, now 65 years old, had to miss the Amsterdam games because of illness, but he sent a message to everyone taking part. Since he was certain he would not be able to attend the Los Angeles Olympics in 1932, the Baron said, "I should be wise to take the present opportunity of bidding you farewell."

PROFESSIONALISM AN ISSUE

Professionalism became the subject of great discussion, and occasional argument, during the 1928 Olympics. There were some complaints about the American system of providing fully subsidized, intensive training programs for college athletes.

There was even greater controversy over the International Soccer Federation's support of payment for "broken time," a plan for continuing a player's salary who had to miss work to participate in sports. Payment for broken time was bitterly opposed by the IOC and many individual nations, especially Great Britain. As a protest, the British team withdrew from the soccer competition.

NURMI LEADS THE FINNS
TO NEW HEIGHTS

On the track, the Flying Finn, Paavo Nurmi, was back again to try to defend his "title" as the world's greatest distance runner. But at age 32, he found himself unable to repeat his previous successes. There was simply too much distance to cover in too short a time: the 10,000 final, which followed the opening ceremonies on Sunday, a 5000 heat on Tuesday, a 3000 steeplechase heat on Wednesday, the 5000 final on Friday, and the steeplechase final on Saturday.

Nurmi was able to win the 10,000 in Olympic record time, and he finished second in the 5000 and the steeplechase behind fellow Finns Ville Ritola and Toivo Loukola. Some historians insist that Nurmi could have won all three races, but Finnish officials had determined in advance the outcome of each race.

Nurmi and Ritola made life difficult for Edwin Wide, Sweden's outstanding distance runner. Wide finished behind the Finns on four different occasions in the 1924 and 1928 Olympics. Wide's one silver and three bronze medals would all have been gold had it not been for Paavo Nurmi and Ville Ritola.

DISAPPOINTING U.S. PERFORMANCES

There was a decided contrast between the successes of the Finnish runners and the unexpected decline of the American track and field team, which made its most dismal showing since the revival of the Olympics. Critics credited the failure of the U.S. team to a combination of "overeating and overconfidence."

In response to the criticisms which were appearing daily in American newspapers, the ever-optimistic Douglas MacArthur sent a cable, reprinted in the *New York Times*, which said: "The athletes had a specially prepared menu prescribed by the dietician who accompanied the team to Amsterdam."

He did not, however, mention if the dietician also prescribed the sizes of the portions.

ANOTHER TARZAN

The silver medalist in the shot put was American Herman Brix, who was in the lead for the gold medal with an Olympic record during the first rounds of the competition. But his mark of 51 feet 8 inches was surpassed in the final round by teammate John Kuck, who broke both Brix's Olympic record and the world record, with a put of 52 feet $3/4$ inch. Herman Brix later became Bruce Bennett and starred in several Hollywood movies, even appearing once as Tarzan.

A TRUE IRISH VICTORY

The hammer throw was again won by someone who was born in Ireland, but this time it was an Irish citizen, Patrick O'Callaghan. From 1900 through 1920, each winner had been an Irish-born U.S. policeman. The Irish-American winners were John Flanagan in 1900, 1904, and 1908, Matt McGrath in 1912, and Pat Ryan in 1920.

O'Callaghan, who was to take the title again four years later, was coached by the three-time gold medalist Flanagan, who had retired from the New York Police Department and returned to Ireland.

THE BIZARRE WOMEN'S 800

There were only five track and field events for women—100 meters, 800 meters, the sprint relay, high jump, and discus. In the 800 meters, the meet organizers' worst fears were realized. Many of the competitors (some of whom had never run the distance before) were so exhausted at the end of the race that they began collapsing on the track, some of them before reaching the finish line.

Because of that bizarre finish and the public's response to it, the IOC decided to drop the 800 meters from the women's program. The president of the IOC, Count Henri Baillet-Latour, even suggested eliminating all women's events from the Olympics, but the other IOC members did not agree with him.

It would be 32 years before the women's 800 meters would return to the Olympic Games.

FALSE STARTS

In the women's 100 meters, Myrtle Cook of Canada and Leni Schmidt of Germany were disqualified before the race began for having two false starts. The two sprinters responded with completely different emotions.

Cook sat near the starting line and sobbed uncontrollably. Schmidt swore and shook her fist at the starter.

A SURPRISE FINISH

Johnny Weissmuller again emerged as the star of the swimming pool, repeating as gold medalist in the 100-meter freestyle and as a member of the 4 x 200 relay. When Weissmuller decided not to swim the 400, it was generally accepted that the 400 final would be a two-man affair between Arne Borg of Sweden and Andrew "Boy" Charlton of Australia. Borg and Charlton had finished second and third behind Weissmuller in the previous Olympics.

Throughout most of the race, Borg and Charlton were swimming at a relatively slow pace, each watching the other carefully, playing a cat and mouse game. After the final turn, Charlton outswam Borg in a furious sprint to the finish. Both were shocked to see that Alberto Zorilla of Argentina, who, swimming unnoticed in an outside lane, had finished a full two seconds ahead of Charlton to win the gold medal.

**The women's 800 meters.
Winner Lina Radke of Germany in front.**

A MAJOR JUDGING ERROR

A mixup in the judging of the high dive event caused a long delay in the victory ceremony. Farid Simaika of Egypt was declared the winner, based on total points, and he took the victory stand as the Egyptian flag was raised and the anthem was played. Then the officials realized the finish should have been based on judges' placings, not on total points. They interrupted the anthem, lowered the flag, and apologized to Simaika. Peter Desjardins of the United States, who was not even present, was declared the winner.

COMPLAINTS IN WRESTLING

There were endless controversies over the officiating in the wrestling competitions. The Americans, in particular, complained that the rules had been changed to favor other nations. In the U.S. Olympic Committee's report, authored by Douglas MacArthur, it says: "With rules interpreted as they have been in former Olympic

Games, the U.S. wrestling team should have won at least six championships. Every man, without exception, took his man to the mat, only to be eliminated by decisions that had never been allowed in Olympic competition before and which all admitted should never be allowed again. In the face of such conditions, it is a wonder that anyone won."

MORE UNSPORTSMANLIKE CONDUCT

The ugly scenes that marred the boxing events in the Paris Olympics were repeated and even intensified in Amsterdam. The fans, and even some of the boxers themselves, hooted their disapproval when they disagreed with a decision, which was often. After one match, in which Piero Toscani of Italy won a controversial decision over Jan Hermanek of Czechoslovakia, the spectators rioted, culminating in a brawl between police and spectators.

After another match, the Hungarians and the Dutch threatened further violence. The Argentineans stormed the ring, as they had done in Paris, when one of their favorites lost. The vice president of the International Boxing Federation called it a "scandalous travesty." A *London Daily Telegraph* reporter wrote: "It was as if there were no sanity; only men, wild-eyed and raucous of voice."

THE GAMES COME TO A CLOSE

The closing of the Olympic Games included the awarding of medals to the victorious athletes. Queen Wilhelmina gave out the gold medals, Prince Hendrik the silver, and IOC president Count Baillet-Latour the bronze.

After the Games, Douglas MacArthur issued a glowing, optimistic, somewhat exaggerated report on the performance of his American team.

Selective in his recollections of the events in Amsterdam, he wrote: "The team proved itself a worthy successor of its brilliant predecessors."

Olympiad X
LOS ANGELES, 1932

MUCH TO OVERCOME

Los Angeles had been chosen as the site of the 1932 Olympics at the IOC meeting in Rome in 1923, giving the organizers an unprecedented nine years in which to prepare. Los Angeles was anxious to show that Southern California was as capable of staging the Olympics as any of the European cities.

But by 1930, the world was plunged into a grim economic depression, and with the growing political tensions in Europe and Asia, there were many who felt the Los Angeles Games should be canceled. Even the U.S. Olympic Committee was having trouble raising the funds to transport American athletes from other parts of the country to Los Angeles.

The spirit and the tenacity of William May Garland and his fellow Los Angeles organizers and the support of the world's Olympic committees prevailed, however. Los Angeles was able to stage the first of the expensive, highly-organized spectacles that have since typified the Olympics.

FEWER TEAMS, BUT LARGER CROWDS

Because of the relative isolation of Los Angeles at that time and the effects of the depression, there were fewer participants than in any of the five previous Olympics, but the games drew the largest audiences in Olympic history. The 105,000-seat stadium and the other sports venues were at least half-filled every day and attracted capacity crowds for several events.

ATTRACTING FOREIGN NATIONS

The Los Angeles organizers had come up with a bold plan to encourage nations to come to the Olympics who might otherwise have had to stay at home because of a lack of funds. They constructed the first-ever complete Olympic village and they offered lodging, food, transportation, and the use of training facilities for $2 per day for every competitor. They also made arrangements with steamship and rail companies to offer reduced fares for Olympic teams.

The organizers remained uneasy about their plan until the spring of 1932, when they began to hear from Olympic committees from around the world. Japan would send 150 competitors, Great Britain would send 100, Italy 100, France 100, Germany 90. In all, 36 foreign nations said they would attend.

FILLING THE SEATS

The next objective was to attract spectators. But that problem was solved as soon as the athletes began arriving at the various ports around the United States. Newspapers and radio stations became immediate advocates of the Olympics, the public began scrambling for tickets, and financial success was assured.

MANCHUKUO DENIED ENTRY

As always, there were political squabbles. In September of 1931, Japan had invaded Manchuria, forming the puppet nation they called Manchukuo.

Japan sent forms to the Los Angeles organizers, entering Manchukuo in the Olympic Games. The Los Angeles organizers refused the entry, ruling that Manchukuo was not a member of the family of nations. The IOC agreed with the decision.

NURMI RULED INELIGIBLE

The great Paavo Nurmi of Finland, winner of nine gold medals in three previous Olympics, arrived in Los Angeles for the Games, hoping to enter the 10,000 and the marathon, but he had to be content to be a spectator.

Despite the protests of the Finnish officials, it was ruled that Nurmi had received excessive expense money during a European tour and could no longer be classified as an amateur. (One official reportedly remarked that Nurmi had the lowest heartbeat and the highest asking price of any athlete in the world.) The Los Angeles organizers were disappointed, since they had been counting on Nurmi to help build gate receipts.

THORPE ATTENDS

Another former Olympian attending the Los Angeles Games was the great decathlon and pentathlon champion of the 1912 Games, Jim Thorpe. Some accounts say he stood outside the stadium before the opening ceremonies, unable to pay the $3 admission price. He was recognized by some journalists who got him into the pressbox where, according to one account, he "wept openly."

In the movie, *The Jim Thorpe Story,* on which he served as technical advisor, Thorpe was given a ticket by his college coach, Pop Warner, and the two sat together through the opening ceremonies. In the film, Thorpe stayed in his seat until nightfall, long after everyone else had left the stadium.

THE BRAZILIAN ODYSSEY

Brazil's Olympic team did not have enough money to get to Los Angeles, so the Brazilian government offered the team a ship and 50,000 bags of coffee to sell in the ports along the way. However, the price of coffee was in decline at that time and sales were paltry. When the ship reached Los Angeles, only 24 of the Brazilian athletes disembarked. They were the only ones who could afford the $1 per head landing tax.

The crew and the other 45 athletes set sail again to try to locate coffee customers. The ship finally returned to Los Angeles after more unsuccessful attempts to sell the coffee, picked up the 24 athletes who had already participated in the Olympics, and returned to Brazil.

HOMES FOR THE ATHLETES

The Olympic village, consisting of 550 prefabricated two-room cottages, was built to house 1,300 male athletes and 900 coaches, trainers, and managers. There were also 40 kitchens and dining rooms, a lounge, a library, a post office, a hospital, a fire station, and an open-air theater where films of the previous day's events were shown. The entire village was surrounded by a high fence, which was patrolled by cowboys on horseback. Situated on a quiet hill near the ocean, the village was only a ten-minute ride from the stadium.

The 127 women competitors had the exclusive use of The Chapman Park Hotel on Wilshire Boulevard, where they also paid only $2 per day.

MORE INNOVATIONS

Besides the introduction of the Olympic village, there were several other innovations in Los Angeles. Free bus service between venues, a victory stand for award ceremonies, and teletype communications for the press were all introduced at Los Angeles.

SECURITY AT THE VENUES

Security was not an important issue at the Los Angeles Olympics. Only 200 police officers were hired for security and crowd control during the time of the Games. (When the Olympics returned to Los Angeles in 1984, 20,000 security officers were hired, at a cost of $100 million.)

THE OPENING CEREMONIES

A crowd of 105,000 spectators filled the new Coliseum to capacity for the opening ceremonies, which lasted two hours. The ceremonies began with the singing of *The Star Spangled Banner* by a massed chorus in white robes, followed by the entrance and the march-by of the Olympic athletes, country by country, into the stadium.

The veteran Hawaiian swimmer, 41-year-old Duke Kahanamoku, marched with the U.S. team for the final time, but not as a member of the swimming team. He was a reserve member of the water polo team. The U.S. won the bronze medal in water polo, but Kahanamoku was not called upon to compete.

The flagbearer for the Chinese team, sprinter Cheng Chun-liu, was the only participant from China. Cheng represented 400 million Chinese people.

President Herbert Hoover, who was busy campaigning for reelection, sent Vice President Charles Curtis to represent him. A number of Olympic history books say it was the first time the host country's head of state did not attend. However, Theodore Roosevelt definitely did not attend the 1904 Olympics in St. Louis, and there is no record that France's president, Emile Loubet, attended the Paris Games in 1900.

Curtis declared the Games officially open, the torch at the top of the stadium's peristyle was lit electronically, and the Olympic oath was taken for all of the competitors by an American fencer, Lieutenant George Calnan, who had participated in four Olympic Games. Then the chorus sang *Hymn Olympique* as the athletes marched out of the stadium.

At the request of the public address announcer, the audience remained seated for an additional ten minutes so the athletes could be transported back to their living quarters without any traffic problems.

THE AMERICANS PREVAIL ON THE TRACK

The U.S. track and field team, anxious to atone for its disappointing showing in the 1928 Games, was overwhelmingly dominant, winning 16 of the 29 events, breaking 15 Olympic records and 8 world records. No other nation won more than three gold medals.

THE "BABE"

The star of the 1932 Olympic Games was an 18-year-old schoolgirl from Texas named Mildred Ella Didrikson. Didrikson was much better known as Babe, a nickname she had been given by schoolmates because she could hit a baseball like Babe Ruth. (One historian says the preferred family spelling was Didriksen. It is true the family name was Didriksen, but Babe herself insisted on spelling it Didrikson. Her name had been spelled incorrectly on school records and she refused to correct it. Her friends and family explained it away by saying that Babe simply did things to be different.)

A month before the Olympics were to open, Didrikson was the lone entrant representing her employer, the Employers Casualty Company of Dallas, in the national track and field championships in Evanston, Illinois. In the meet, which was also the U.S. Olympic Trials, Didrikson won the shot put, javelin throw, long jump, baseball throw, and 80-meter hurdles, tied for first in the high jump, and finished fourth in the discus throw. Two of her performances were American records.

Didrikson scored 30 points to win the national team championship by herself. The 22-member Illinois Women's Athletic Club finished second with 22 points.

Needless to say, Babe Didrikson was

Babe Didrikson

well-known to sports fans and sports writers when she arrived in Los Angeles. She had also been an All-American basketball player and she had participated in many other sports before becoming a sensation in track and field. One journalist who was curious about Didrikson's great versatility and her ability to excel in every sport she had tried, asked her, "Is there anything at all you don't play?"

"Yeah," she answered, "dolls."

In later life, of course, as Babe Didrikson Zaharias, she went on to an outstanding career as a professional golfer. She died of cancer at the early age of 42.

Women were limited to only three events in the Olympics. In the javelin, she won the gold by 8 inches, setting a new American and Olympic record. In the hurdles, she won in a photo finish, setting a world record.

In the high jump, Didrikson tied for first with teammate Jean Shiley, at 5 feet 5 inches, a world record—both clearing on their second attempt. They each failed three times to clear 5 feet 5³/₄ inches, so a fourth attempt (jump-off) was given.

Both cleared it, but the judges ruled that

Didrikson's jump was an illegal "dive," with her head clearing the crossbar slightly before her feet cleared. Shiley was awarded the gold medal, but, interestingly, both were credited with the world record at 5 feet 5 inches, since jump-off clearances (fourth attempts) were not allowed for record purposes. One historian wrote of the disallowed clearance: "It was a preposterous decision!"

WALSH RETURNS TO WALASIEWICZ

Stella Walsh, a Polish immigrant living in Cleveland, Ohio, who was the top female sprinter in the United States, was asked if she would compete as a member of the U.S. track and field team. Even though she was seeking U.S. citizenship at the time, she elected to compete for her native Poland under her original name, Stanislawa Walasiewicz. She won the gold medal in the 100 meters, equaling the world record, and finished sixth in the discus throw.

A DISTANCE RACE CONTROVERSY

The partisan U.S. crowd voiced vigorous disapproval over the finish of the 5000-meter run. Unheralded Ralph Hill of the U.S. had moved up on the favorite, Lauri Lehtinen of Finland, and was attempting to pass him in the final lap. The Finn began to run wide, forcing Hill to break his stride.

Then Hill tried to pass on the inside, but he was cut off again. At the finish tape, the American lost the race by such a small margin that the two were both timed in 14 minutes, 30 seconds, a new Olympic record. The booing of the crowd continued until the public address announcer said, "Remember, please, these people are our guests." The announcer was journalist and Olympic historian Bill Henry.

The next day, during the awards ceremony, Lehtinen stood on top of the victory stand to receive his gold medal. He reached down to Hill, who was on the second step, and tried to pull him up to share the top position.

Hill declined politely. Then Lehtinen pinned a small Finnish flag on Hill's shirt, to the delight of the crowd.

TOO CLOSE TO CALL

The 110-meter high hurdles final was so close that the finish line motion pictures were viewed, but not until after the medals had already been awarded. The films showed that American Jack Keller, who had received the bronze medal, had actually finished in fourth place behind Britain's Don Finlay. Keller went to the British quarters so he could personally present the medal to Finlay.

ANOTHER PHOTO FINISH

In the final of the 100 meters, the race for first was so close that officials waited until the motion picture film was developed before announcing that Eddie Tolan had beaten Ralph Metcalfe by two inches. Years later, Metcalfe said, "I'll never believe I really lost." (One Olympic history book says, without further explanation, that Metcalfe "reached" the finish line first, but Tolan "crossed" the finish line first.)

AN UNEXPECTED HANDICAP RACE

In the 200 meters, U.S. sprinters Eddie Tolan, George Simpson, and Ralph Metcalfe swept the medals. After the race it was discovered that Metcalfe's lane had been mismeasured and he had run farther than anyone else. At the time, Metcalfe refused to ask for a rerun, but years later, when he was serving as a member of Congress, Metcalfe remarked privately that he should have been the Olympic champion.

AN EXTRA LAP

In the 3000-meter steeplechase, Finland's Volmari Iso-Hollo set an Olympic record of 9:14.6 in the preliminaries, but managed only 10:33.4 in the final, even though he won easily. It was discovered that a substitute official had miscounted the laps and everyone had run an additional lap.

The error may have cost America's Joe McCluskey the silver medal; he was second at the 3000 mark, but was passed by Tom Evenson of England during the extra lap. Evenson offered to trade medals with McCluskey, but McCluskey said he was happy to have the bronze.

A WORLD RECORD FOR SECOND PLACE

Because of the rules in force at the time, Glenn Hardin of the United States became the world record holder in the 400-meter hurdles, even though he didn't win the race. Bob Tisdale of Ireland beat Hardin to the tape to win the gold medal. Since he had knocked over a hurdle, however, the world record was awarded to Hardin, whose second-place time was also under the previous record.

AN UNMEASURED "RECORD"

A French discus thrower, Jules Noël, may have had the longest throw in the discus competition, but he didn't even win a medal. Noël got off one magnificent throw which, according to many spectators, was the best throw of the competition by far. But all of the judges were watching the pole vault competition at that moment and no one saw where the discus landed.

The embarrassed judges allowed Noel an additional throw, but he couldn't match his previous "best effort." Noël finished fourth.

During the discus competition, Noël returned to his dressing room between throws to drink wine with his teammates. It was the height of prohibition in the United States, but the French had been given permission to bring in thousands of bottles of wine during the period of the Olympic Games, since wine was considered to be part of a Frenchman's regular diet.

ANOTHER FUTURE MOVIE STAR

In the pool, the young Japanese swimmers dominated in the swimming events. The only person to break the Japanese dominance was American Clarence Crabbe, who won the 400 meters in Olympic record time. "Buster" Crabbe, as he was better known, later became a film star, and was another movie Tarzan for a short time before moving on to portray space travelers Buck Rogers and Flash Gordon, among other roles.

A REAL CRASH DIET

A 29-year-old Swedish wrestler, Ivar Johansson, performed an amazing double, winning gold medals in both the middleweight division of freestyle wrestling and the welterweight division of Greco-Roman wrestling. It was a difficult double victory because Johansson weighed 169 pounds when he won the middleweight title at 1:00 P.M. on August 3, but could weigh no more than 159 pounds when he entered the first rounds of the welterweight division the next morning. Johansson was able to lose the weight by taking hot baths, sitting in a sauna, and electing not to eat or drink.

Buster Crabbe

ESCAPE FROM THE HOSPITAL

A New Zealand cyclist, Ron Foubister, was taken from the Olympic Village to a Los Angeles hospital with suspected appendicitis. As the doctors were conferring over the diagnosis, Foubister was put on a liquid diet, which he didn't care for.

Dressed in his pajamas, Foubister slipped out of the hospital, took a taxi back to the Olympic village, changed into his clothes, and had a meal of steak and eggs, topped off with a large helping of ice cream. Then he went out for a long training ride. The next day, the *San Francisco Examiner*, reporting on Foubister's experience, said, "You can't keep a good New Zealander down!"

IN PURSUIT OF THE REFEREE

Members of the Brazilian water polo team had a major disagreement with a Hungarian referee during an early round match against Germany. When the referee penalized the Brazilians for committing a foul, the Brazilians climbed out of the pool and verbally, then physically, attacked the referee, who ran up into the stands. The police were summoned to call off the angry Brazilians, who were required to forfeit their remaining games.

THE BRAWLERS END UP IN PRISON

There was a small revolution and a minor brawl among the Argentineans in the Olympic village during the games. Besides fighting among themselves, the athletes accused the team manager of being dictatorial and refused to cooperate with him. The trouble continued after the Games, with arguments and fights breaking out on the ship as the team sailed back to Argentina.

The ship's captain was forced to put the entire team under armed confinement until they reached Buenos Aires. As soon as they docked, the more militant of the athletes, including Santiago Lovell, the heavyweight boxing gold medalist, were taken to prison.

THE GAMES COME TO A CLOSE

When the Los Angeles Olympics came to a close and the records were compiled, it was agreed that these were among the most successful of Olympic Games. There were many outstanding achievements. Problems were minimal. And despite the economic conditions, the Games were profitable, earning the organizers almost $1 million in profits.

A crowd of more than 100,000 attended the closing ceremonies at sundown on August 14. The Olympic chorus sang *Aloha,* the Olympic flag was lowered, trumpeters played *Taps,* and the Olympic flame flickered and then disappeared.

Olympiad XI
BERLIN, 1936

THE NAZIS EMERGE

When it was announced in 1931 that Berlin would be hosting the Olympic Games five years later, Germany's fledgling Nazi party called the event "an infamous festival dominated by Jews." But after the Nazis came to power in 1933 and the Games neared, it became evident to the new German chancellor, Adolf Hitler, that the Olympics could have enormous propaganda value for the Germans.

Thus, Hitler decided to spare no expense in making the "Nazi Olympics" the best organized and most efficiently run Games ever. Government money was spent lavishly to make these Olympics memorable, for the glory of sport, and, of course, for the glory of Hitler's Third Reich.

GROWING DISCRIMINATION

As Hitler's power grew, the Jews in Germany began facing increasing hostility and persecution from the Nazis. Jewish businesses and professions were openly boycotted. Jewish citizens were subject to attack and harassment. On two occasions, Germany was called before the League of Nations to answer charges of discrimination against Jews and other "non-Aryans." Germany solved that problem by dropping out of the League of Nations.

The head of the German Olympic Organizing Committee, Dr. Theodor Lewald, was of Jewish descent—his paternal grandmother was a Jew. The Nazis first forced Dr. Lewald to resign from the national sports committee. Then they attempted to have him removed from the German and International Olympic Committees. The IOC members, however, stood behind Lewald and threatened to cancel the Games unless they were to be entirely nonpolitical in character and organized in the spirit of the Olympic ideal. Reluctantly, Hitler agreed to the terms.

THREATS TO BOYCOTT

Movements to boycott the Games because of the persecution of Jews began in France in 1933, an idea that spread quickly to many of the other countries of the world. In Great Britain, the debate carried all the way to the House of Commons. Strangely, it was a noted Jewish athlete, 1924 Olympic 100-meter champion Harold Abrahams, who convinced the British Amateur Athletic Association that Britain should attend.

Nowhere was the fight to boycott the Olympics greater than in the United States. A request that the United States withdraw from the Games was debated in the U.S. Senate. A proposal to discourage the use of public funds to finance the trip was introduced in Congress.

As opposition to U.S. participation began to mount, Avery Brundage, head of the U. S. Olympic Committee and a member of the IOC executive committee, was sent to Germany on a special fact-finding mission. His pronouncement on his return that "Jewish athletes in Germany are not being discriminated against" raised a further furor among those pressing for a boycott.

But when a vote was taken at the national convention of the Amateur Athletic Union in 1935, the motion to participate in the Games passed by a narrow 58-56 margin. The boycott proponents stormed out of the meeting, and Brundage immediately announced: "The United States will go to the Olympics, no matter what."

NAZI CONCESSIONS

As the Games approached, a number of concessions were made by the Nazis. Anti-Semitic signs were removed from the streets. Token Jews were asked to join the German Olympic team, including champion fencer Helene Mayer, who was living with her parents in California at the time. And a Jew, Wolfgang Fürstner, was selected to design and construct the Olympic village. In fact, in order to influence world opinion, the entire anti-Semitic campaign was muted for the duration of the Games.

BRUNDAGE VS. JARRETT

One of the most publicized incidents associated with the 1936 Olympics was the decision by Avery Brundage to drop Olympic champion swimmer Eleanor Holm Jarrett from the Olympic team. Jarrett, who had become a film actress and night club singer after setting an Olympic record in the backstroke in the 1932 Games, was accused of drinking, smoking, shooting craps, disregarding curfews, and generally carousing on the nine-day voyage to Europe. Jarrett didn't help her case when she announced, "I trained on champagne and caviar."

The incident was a cause célèbre, both in Europe and at home. She received numerous telegrams of support from fans in the U.S. A petition asking clemency was signed by 220 of her Olympic teammates.

But Brundage was adamant. Jarrett had been warned several times, had been put on probation, had been given "one more chance," and, according to Brundage, "had been drinking for a week since my last warning." Jarrett, who had not lost a race in seven years, was off the team.

During the Berlin Olympics, Jarrett served as a news service correspondent, but she said later all of her articles were ghostwritten by Paul Gallico, a writer with the *New York Times*. During the Games she had a meeting with Adolf Hitler, and reported later: "He said if I'd been on the German team, they'd have kept me on the team and then punished me after the Olympics—if I had lost!"

THE VILLAGE

Berlin's Olympic village, covering 134 acres and designed to house 4,000 athletes, was a stunning model city of brick and stucco cottages, swimming pool, library, hospital, theater, and 38 dining halls. Later, the entire complex would be turned into an officers' club for the military. Each cottage was named for a German city, which caused some amusement among the Australians when they were assigned to Worms House.

On display in the beautifully-landscaped village, amid the modern structures, was one of the small, plain wooden cottages the Americans had used as part of their Olympic village four years earlier. The Germans had purchased the building after the 1932 Games in Los Angeles and moved it to Berlin to contrast it with Germany's far more impressive village.

RECORD CROWDS

More than four-and-a-half million tickets were sold for the various events, with virtually all of the venues drawing capacity crowds every day. Even exhibition sports drew record numbers. The baseball exhibition game, which featured two unknown U.S. amateur teams, drew more than 100,000 spectators, the largest crowd ever to witness a baseball game up to that time— even in the World Series.

For the first time, there was television coverage of the Olympic Games. German citizens who were not able to get tickets to the Games could view the Games on screens set up in 25 movie theaters in Berlin and other theaters throughout Germany. More than 160,000 people crowded the theaters daily to watch the Olympic events.

THE FIRST TORCH RUN

For the first time, a flame ignited by rays of the sun at Olympia, Greece, was relayed by torch to the site of the modern Olympic Games. The torch was carried by 3,075 runners, each covering one kilometer of the route through Greece, Bulgaria, Yugoslavia, Hungary, Austria, Czechoslovakia, and Germany. Although several modes of transportation have been incorporated into the torch relay since 1936, the practice of transporting the flame from Greece to the site of the Olympic Games has continued to this day.

The ceremony at Olympia takes place before the Temple of Hera, at the site of the ancient Olympic Games. During the ceremony, no one is allowed to enter the sacred area except the high priestess, who kindles the flame, and the vestals who assist her. The flame is kindled by using a parabolic mirror which concentrates the rays of the sun on twigs from nearby trees.

Once the fire has begun, it is carried to the site of a public ceremony, where it is handed to the first of the relay runners.

Many Olympic books and newspaper articles have said the Olympic flame is ignited on Mount

Olympus and is relayed from there. However, Mount Olympus is approximately 300 miles north of Olympia and has never had any connection with the Olympics, either ancient or modern.

POMP AND CEREMONY

A capacity crowd of 110,000 people, including 3,000 journalists, jammed the stadium for the opening ceremonies. There were more flags with Nazi swastikas than Olympic flags outside the stadium, but most of the swastikas and Nazi slogans inside the stadium had been removed at the insistence of the IOC. Most accounts say there were no swastikas inside the stadium, but there were swastikas on the German national flags, the German participants' uniforms, and on the huge Olympic bell which had been cast especially for these Olympics.

The Olympic bell, which is still on display outside the Berlin stadium, shows there are swastikas on both sides of the phrase, *Ich rufe die Jugend der Welt* ("I call the youth of the world"), which circles the base of the bell. The swastikas on the bell had been filled in with metal by the Allies after the war, to make them appear to be squares, but "vandals" have since chiseled the metal out, making the swastikas visible again.

The traditional parade of the teams began, with Greece the first country to enter the stadium. At the head of Greek team marched a 65-year-old man dressed in his native Greek costume. The spectators did not realize until later that he was Spiridon Louis, the winner of the first marathon in the 1896 Olympics in Athens.

As the teams marched in front of the reviewing stand, their various salutes brought contrasting reactions from the partisan German audience. The Canadian and French teams gave the straight-arm Olympic salute, similar to the Nazi salute, and received ovations from the crowd. Britain's curt "eyes right" was received with stony silence, and the United States' refusal to dip the flag was greeted with foot stomping and whistles of disapproval. The political implications were obvious.

The 500-member German team marched in last, wearing solid white military uniforms. The crowd broke into a chorus of the German anthem, *Deutschland Über Alles*, as the German athletes, looking more like soldiers than athletes,

took their places in the infield.

Following Hitler's one-sentence declaration that the Olympic Games were open, the Olympic flag was raised, along with the flags of all nations around the perimeter of the stadium, and 20,000 carrier pigeons— symbolizing doves of peace— were released. (The top pigeon breeders in Germany had submitted 80,000 of their finest birds; the best 20,000 were selected for the opening ceremonies.) All of the pigeons, except one, returned to their owners. The lone dissenter took up residence in the stadium and was seen flying around daily during the Games.

The final torchbearer, blond and "Aryan-looking" Fritz Schilgen, entered the stadium and ran down a long flight of steps leading to the track. He ran the length of the stadium, on the track, with the torch held high, and ran up the steps at the opposite end of the stadium to a large steel urn. There he touched the torch to the urn, which was immediately crowned in flame. The huge crowd roared its approval.

Then it was announced that Spiridon Louis, the winner of the first Olympic marathon race, was on the infield. He was escorted to Hitler's box, where, in one of the most moving moments of these ceremonies, Louis presented Hitler with an olive branch from the sacred grove of Olympia, a stark symbol of peace. Louis was dressed in his native Greek costume. Hitler was dressed in his military uniform.

HITLER'S INTEREST IN THE GAMES

To everyone's surprise, Hitler attended most of the track and field final events, showing great enthusiasm, rocking back and forth nervously, and often jumping to his feet. He was so much a part of the show that when he was late arriving one day, the 1500-meter final was delayed until he could get to his seat.

ARYAN SUPREMACY QUASHED

The U.S. dominated the track and field events, thanks largely to the ten black athletes on the team who won six gold, three silver, and two bronze medals. Referred to as "African Auxiliaries" by Joseph Goebbels, Germany's propaganda minister, the ten athletes scored more victories than every other nation in the track and field competition, including the rest of the U.S. team.

58

From his box in the stadium, Hitler was forced to watch a living denial of the Nazi theory of Aryan superiority.

A CORDIAL WELCOME

The black Americans were treated surprisingly cordially during their stay in Germany. Mack Robinson, the 200-meter silver medalist and older brother of future baseball star Jackie Robinson, tellingly said later, "In Germany the people treated us very well. What was difficult was returning to the United States and again having to sit in the back of the bus as a second-class citizen."

J.C. OWENS

America's Jesse Owens—winner of four gold medals—emerged as the hero of the Games. In nine of his twelve appearances in preliminary and final events, he either broke or tied Olympic records, and on five of those occasions he bettered world records. He won gold medals in the 100, 200, long jump, and 400-meter relay.

Born James Cleveland Owens in Danville, Alabama, Jesse Owens was known as J. C. by his family and friends until the Owens family moved to Cleveland, Ohio, in 1922. When the nine-year-old told his new teacher his name was J.C., she thought he said Jesse. The name stuck.

THE FAMOUS "SNUB"

The popular fable that Jesse Owens was "snubbed" by Adolf Hitler has lived on, despite the efforts of Owens at the time, and historians later, to dispel it. As historian Bill Henry has written: "The fable persists that Hitler refused to shake hands with Owens, though the fact is that he never had the opportunity."

The story goes that Hitler left the stadium early so he would not have to congratulate Jesse Owens after Owens won one of his gold medals.

However, Hitler's famous departure from the stadium was made on August 2, the first day of the track and field competition and the day before Owens won his first gold medal.

Hitler had congratulated the winners in the shot put (a German), the first three finishers in the 10,000-meter run (three Finns), and the first two finishers in the women's javelin (both Germans). The other final event of the day, the high jump,

required a jump-off to decide second, third, and fourth place, and was not completed until after dark, almost four hours after the event had begun.

Hitler, who had overstayed his intended time in the stadium, left before the high jump was completed, and so was not present to congratulate the eventual winner, Cornelius Johnson, a black American.

Newspapers everywhere carried the story about Hitler's snub of a black American athlete. A headline in the *New York Times* read, "Hitler Ignores Negro Medalists." The "negro medalists" were Cornelius Johnson and Dave Albritton, the two U.S. high jumpers. Later, after Owens became the star of the Olympics, the story was altered to say that Hitler had snubbed Jesse Owens.

The day after the high jump competition, Hitler was informed by Count Henri de Baillet-Latour, the president of the IOC, that as merely a guest of honor at the Games, Hitler would either congratulate all winners or none. Because his schedule would not allow him to be present for all the Olympic events, Hitler chose not to congratulate any more winners publicly.

According to Owens, Hitler was not able to offer him personal congratulations, but he did pay Owens a special tribute by standing and waving to him at one point. Owens was quoted at the time, "When I passed the Chancellor he arose, waved his hand at me, and I waved back at him. I think the writers showed bad taste in criticizing the man of the hour in Germany."*

After the Olympics, when asked about the snub, Owens responded, "People kept writing that Hitler snubbed me. If he did, I never noticed." Jesse Owens continued to deny the snub story until World War II broke out and it became extremely popular for Americans to denigrate Hitler. Then he stopped denying the story.

It must be remembered that Jesse Owens and his teammates were not concerned with the politics of Nazi Germany in 1936. They had had no reason to harbor a dislike for Adolf Hitler, any more than they would for white supremacists in America, who were common at that time. Few could foresee the horror that Hitler would unleash on the world three years later. Not until the late 1930s did it become routine for Americans to be rabidly anti-Hitler.

JESSE'S LATER RECOLLECTIONS

More than 40 years later, Jesse Owens co-authored two books about his experiences at the 1936 Olympics. In both books he wrote that Hitler had snubbed him by not being present for the long jump preliminaries on August 4, two days after Hitler had been accused of snubbing Cornelius Johnson. (It should be noted, first, that Hitler attended few, if any, preliminary events. Second, if Hitler's absence was a snub of Owens, he was also snubbing Long, the German long jumper who had the best chance of outjumping Owens for the gold medal.)

In one of the accounts, Owens wrote: "I looked at Hitler's box. Empty. His way of saying that Owens was inferior." In the other, he wrote: "He'd already snubbed me once by refusing the Olympic Committee's request to have me sit in that box." Hitler was present throughout the long jump finals later that day, where he watched Owens beat Long to win his second of four gold medals.

In a 1974 interview, Owens said, "I wasn't invited up to shake hands with Hitler, but I wasn't invited to the White House to shake hands with the President, either."

INSTANT FAME

Owens was surprised and pleased by his growing popularity with the German fans during the Olympics. When he competed, the crowd would chant, "Yes-See Oh-Vens, Yes-See Oh-Vens!" The mobs of autograph seekers waiting outside the Olympic village grew larger every day. At first he enjoyed the attention, but eventually the strain of signing countless autographs began to worry Owens and his coaches. It was then that the other black American athletes, who were often mistaken for Owens anyway, were given permission to sign Owens' name when they were asked for his autograph.

THE LUZ LONG FABLE

Another tale from the 1936 Olympics that has been told and retold is the story about the advice Jesse Owens received from his German opponent, Luz Long, that enabled Owens to qualify for the finals of the long jump and led to his eventual victory. The story, which has been included in many Olympic history books, was a fabrication.

According to the *New York Times* of August 5, Owens fouled on his first two of three qualifying jumps, although Owens himself wrote later that his second jump was not a foul. In either case, if Owens fouled or failed to reach the qualifying distance on his third and final jump, he would be eliminated from the competition.

Owens and Long on the victory stand.

The story goes that Long suggested that Owens make a mark (or place a towel, according to some accounts) a foot in front of the takeoff board and jump from behind that mark. Since Owens was jumping consistently over 25 feet and the qualifying distance was only 23 feet 5$^1/_2$ inches, he would then be able to better the qualifying mark while ensuring there would not be a foul. Owens followed Long's advice and, according to the accounts of the day, qualified easily, although several sources say, incorrectly, that he qualified by only one-sixteenth of an inch.

The *Times* article says: "The situation was getting to be alarming by this time. Owens had only one more jump left to stay in the competition. So, on his last attempt, he sprinted carefully, left the ground with a half-foot clearance at the takeoff and went past 25 feet to safety."

Although it is a wonderful story, researchers have never been able to find any evidence that Long and Owens talked at all before Owens' final jump. Not one observer that day could recall seeing Long and Owens together. Grantland Rice, who was at the time the best-known sports journalist in America, was in the pressbox with his binoculars trained on Owens the entire time between his second and third jumps, "searching for some telltale sign of emotion." He did not see Owens and Long talking. And he did not see anyone make a mark or place a towel near the take-off board.

Owens himself finally settled the matter late in his life, when he admitted that he and Long never spoke to each other until after the long jump competition was completed later that day.

THE RELAY SELECTION CONTROVERSY

Jesse Owens' fourth gold medal was in the 400-meter relay. Originally, Owens and Ralph Metcalfe had not been selected for the relay, since it was likely the team would win easily without them. It had been decided weeks before that the team would be made up of Frank Wykoff, Foy Draper, Marty Glickman, and Sam Stoller. But at the last minute, Glickman and Stoller were dropped from the team and Owens and Metcalfe were added.

Since Glickman and Stoller were the only Jews on the U.S. team, there were immediate charges that they had been dropped to appease the Nazis. Of course this was denied by U.S. coaches and officials, but Glickman, who later became a noted sportscaster, never thought there was any other reason, believing Avery Brundage engineered their removal.

"To have had two Jewish athletes on the winning podium," Glickman said later, "would have been too much for Hitler, Goebbels, and Brundage. Avery Brundage was an American Nazi." (It was true that Brundage was very active in the America First Committee, an organization sympathetic to the Nazis. He is reported to have resigned from the organization on December 8, 1941, the day the United States declared war on Germany.)

Many of the Olympic history books and the motion picture, *The Jesse Owens Story*, say that Owens did not want to run in the relay.

At a team meeting with the coaches, Owens is quoted as saying: "Coach, I've won my three gold medals. I'm tired. Let Marty and Sam run. They deserve it." However, years later Metcalfe recalled that Owens "didn't say a word. I guess he wanted number four that bad."

Glickman and Stoller were the only U.S. Olympic team members who did not get to participate in the Games.

AN ABRUPT END TO A BRILLIANT CAREER

When the Olympics were over, invitations poured in for Jesse Owens to compete in European track meets before returning home. America's AAU, anxious to raise money to help pay for the trip to Berlin, signed contracts for him to compete in a long series of meets.

Jesse ran in competitions daily for the next week, and then announced he was tired and was going home. "I've lost six pounds being circused all over Europe," he said. "I'm burned out and tired of being treated like a head of cattle."

The AAU insisted Owens stay to run a series of races in Sweden, but he refused. The autocrats felt their authority could not be brooked and suspended Owens for life. Thus ended Jesse's shining track career. He had one year of eligibility remaining at Ohio State, but he did not return to school.

HITLER TAKES A LIKING
TO HELEN STEPHENS

Adolph Hitler took an immediate liking to Helen Stephens, the six-foot Missouri farm girl who defeated Poland's defending Olympic champion, Stella Walsh, in the women's 100-meter dash. After the race, Hitler invited Stephens to his private quarters in the stadium, out of sight of spectators. When she arrived, he hugged and pinched her, and then invited her to spend a weekend with him. She demurred, instead offering him "a good old Missouri handshake" and asked for his autograph.

AN EARLY SEX TEST

It is ironic that Helen Stephens was forced to submit to a sex test later in the Games after a Polish journalist accused her of really being a man. She underwent the test, which proved that she indeed was a woman.

Her longtime sprint rival, Stella Walsh, who was still competing for Poland under the name Stanislawa Walasiewicz, was not required to submit to the same test. It was not until 1980 that the truth about Walsh was finally known. She was killed in a freak shooting accident in Cleveland, Ohio, and the autopsy showed that she had male sex organs.

ANOTHER APE MAN

The decathlon winner was a car salesman from Colorado, Glenn Morris. Because of his world record performance and good looks, Morris was offered a Hollywood contract to play (you guessed it) Tarzan. Morris was the fourth Olympic medalist to portray Tarzan on the screen, following Johnny Weismuller, Herman Brix (Bruce Bennett), and Buster Crabbe.

Helen Stephens wins the 100 meters (Stella Walsh at far left).

SHARE AND SHARE ALIKE

In the pole vault, which was won by American Earle Meadows after 14 hours of competition, Japanese athletes Shuhei Nishida and Sueo Oe finished in a tie for second. Since there were not two silver medals available for them, they decided to share the silver and bronze medals by having a jeweler saw them in half and having the halves fused together. Each medal became half silver and half bronze.

UNDER THE JAPANESE FLAG

Korean runners finished first and third in the marathon, but they had to suffer the humiliation of competing as Japanese citizens, since Korea was occupied by Japan at the time. They had to wear Japanese uniforms and even were forced to adopt Japanese names. Competing as Kitei Son and Shoryu Nan, the two Koreans, whose real names were Sohn Kee-chung and Nan Seung-yong, participated in a silent protest during the awards ceremony. They bowed their heads as the Japanese anthem was played and the Japanese flag was raised.

At the 1948 Olympics, the first Games held after Korea had regained its independence from Japan, Sohn Kee-chung was the flagbearer for South Korea as the teams from around the world marched into the stadium in London. At the 1988 Olympics in Seoul, South Korea, Sohn was selected to be the final torch bearer, bringing the Olympic flame into the stadium. At the age of 76, Sohn completed several jumps for joy as he rounded the track.

A FINE FOR FOULING

In the final of the 1,000-meter sprint cycling race, Arie van Vliet of the Netherlands was overtaking the leader, Germany's Toni Merkens, and heading for certain victory, when the German swerved to the right, committing a flagrant foul and forcing van Vliet to finish second. The protest filed by officials from the Netherlands was upheld by the officials. However, instead of issuing a disqualification, the committee decided to fine the German 100 Deutchmarks and award him the gold medal! (Essentially, they gave him a traffic ticket.) The silver medal went to van Vliet.

BASKETBALL INTRODUCED

For the first time ever, the North American game of basketball was officially included in the Olympic program, but the Olympic organizers added some rules to the game that left the Americans dismayed, including one that limited participation to players who were shorter than six feet, three inches tall.

After vigorous protests from the U.S. team, which would have lost three of its best players, the rule was withdrawn.

The basketball games were played outdoors on clay and sand tennis courts. The final game, which the U.S. won over Canada, was played in the rain, on a court that became a quagmire of mud. During the second half, there was more than an inch of water on the surface, making it impossible to dribble. Sliding around in the mud and water, each team was able to score only four points in the second half. The final score was 19-8.

SOCCER HOOLIGANISM

In the soccer quarterfinal match between Peru and Austria, the score was tied 2-2 in the second overtime period when a group of frenzied Peruvian fans rushed onto the field and assaulted an Austrian player. In the confusion, Peru scored two quick goals for a 4-2 victory. After a protest was filed by the Austrians, the officials ordered the game replayed two days later—in a locked stadium with no spectators.

The Peruvians not only failed to show up for the rematch, they withdrew all of their participants from the Olympic Games and returned home. Colombia, in support of her South American neighbor, also withdrew from the Games. In far-off Peru, angry citizens threw rocks at the German Consulate and longshoremen refused to unload German ships.

THE OLYMPIC OAKS

Among the awards presented to gold medalists were one-year-old potted oak trees, to be replanted in the home nations of the winners. (See victory stand picture, p. 60.)As the first century of Olympic history comes to a close, 16 of the 130 Olympic oaks are still growing, in eight different countries.

Two of Jesse Owens' trees, towering to 60 feet, are still alive. One is next to the track at James Ford Rhodes High School in Cleveland, Ohio. The other, which was shared by his fellow relay teammates, is at the University of Southern California in Los Angeles.

The oak tree that was presented to Jack Lovelock of New Zealand for the 1500-meter run barely survived the trip from Germany. Because the tree experienced two consecutive spring seasons, its bark became brittle and it nearly died. Under the watchful eye of the curator of the Christchurch Botanical Gardens, the tree spent a year being nursed back to health in a greenhouse. Although Lovelock died 13 years later, at the age of 39, his oak tree is still thriving at the site where he began his running, Timaru Boys High School.

ON TO TOKYO

At the end of the final day of competition, the flame was extinguished, the Olympic flag was lowered, and the Berlin Olympic Games—the best organized and certainly the most political Games to date—came to an end. Over the loudspeaker system came the announcement: "I call the youth of the world to Tokyo."

**Marathon winner Sohn Kee-chung
at the turnaround point.**

Olympiads XII and XIII
TOKYO and HELSINKI, 1940;
LONDON, 1944
Canceled because of World War II

THE END OF AN ERA

When the 1936 Berlin Olympic Games came to a close, no one knew it would be 12 long, cheerless years before the world would see another Olympic festival. However, the cancellation of the 1940 and 1944 Olympics would be an experience the Olympic founder, Baron Pierre de Coubertin would not have to endure. He had died in 1937 at the age of 74.

DE COUBERTIN'S HEART
SENT TO OLYMPIA

De Coubertin, who had authored the revival of the Olympic Games and had devoted a lifetime to preserving the ideals of the Olympic movement, was buried in Lausanne, Switzerland. But, at his request, his heart was sent to Olympia, Greece, and placed in a marble monument there. The box in which the heart was shipped, complete with notes and red hearts penciled on the wrapping, is still on display in the Olympic Museum in the village of Olympia.

TOKYO IS SELECTED

The 1940 Games were awarded to Tokyo at a meeting of the IOC during the Berlin Olympics in 1936. Two cities—Tokyo and Helsinki—were contenders to host the Games, but the Japanese offered an additional incentive that swayed the vote—a sum of 1.5 million yen to be provided to foreign teams to reduce their travel and lodging costs. One-third of the cost would be borne by the Japanese government, one-third by the city of Tokyo, and one-third by public subscription.

ELABORATE PLANS

As soon as the announcement was made that Tokyo would host the 1940 Olympics, Japanese officials, aided by a nucleus of Germans who had worked on the Berlin games, began making elaborate plans. They even announced that the Olympic flame would be relayed from Olympia, Greece, to Tokyo by a series of runners, with airplanes stationed to carry the torch over bodies of water.

JAPAN FORCED OUT

In 1937, with just three years to go before the opening of the Tokyo Olympics, the Japanese invaded China, seizing Shanghai and Nanjing, and thus escalating the 2nd Sino-Japanese War. Tokyo continued plans to host an extensive Olympic program until July of 1938, when the Japanese government, too busy with their burgeoning war effort to worry about the Olympics, ordered a halt to the preparations. Immediately the IOC turned to tiny Finland.

FINLAND TAKES OVER—TEMPORARILY

The Finns, realizing the enormity of the task, agreed to host the games in Helsinki. With the help of the same Germans who had gone to Japan, the Finns designed and constructed a magnificent stadium not far from the center of town, complete with a tall, slender tower for the Olympic flame. But when Finland was invaded by the Soviet Union in 1939, the 1940 Olympics had to be canceled.

THE FLAME BURNS IN LOS ANGELES

On the day the opening ceremonies for the 1940 Olympics would have been held, the Olympic flame was relit at the top of the peristyle in the Olympic stadium in Los Angeles. The flame continued to burn throughout the time the Games would have been held in Helsinki.

HITLER'S OLYMPIC DREAM

In late 1940, members of the German Olympic Committee met with IOC president Henri de Baillet-Latour to tell him of Adolf Hitler's plans for the postwar Olympic Games. Hitler, who recognized the great propaganda value of the Olympics, had dreamed up a grandiose plan for the "Nazi Olympics," which would be staged permanently in Germany. He had already met with an architect who was to design a 450,000-seat stadium in Nuremberg. Needless to say, the IOC did not look upon this plan with much favor. Of course, if the outcome of World War II had been different, the IOC wouldn't have had much choice in the matter.

ANOTHER CANCELLATION

After the 1936 Olympics closed, there were eight candidates for the 1944 Olympics, but four of the cities had to withdraw because of the impending war. In 1939, the IOC met and awarded the 1944 Olympics to London over Detroit, Lausanne, and Rome.

In the early 1940s, with most of the world at war, the second successive Olympic Games had to be canceled.

Olympiad XIV
LONDON, 1948

ANOTHER OLYMPIC REVIVAL

When World War II came to an end in 1945, the IOC met and agreed the Olympic Games should be resumed in 1948. The meeting was chaired by Sigfried Edstrom, who had managed the affairs of the IOC from neutral Sweden during the war. Since the IOC president, Count Henri de Baillet-Latour, had died in Brussels during the German occupation, an election was held to select new IOC officers. Edstrom was elected president and America's Avery Brundage was elected vice president.

Early in 1946, the IOC awarded the 1948 Games to London, even though the city was struggling to recover from five years of the horrors of war, including extensive periods of heavy bombing and rocket attacks by the Germans. Even as the decision was made for London to host the Olympics a little more than two years later, the British were trying to rebuild their city and were continuing to suffer shortages of food, clothing, housing, and public transportation. Naturally, with austerity a necessity and almost everything rationed, there were those who thought hosting the Olympic Games was a frill the country could not afford.

LONG ON SPIRIT, SHORT ON FINANCES

The British government and the Londoners took on the Olympics with the same indomitable spirit that had become legendary during the war.

Using many existing facilities and donated equipment, some of it makeshift at best, the Londoners spent very little money on the project. In just two weeks, a temporary cinder track was installed in the Empire Stadium at Wembley, where greyhounds usually raced.

The athletes were quartered in nearby military camps and school buildings. The majority of the visiting athletes found the housing adequate, although some complained of drafty rooms, a lack of hot water, and the unavailability of eggs, steak, and milk.

THE U.S. QUARTERS

The American men were housed at a Royal Air Force base in Uxbridge, ten miles from the stadium, where they stayed in barracks, four to a room. The women stayed in dormitories at Southlands College. The U.S. athletes had access to a practice track, post office, bank, movie theater, barber shop, and medical and dental clinics. Because food was so scarce in England, the Americans received tons of fresh food, flown in daily from the States.

GROWING PARTICIPATION

A record 59 countries participated in the London Games, but World War II's "aggressor nations," Germany and Japan, were not invited. Almost all of the participating countries from Europe had suffered great losses of life and property during the war that affected their Olympic teams; only neutral nations Sweden and Switzerland had survived the war without serious harm to their sports programs.

ISRAEL RULED OUT

Israel had achieved national status in May of 1948 and should have been eligible to participate in the 1948 Games. However, the IOC, citing a "technicality," ruled that Israel would not receive an invitation. The reason for this decision, of course, was to avert a threatened boycott by the Arab countries.

U.S. TRYOUTS

The American teams were selected at "Olympic tryouts" held at various sites around the country early in the summer of 1948. The decathlon tryouts were held in Bloomfield, New Jersey; the tryouts for the rest of the men's track and field team were held in Evanston, Illinois. In the American system of team selection, the top three finishers in each event make the team, while those who do not finish in the top three are out, no matter how they had performed previously.

Unfortunately, several of the top U.S. athletes failed to finish in the top three in their events.

Dean Cromwell, the head coach of the U.S. team defended the selection process: "If an athlete must be at his peak on a given day in London, why also should he not be required to produce a championship performance at a specific moment in Evanston?" Cromwell pointed out that the athletes who made the teams thought the method was fair; those who were eliminated thought it was unfair.

DILLARD FAILS TO QUALIFY

The most outstanding athlete to fail to qualify for the Olympic team in his event was Harrison "Bones" Dillard, who had set the world record in the high hurdles earlier in the year, had won 82 consecutive races over a 13-month period, and was considered America's most certain winner in London.

But in the race in Evanston, Dillard's timing was off, he knocked down a succession of hurdles, and he failed to finish the race. Fortunately, Dillard had qualified for the 100 meters with a third place finish the previous day, so he did make the team—barely.

YOUNG MATHIAS SURPRISES

Another surprise at the tryouts was the success of the 17-year-old California high school junior, Bob Mathias, in the decathlon.

Participating in the ten-event contest for only the second time in his young life, Mathias surprised everyone—including himself—by outscoring the three-time national decathlon champion, 24-year-old army veteran Irv "Moon" Mondschein. Mathias won with the highest point total that had been scored by anyone since 1940.

Mathias was described by some as "a lazy-looking kid" because of his uncanny ability to relax. While other athletes, including Mondschein, paced back and forth nervously between events, the low-key Mathias would wrap himself in blankets and fall asleep.

A "ROUGH" CROSSING

Young Bob Mathias had his problems during the team's ocean voyage from New York to England aboard the S.S. America. First he suffered a two-day bout with sea sickness. Then he had to endure the antics of his high-strung cabinmate Mondschein, who would flip on the lights in the middle of the night and engage in an energetic calisthenics routine. This was not conducive to a good night's sleep for the teenager.

Years later, when recalling the ocean crossing, Mondschein remarked that he would go up on deck every day and do an exhausting workout. Then he'd return to the cabin and see Mathias lying in his bunk, reading and eating snacks. Mondschein was sure that shy, quiet Mathias did not have the maturity or experience to be a threat to him in London.

THE TORCH TRADITION IS CONTINUED

The British organizers did not attempt to match the elaborate and expensive Olympic carnival that Berlin had put on in 1936, but they did borrow a few ideas from the Germans. One was the lighting of the Olympic flame at the Temple of Hera at Olympia, Greece, and the relaying of the Olympic torch across Europe to London.

The flame was relayed first to Lausanne, Switzerland, to the grave of Pierre de Coubertin at the Bois-de-Vaux cemetery, and then relayed across France, Luxembourg, and Belgium, where it crossed the English Channel by ferryboat.

The organizers also announced that the British anthem, *God Save the King*, would be played only twice during the Games—once during the opening ceremonies and once during the closing ceremonies. They also commented, tongue-in-cheek, that the anthem would be played exactly 478 fewer times than *Deutschland Über Alles* had been played at Berlin.

NO SUNDAY EVENTS

The British, wishing to avoid the controversies that plagued some of the earlier Olympics because of Sunday competitions, scheduled no activities for the Sunday that fell in the middle of the 1948 schedule. The Olympics closed down completely at the close of the Saturday events and were resumed again on Monday.

AN IMPRESSIVE OPENING

Wembley Stadium was filled to capacity for the opening ceremonies, which began at 2:00 P.M. on July 29, in 93-degree heat. Following a trumpet fanfare by the Household Cavalry, the massed bands marched and played, with typical British pomp and pageantry.

King George VI stood at attention for more than an hour as the teams of athletes marched into the stadium, past the reviewing stand, and onto the infield. The King declared the Games open, there was another trumpet fanfare, and then 7,000 pigeons were released. (One reporter remarked that it probably wasn't wise to release that many pigeons in the presence of so many hungry people.)

The five-ringed Olympic flag, which had been taken from Amsterdam to Berlin for the 1936 Olympics, had disappeared in Berlin during the war. It was discovered unharmed, after the war, amid the ruins of Berlin by members of the British army. The flag, which first flew in Antwerp after the first great war, was now raised in Wembley Stadium following the second great war.

The Olympic torch, at the end of its 12-day journey from Greece, was carried into the stadium by Cambridge student John Mark. Mark ran around the track and up the steps to the peristyle, held the torch high for all to see, and then touched the torch to the large metal urn, igniting the Olympic flame.

RADIO AND TV COVERAGE

Radio coverage of the Olympic events was extensive throughout Great Britain and television brought the drama of many of the Olympic events into British homes for the first time. Although there were only 80,000 TV sets in Britain in 1948, it was estimated that more than 500,000 people saw the Games via shared TV sets.

BLANKERS-KOEN STARS

The star of the 1948 Olympics was Fanny Blankers-Koen of the Netherlands, who had run on the Dutch relay team in 1936 as Francina Koen, an 18-year-old schoolgirl. Now back as a mature 30-year-old mother of two, she became the first woman to win four gold medals in the Olympics.

Blankers-Koen's victories in the 100 and 200 meters were convincing, but she had close calls in the 80-meter hurdles and the 400-meter relay.

In the hurdles, the battle was between Blankers-Koen and a London ballet instructor, Maureen Gardner, who was personally coached by Britain's head coach, Geoffrey Dyson. At the

Fanny Blankers-Koen

gun, Gardner took an immediate lead, with Blankers-Koen struggling to catch up. At the sixth hurdle, when she was pulling up even with Gardner, Blankers-Koen hit the hurdle, stumbled slightly, and then the two raced, side-by-side, to the finish line. The finish photo showed that Blankers-Koen had won narrowly, but both women were credited with the Olympic record.

AN OLYMPIC ROMANCE

It seemed to some observers that the British team's coach, Geoffrey Dyson, was spending more time coaching Maureen Gardner than he was the

69

rest of the team. He was seen with her daily at her practice sessions, and he had even fashioned special collapsible hurdles for her. The reason became clear after the Olympics when they announced they were going to be married. Dyson was to continue as head coach of the British team through three more Olympics.

ANOTHER COME-FROM-BEHIND VICTORY

In the women's 4x100 relay, Blankers-Koen, running the final leg, had another come-from-behind assignment. The Dutch team was in fourth place when she took the baton. Blankers-Koen began overtaking the other anchor runners, first passing her hurdles rival, Maureen Gardner of Great Britain, and then Patricia Jones of Canada, and finally, just before the tape, Joyce King of Australia. The Netherlands team won by one-tenth of a second and Blankers-Koen won her fourth gold medal.

DRAMA IN THE MARATHON

The marathon produced another human drama, as Olympic marathons had done so many times before. A 21-year-old ex-paratroooper from Belgium, Etienne Gailly, had led most of the way, but he had been passed by Delfo Cabrera of Argentina as they approached the stadium.

Inside the stadium, the public address announcer was receiving reports on the progress of the race by radio, and he was relaying the information to the 70,000 spectators in the stands. Suddenly the announcer said, "Gailly has passed Cabrera with a sudden burst of speed and he is about to enter the stadium."

The eager crowd was anxious to welcome the young Belgian back from his 26-mile run through the streets of London. All eyes were on the gate where the marathoners would first appear. But what they saw left them in stunned silence. Gailly staggered into the stadium in a state of semi-consciousness, barely able to put one foot in front of the other. He was passed first by Cabrera, and then by Tom Richards of Great Britain.

Gailly managed to keep moving somehow and he finally staggered across the finish line, much to the relief of the empathetic crowd, which was much more interested in Gailly's struggle than the efforts of the gold and silver medal winners.

When the medals were awarded to the mara-thon runners later, only Cabrera and Richards were present. When the crowd saw the third place step was vacant, the rumor that Gailly had died quickly spread throughout the stadium. But Gailly was very much alive, recovering from his ordeal, but still too exhausted to participate in the awards ceremony.

A SPRINT SURPRISE

The favorites in the 100-meter final were the USA's world record holder at 100 yards, Mel "Pell Mell" Patton, his U.S. teammate Barney Ewell, who had equaled the world record for 100 meters, and an American-trained college student from Panama, Lloyd LaBeach, who had also matched the 100-meter world record.

Ewell was in lane two, between the other pre-race favorites, Patton in lane one and LaBeach in lane three. When the gun fired, Ewell, who considered it a three-man race, pulled away from his two rivals, crossed the finish line ahead of them, and began to dance around on the infield, thinking he had won. But Harrison Dillard, the displaced hurdler in the outside lane, had come off the blocks first, had streaked down his lane where Ewell did not notice him, and had finished inches ahead.

The race was close, but the judges all agreed that Dillard—who had not been given a chance by the prognosticators—had won in one of the greatest upsets in Olympic history. A new photo-finish device, which was in use for the first time at these Olympics, showed that Dillard was the clear winner, with Ewell second and LaBeach third. Patton, who finished fifth and thought he had no chance in the 200 meters, commented that his running career was over.

PATTON COMES BACK

The 200-meter field was touted as the finest ever assembled. In the final were Barney Ewell, Mel Patton, and Cliff Bourland for the U.S., Lloyd LaBeach from Panama, and Herb McKenley and Les Laing from Jamaica.

Most impressive in the preliminaries were Bourland and McKenley, but it was Patton and Ewell who headed the field as they came out of the turn in the final. Patton had a two-meter lead at that point, but Ewell was gaining as they headed down the stretch. Patton managed to hold him off at the finish and won the gold medal, even though both runners were clocked in 21.1 seconds. LaBeach finished third.

A SERIES OF UPSETS

In the track events, the favorites in three different races were all defeated by their own countrymen. Mel Patton lost to Harrison Dillard in the 100, Herb McKenley of Jamaica lost to Arthur Wint in the 400, and Lennart Strand of Sweden lost to Henry Eriksson in the 1500.

LOSSES BECAUSE OF THE RULES

The rules for deciding ties proved to be a curse for high jumper Dorothy (Odam) Tyler of Great Britain. In two Olympics she had achieved the same height as the gold medal winner, but received the silver medal because of the rules. In the Berlin Olympics she lost in a jump-off, but under the current rules, Tyler would have won the gold. In London, 12 years later, she had one more miss at the winning height, and again took silver.

A BOLD PREDICTION

In the discus throw, America's hope was Fortune Gordien, who had been throwing near the world record consistently prior to the Olympics.

However, Gordien finished third behind two Italians who, according to Coach Dean Cromwell, did not have as much speed or as perfect a pivot as Gordien.

Admitting "we are still learning in this event," Cromwell made a bold prediction: "I can see no reason why the world record won't eventually be advanced to more than 190 feet, probably to 200 feet." (The winning distance in the Olympics has not been less than 200 feet since 1960.)

HAMILTON'S "ULTIMATES"

Cromwell's prediction was reminiscent of the track and field "ultimates" created in 1934 by another Olympic coach, Brutus Hamilton. Hamilton predicted the absolute human limits in each of the track and field events, including 46.2 in the 400 meters, 3:45 in the 1500 meters, 6 feet 11¼ inches (2.11 meters) in the high jump, 15 feet 1 inch (4.60 meters) in the pole vault, and 57 feet 1 inch (17.4 meters) in the shot put. All of Hamilton's ultimates except three are below the standards required just to enter the Olympics today.

A GRUELING TEN EVENTS

The decathlon, that two-day, ten-event test of speed, strength, and endurance was contested under the very worst of conditions—some caused by the weather and some by what Coach Cromwell called "haphazard and unknowing officiating." It rained steadily the first day and it continued to pour the second day. Add the long delays and the continual errors made by officials and it is a wonder that there were any decent performances at all.

The rain and the delays took their toll on most of the athletes, but young Bob Mathias didn't seem affected. He managed to stay calm and relaxed while the others stewed and fidgeted.

At the end of the first day, after completing the 100 meters, long jump, shot put, high jump, and 400 meters, Mathias was in third place. Irv Mondschein, whose best event normally was the high jump, had done poorly in that event and was well behind the leaders.

The next day, in a constant pouring rain, the competitions began at 10:30 in the morning and ended for Mathias at 10:35 that night. He had little to eat and he emerged from his blankets only long enough to run, jump or throw.

It was so dark at the end of the pole vaulting competition that a white handkerchief was tied to the crossbar so the vaulters knew where it was.

The javelin foul line could only be seen because of an official's flashlight. When the final event, the 1500-meter run, was started on the backstretch of the track, all the spectators could see through the falling rain was the flash of the starter's gun.

Mathias was dogtired before the 1500 meters began, but he had built up enough points so that a fast race wasn't necessary. He plodded through the race, staggered across the finish line, and became the youngest track and field athlete to win an Olympic gold medal.

Mathias, who lost 15 pounds during the competition, vowed he would never participate in another decathlon. When asked by a reporter what he was going to do to celebrate, Mathias replied, "Start shaving, I guess."

WALKING CONTROVERSIES

The 10,000-meter walk was marred by constant warnings and eventual disqualifications of several walkers for "lifting"—not having at least one foot on the ground. There was so much confusion and squabbling that American coach Dean Cromwell was prompted to remark, "Walking races, as well as such other events of extreme controversy as boxing and water polo, should not be a part of the Olympic Games program."

ANOTHER QUESTION OF AMATEURISM

In the equestrian events, an unusual disqualification took place in the team dressage, which at the time was open only to officers in the military.

Though Sweden won the event easily over France, it was discovered more than a year later that one of Sweden's riders, Gehnall Persson, was an enlisted man. Before the Games, Persson was commissioned an officer, but after the Games he returned to his former rank. The team was disqualified and lost its gold medals.

THE JAPANESE SHOW THEIR STRENGTH IN SWIMMING

Uninvited Japan, a world power in swimming since the 1932 Games, staged its national swimming championships to coincide exactly with the Olympic Games in London. As the 400-meter and 1500-meter events were being contested in London, the Japanese were swimming the identical events in much faster times. In those two events, the Japanese bettered world records, but the new marks were never accepted because Japan did not belong to the International Swimming Federation.

A NEAR-DROWNING

Denmark's Greta Andersen, who had won the women's 100 meters freestyle five days earlier, collapsed and sank during the third heat of the 400 freestyle. Nancy Lees of the U.S., who had raced in the previous heat, and Elemér Szathmáry of Hungary, jumped in to hold Andersen's head above water until the race ended. The Danish girl was carried to the dressing room unconscious, but she recovered quickly after receiving medical treatment.

RACING IN THE DARK

The cycling events were held at Herne Hill, a cycling track that had ample seats for spectators, but had no electricity. Normally electricity would not have been necessary, but on the last day of cycling, the events were so far behind schedule that the final of the 2000-meter tandem race was contested in almost total darkness. The crowd could not distinguish between the British and Italian cyclists on the backstretch, but they could see the shadowy figures of the tandem bicycles in a photo finish, where the Italians won by a mere 6 inches. The journalists covering the event had to light matches to complete their reports.

A MISFIRE IN SHOOTING

Entered in the pistol shooting competition was Hungary's Károly Takács, a former army sergeant who had lost his right hand in a grenade explosion during the war. Takács had since taught himself to shoot left-handed so he could compete in the Olympics.

During the competition, his gun went off accidentally while he was reloading and the judges ruled it a failed shot. After lengthy deliberation, Takács was allowed to shoot again and he went on to score a record 580 points to win the gold medal.

A BREAK IN THE WEATHER

The weather throughout the Games ranged from stifling heat and humidity to light and heavy rainstorms, without much in between. It is surprising with weather conditions at such extremes that there were so many outstanding performances.

Finally there was a perfect day for the Olympics—no insufferable heat and no rain; just warm sunshine. It was the day of the closing ceremonies.

The Olympic flag was lowered and prepared for its transfer to Helsinki, the flame died out, and the London Games were over. However, there was one political addendum. Some of the athletes from Hungary and Czechoslovakia announced they were not going home. They asked the British government for political asylum.

Olympiad XV
HELSINKI, 1952

A TWELVE-YEAR DELAY

In 1947, the IOC awarded the 1952 Olympics to Helsinki. It was a tribute to Finland for its courageous attempt to stage the 1940 Olympics after Tokyo had given up the project in 1938. The Olympic stadium, constructed for the 1940 Games, was already in place, and *sisu*, the Finnish word for indomitable spirit, was everywhere in the tiny nation.

Finland was a mystery country to most of the rest of the world, nestled away in the far northeastern corner of the free world. The northernmost portion of the USSR's "iron curtain," which separated the Soviet Union from Western Europe, was also Finland's eastern border.

FUNDRAISING BY TELEVISION

The United States Olympic Committee was quick to put together an outstanding Olympic team, but was slow in raising funds to send the team to Helsinki. Using slogans urging donations to the Olympic fund so "we can beat the Russians," the USOC found itself $500,000 short of its goal with just two weeks before the U.S. team's departure.

Suddenly two surprise boosters—entertainers Bob Hope and Bing Crosby—came to the rescue. They hosted a 15-hour all-star Olympic telethon which brought in enough money to cover the 1952 Olympic shortage and give the IOC a head start for 1956.

THE RUSSIANS ARE COMING

Athletes from the Soviet Union entered the Olympics for the first time in 1952, but Soviet officials announced they would only do so if they would be allowed to have their own Olympic village, separating their athletes from those from the West. The Soviet spokesman explained they did not wish their athletes to be "contaminated." In a surprise move, the IOC approved the separate village, even though it was, to even the most casual Olympic observer, a violation of the Olympic spirit.

The Soviet Union had sent observers to the 1948 Olympics in London and had spent the following four years preparing for their first-ever Olympic appearance. There was no doubt about their seriousness when their train, with 370 athletes aboard, arrived in Helsinki.

The Soviets settled into their own Olympic village, which they shared with fellow East bloc countries Bulgaria, Czechoslovakia, Hungary, Poland, and Romania. Surrounded by a high barbed wire fence, the Soviet village was closed to all outsiders at first. But two days after the Games had opened, in a sudden turnaround, the Soviets began allowing the press and other authorized visitors, including American athletes, to visit their village.

MYSTERIOUS NO-SHOWS

Several Soviet athletes, including world-ranked shot putter/decathlete Heino Lipp of Estonia, were expected to be entered in Helsinki, but they did not make the trip. It was obvious that the Soviet hierarchy, wary of potential defections, did not bring any athletes they considered "politically unreliable."

POLITICS AGAIN

Mainland (Communist) China and Nationalist China (Taiwan) each had members serving on the original Chinese Olympic Committee. When each nation requested that it be the Olympic entry representing China, the IOC was faced with an international dilemma. Waffling on the decision, the IOC finally accepted both. Nationalist China stomped out in disgust, leaving Mainland China, with no athletes present, to be the sole Chinese representative.

EAST GERMANY IS REJECTED

East Germany petitioned the IOC, asking to

be accepted into the Olympic Games as a separate nation. But the IOC, not wishing to create an incident, continued to recognize West Germany as the sole country representing the German nation.

AN INDIRECT ROUTE FOR THE TORCH

The Olympic flame was forced to follow a rather unorthodox route from Greece to Finland. Originally the torch was scheduled to be relayed by thousands of runners along the most direct route, through the Soviet Union.

However, the Soviets refused permission for the torch to enter their country and the plans had to be changed.

The torch was relayed from Olympia to Athens, where it was transferred to a miner's lamp and flown to Copenhagen, Denmark. From there it was taken to Sweden by boat and then was carried all the way to the Arctic Circle by runners, motorcycles, and automobiles.

North of the Arctic Circle, native Laplanders combined the Olympic flame with a flame they created at midnight from the rays of the midnight sun.

Then the torch was relayed by Finnish runners the length of Finland, from north to south, to Helsinki.

FULL HOUSE FOR THE OPENING

The 70,000-seat Olympic stadium was filled to capacity as the teams from 67 nations marched into the stadium in a steady, light rain. The Finnish president, Juho Passikivi, proclaimed the Games open, a cannon fired 21 times, thousands of pigeons were released, and it was time for the Olympic torch to enter the stadium. The rain-drenched crowd waited patiently. The identity of the final runner had been a closely-guarded secret—even from the members of the IOC.

Then, out of the tunnel ran the torchbearer, a balding 55-year-old runner who brought the entire crowd to its feet. It was the greatest of all Finnish Olympic gods, Paavo Nurmi. Even though he was suffering from advanced rheumatism, he looked like the Nurmi of old, running with steady, bounding strides. As the ecstatic crowd both cheered and cried, Nurmi ran one lap before transferring the flame to a large urn beside the track.

Although the partisan Finns couldn't have been happier to be able to watch their Olympic hero on the track once again, some members of the IOC, who had not been told Nurmi would bring the Olympic flame into the stadium, were furious. The IOC still considered Nurmi a professional, since he had been banned from the Olympics 20 years earlier for accepting excessive expense money.

AN UNKNOWN CAUSE

During the opening ceremonies, a woman, described as overweight and dressed in a long white robe and heavy black boots, jumped out of the stands and ran around the track. At first it was thought she was part of the opening ceremonies ritual, but it turned out she was demonstrating for an unidentified cause.

After running a half-lap, she ran up the steps to the officials' microphone, but was so winded she could say only one word. Some say the word was "Friends." Others say it was "Peace." Before she could say more, the police took her away.

PHOTO FINISH

The 100-meter final produced the closest finish in Olympic history. The finish photo showed that the lightly-regarded American Lindy Remigino (named for aviator Charles "Lucky Lindy" Lindbergh) was 4 millimeters (less than one-eighth inch) ahead of Herb McKenley of Jamaica at the tape. A total of 14 inches separated the first and fourth place finishers.

IN A RUT

In the 800 meters, America's Mal Whitfield, the smooth-striding Air Force sergeant, repeated as Olympic champion. In 1948, Whitfield had defeated Arthur Wint of Jamaica in 1:49.2, a new Olympic record. In 1952, Whitfield defeated Wint again in 1:49.2, equalling the Olympic record. Wint was not as consistent as Whitfield. He ran 1:49.5 in 1948 and 1:49.4 in 1952.

LUXEMBOURG'S FIRST GOLD

Little-known Josef Barthel won the 1500 meters in a major upset over a field of world-ranked runners, winning the first-ever gold medal for tiny Luxembourg. The organizers had to delay the awards ceremony briefly until they could locate the sheet music for Luxembourg's

Barthel on the victory stand.

national anthem. When the anthem was played and the flag of Luxembourg was raised on the flagpole, Barthel stood on the victory stand, sobbing uncontrollably.

PAIN IN MOTION

Emil Zátopek was not only the greatest distance runner of his day, it seemed to the spectators as though each step might be his last. His facial contortions and unorthodox body movements made him appear to be suffering great pain as he grimaced in apparent agony with every step.

In Helsinki, Zátopek put on such an amazing display of distance running that Britain's Roger Bannister described him as "the greatest athlete of the postwar world." Following up on his victory in the 10,000 meters and his second place finish in the 5,000 at the 1948 Games, Zátopek began his Helsinki assault by winning the 10,000 by almost 100 meters in Olympic record time. It was an amazing feat when you realize the next five runners were also under the old record.

Four days later, he won the 5,000 meters, breaking the Olympic record by nine seconds. After the finish, Zátopek's wife, Dana, celebrated

his win briefly. Then she went to compete in her event, the women's javelin throw, which she won, breaking the Olympic record by almost 16 feet. The Zátopeks had won gold medals the same day. (Note: Emil and Dana were also born on the same day—September 19, 1922.)

Three days later, Zátopek won the marathon, a race he had never run before, finishing two and a half minutes ahead of the second place finisher. "The marathon," Zátopek said afterwards, "is a very boring race."

Zátopek had shoe problems in Helsinki that almost kept him from capturing the marathon title. His running shoes were completely worn out after the 5,000 meters, so he bought a pair of Finnish-made Karhu shoes. But the Karhu shoes were uncomfortably stiff and tight—not the sort of shoes that will carry a runner for 26 miles.

Zátopek went to Fred Wilt, a U.S. distance runner he had befriended at the 1948 Games, to see if he could borrow a pair of shoes from him. Wilt, whose shoes were too small for Zátopek, suggested they "grease" the Karhus. The two proceeded to the Olympic village kitchen, where they obtained a small bucket of cooking lard. Then they caked the Karhu shoes with the lard, which softened and stretched the shoes into a perfect fit.

MATHIAS REPEATS

In the two-day, ten-event decathlon, Bob Mathias was obviously stronger and more mature than he was four years earlier when he won the title as a 17-year-old. Still, at the end of the first day he said, "I've never been so tired in my life." The next day he completed the final five events, winning the decathlon by the largest margin in Olympic history and setting a new world record.

During the pole vault competition, Mathias cleared 13 feet, 1$^{1}/_{2}$ inches using a special pole that had been invented for him by his high school coach, Virgil Jackson. Designed to bend yet still support a heavier vaulter, it was the first time a fiberglass pole was ever used in Olympic competition.

TAKING A PLUNGE

In men's swimming, the surprise winner in the 400-meter freestyle was an unknown Frenchman, Jean Boiteux. It was France's first-ever Olympic swimming title. As soon as the race was over, out of the crowd came a fully-dressed man, complete with a beret on his head, who jumped into the pool beside Boiteux. The man, who embraced Boiteux and kissed him on both cheeks, was his exuberant father.

STUDYING CHAMPIONSHIP FORM

The technique of America's two-time Olympic platform diving champion, Sammy Lee, was of particular interest to the Soviet delegation. They discussed his diving technique with him and took both still and motion pictures of his dives.

Afterwards, the Soviets presented him with a Soviet "dove of peace" pin. When Lee was criticized later for wearing the pin, he said, "The purpose of the Olympics is peaceful competition between individuals, to respect each other. That is why the Olympics have meaning for the cause of peace."

A FUTURE PRO CHAMPION

The best of the five U.S. gold medal winners in boxing was 17-year-old Floyd Patterson, who won the middleweight title easily, knocking out his final opponent in just 74 seconds. One of the U.S. boxing coaches said that Patterson's only problem in Helsinki was managing the language differences. Patterson reportedly told the coach, "Every time I get my suit pressed it costs me 300 kilocycles."

In 1956, Patterson became the youngest-ever world professional heavyweight champion. He lost the title in 1959, but in 1960, in a startling comeback, he became the first fighter to regain the world title.

A famous moment in Olympic history: Emil Zátopek sprints away from Alain Mimoun, Herbert Schade and the fallen Chris Chataway to win the 5000 meters.

THE REF TAKES A BEATING

In a bitterly-fought basketball game between Uruguay and France, the Frenchmen were ahead 68-66 with only seconds to go when the referee called a foul on one of the Uruguayan players. The player immediately punched the referee in the eye as the other Uruguayans crowded around the helpless official. One player had the referee in a chokehold while another kicked him. The police intervened and the referee had to be taken to the infirmary for medical treatment.

USA VS. USSR IN BASKETBALL

In the basketball semifinals, the U.S. team defeated the Soviets easily, 86-58. In the final game, with the two teams matched together again, the Soviets decided to slow the game down by stalling. The U.S. led only 4-2 after ten minutes. When the game ended, the Americans had won, 36-25.

Here is the way the basketball competition was described in a book published in the USSR: "In preliminary matches the USSR team beat Bulgaria 74-46, Finland 47-35, and Mexico 71-62. During semifinal matches the USSR outplayed Brazil 54-49, Chile 78-60 and beat Uruguay 61-57 in the final, and being second only to the team of the USA, won silver medals."

KEEPING SCORE

No matter how hard the IOC has tried over the years, they have not been able to stop the nationalistic practice of keeping score in the Olympics.

For some, there seems to be an incessant need to determine—even unofficially—which nations are winning and which ones are losing.

At Helsinki, keeping score became a passion, especially among the journalists. The 1952 Games were turned into a competition, not between individual Olympians, but a dual meet between the USA and the USSR.

THE SOVIET SCOREBOARD

Early in the Olympics, the Soviets didn't pay much attention to the unofficial point totals. But after the ninth day, when they saw their lead over the United States grow to 120 points, they decided to construct a large scoreboard in the

dining room of their village. The scoreboard showed the daily point totals of all nations.

On the last day of Olympic competition, the U.S. won several gold medals and it seemed certain the USA would overtake the USSR in the point totals. Realizing they were not going to finish ahead of the Americans, the Soviets began dismantling the scoreboard, but not before a reporter for a U.S. newspaper saw the scoreboard and sent out the story. The headline read, "Russians caught with their points down."

After the Olympics, the Soviet newspaper *Pravda*, which must have juggled point values until they came out right, announced that the USSR and the USA had finished in a tie, each with 494 points.

SOVIET HISTORY

An Olympic history book published in the Soviet Union presents a different view of the Helsinki Olympics from any of the accounts published in the West. According to the book: "The entry of the USSR to the Olympic movement hallmarked a new stage in the history of the Games. The USSR began to campaign for true democratization of the Olympic movement."

In the chapter on the 1952 Olympics, the USSR is mentioned 29 times. The USA is mentioned only six times.

The description of the 100-meter final is typical: "A rare case occurred at the sprint distance during the men's final: four finishers clocked the same time—10.4—and only the photo-finish placed who was who." There is no mention that the winner was an American, Lindy Remigino.

In the gymnastics events, the book described the scene: "The Soviet gymnasts, the Olympic new entrants, stole the show. Although the top form of 'the beginners' was self-evident, they, nevertheless had to prove their superiority to the judges. The judges meticulously noted every fault of any Soviet competitor, boosting tiny faults to serious blunders.

"Therefore, victory depended not only on the top technique but also on self-composure and the will to win. The athletes had to compete with absolute self-denial, indomitable spirit, and the strongest desire to hear finally the tunes of the USSR anthem."

BRUNDAGE MOVES UP AGAIN

Shortly after the Games closed, Avery Brundage, the Chicago multimillionaire, was elected president of the IOC. The first American to head up the Committee, Brundage won out over Lord Burghley of Great Britain by a vote of 30-17. Thus the dogmatic protector of the strictest codes of amateurism (known to some unaffectionately as "Slavery" Brundage) was about to begin what would turn out to be a stormy 20-year reign as head of the IOC.

Olympiad XVI
MELBOURNE AND STOCKHOLM, 1956

CHANGING SEASONS

In 1949, when Melbourne was selected over nine other cities to host the 1956 Olympics (by a mere one-vote margin), there were serious misgivings—particularly among the nations situated north of the equator.

First there was the question of distance. It would be costly (and inconvenient) for the great majority of the world's Olympic teams to make such a long journey.

Then there was the problem of the reversal of seasons. The Melbourne Games, the first to be staged in the southern hemisphere, would have to take place in November and December, during the Australian summer, a time when northern hemisphere athletes are not usually at their best.

SECURING A STADIUM

The only stadium in the Melbourne area suited for the Olympic Games was the Melbourne Cricket Ground, which had often held 103,000 spectators for cricket and soccer matches. At first, those responsible for the stadium's operation made it clear they didn't want any of the stadium's turf removed to accommodate the Olympic track and field events. The cricket and soccer fans wouldn't approve, they said.

In 1953, with only three years to go before the Games were scheduled to begin, and no other options available, the stadium officials finally relented. They agreed, reluctantly, to approve the use of the cricket ground as the Olympic Games stadium.

A MAJOR SLOWDOWN

As the Games approached, anxiety mounted over whether the venues would be ready on time. Internal bickering and political rivalries brought the Games preparations to a virtual halt. The situation was so bad that IOC president Avery Brundage suggested the Games be moved to Rome where, he said, the organizers were farther along in preparing for the 1960 Games than Melbourne was in preparing for 1956.

When Brundage announced he was going to Melbourne to inspect the Olympic facilities, the Australians told him not to bother. There was nothing to inspect. But Brundage went anyway, and on his return he reported: "Melbourne has a deplorable record of promises upon promises... For years we have had nothing but squabbling, changes of management, and bickering." Then the Melbourne carpenters went on strike.

Finally, the Aussies stopped fighting. In a complete turnaround, they began cooperating to put together what was to become another in a series of very successful Olympic Games. However, the track in the Melbourne Cricket Ground was not installed until two weeks before the opening ceremonies and not all of the training sites were completed in time for the start of the Games.

TWO HOST COUNTRIES

In April of 1953, four years after Melbourne had been selected to host the 1956 Olympics, the Australian government announced that its strict animal quarantine laws would not be relaxed. No matter how important the event, horses would not be allowed to enter the country to participate in the Olympic equestrian competitions.

In a controversial move that was in violation of the Olympic charter, which states that all Olympic events must be held in the same country, the IOC decided, reluctantly and angrily, to have two host cities half a world apart—Melbourne and Stockholm. Stockholm would host the equestrian events during the Swedish summer in June, almost six months before Melbourne would host the remainder of the Olympic events during the Australian summer in November and December.

THE WORLD IN TURMOIL

There was so much turmoil and uncertainty in the world in November of 1956 that there were doubts the Olympic Games could be held. There was even fear of a possible nuclear war.

Israel, with the help of England and France, invaded the Gaza Strip in a dispute with Egypt over the Suez Canal. In protest, Egypt, Iraq, and Lebanon withdrew from the Games.

The Soviet Union moved into Budapest to crush the Hungarian Revolution. In protest, Spain, Switzerland, and The Netherlands withdrew from the Games.

In an ongoing conflict that was almost comical, Communist (Mainland) China withdrew from the Games just two weeks before the opening. Both Chinas had been invited to participate, and after Communist China accepted, Nationalist China turned down the invitation. Then, Nationalist China had a change of heart and accepted the invitation, causing Communist China to withdraw. When Nationalist China arrived at the Olympic village, the Communist flag was raised by mistake. The Nationalists climbed the flagpole and tore the flag down.

There were calls to cancel the Olympics because of the many global conflicts, but Avery Brundage, a longtime proponent of conducting the Olympics despite political hostilities, pointed out that the Olympics are contests between people, not between nations.

UNITED, TEMPORARILY

When the East Germans applied for admission to the Olympic Games again, the IOC decided to allow them to enter, but only if East and West Germany were to participate as a combined team. Both countries agreed, but almost immediately the feuding began. Officials of the two nations not only argued over the selection of athletes, but also over their flag and national anthem. Finally, they agreed to a flag with the black, red, and yellow stripes of both nations, overlapped with the Olympic rings. Beethoven's *Ode to Joy* became their temporary anthem.

THE HUNGARIAN UPRISING

On November 4, 1956, just days before the bulk of the Hungarian Olympic team was scheduled to leave for Australia, the Hungarian nationalist bid to sever ties with the Soviet Union was crushed when Soviet tanks roared into Budapest. The unarmed, rock-throwing Hungar-

ians were no match for the tanks, and in a brutal, bloody showdown, the uprising was put down after 13 days of sporadic fighting. Thousands of Hungarians died in the rebellion and thousands more escaped to Austria.

Some of the Hungarian athletes were already on a ship to Australia when the revolution began. The others had been allowed to cross the border into Czechoslovakia during a brief truce. Three days after the uprising was crushed, the Hungarian team boarded a plane and flew from Czechoslovakia to Melbourne, taking with them the few things they had been able to carry when they left Hungary.

At the Olympic village, the British team "adopted" the Hungarians, providing them with food, clothing, running shoes, pocket money, and even swimming trunks. Because they had left Hungary in such a hurry, the athletes didn't even have matching outfits to wear in the opening ceremonies parade.

After the Olympics came to a close, 45 of the Hungarians decided not to go home, preferring instead to seek asylum in the West.

EARLENE MAKES A HIT

Earlene Brown, the 250-pound Los Angeles housewife who was America's top female shot putter, endeared herself to the Australians during a pre-Olympic meet outside Melbourne—the capital of the state of Victoria.

During the competition, the likeable Mrs. Brown was informed by an excited Australian reporter that she had just broken the Victoria shot put record.

"Shucks, baby," she replied, "I'm sorry. Gee, I didn't really mean to do that." A newspaper reporter, calling her the heroine of the Games, wrote of Earlene Brown: "She is the salt of the athletic earth, and an ode should be composed in her praise." Brown later became a roller derby star, her bulk earning her the name "747" Brown.

THE TORCH JOURNEY

On November 2, the Olympic flame began its 19-day, 13,000-mile journey from Olympia to Melbourne. It was flown from Athens by amphibian plane to Cairns on Australia's northeast coast. From Cairns, the flame was transferred to a torch and relayed by 2,831 runners, each running a mile, to Melbourne in southeast Australia.

The first mile was run by an Australian-born Greek, and the second was run by a native aborigine, who was flown in from the bush to run his mile with the torch.

The final torchbearer was 19-year-old Ron Clarke, Australia's most promising young runner. The torch given to Clarke to carry into the stadium was different from the torch that had been carried to Melbourne from Cairns. "It was a more spectacular one," Clarke explained later. "They wanted one that could be seen clearly on television. And it sparked. People could see the fire dropping off in chunks."

With sparks burning holes in his shirt and singeing his arm, Clarke circled the track, undaunted, holding the heavy aluminum torch high. Then he ran up the stairs to a giant golden cauldron and ignited the flame that would burn throughout the Melbourne Olympics.

PRINCE PHILIP OPENS THE GAMES

In brilliant sunshine, the Melbourne Cricket Ground was jammed with 103,000 people as the 1956 Games were officially opened by the Duke of Edinburgh, Prince Philip. The march-by of the athletes, a trumpet fanfare, a 21-gun salute, and the entrance of the Olympic torch all went without a hitch. When the Hungarian team marched in, not all in uniform because of the circumstances of their arrival, there was a great roar of appreciation from the sympathetic crowd.

NEARLY A STAY-AT-HOME

Prior to the Melbourne Games, Ireland's only sub-four-minute miler, Ron Delany, was not running well. He had been competing for Villanova University in the United States in the spring, but during the summer he had suffered two defeats to England's Brian Hewson.

The Olympic Council of Ireland was not certain Delany should be sent to Melbourne, but finally decided he could go. Delany didn't disappoint them. He came from behind in the final stretch of the 1500 meters and won in Olympic record time.

KEEPING SCORE

Attempting to emphasize the basic tenet that Olympic competitions are between individuals,

not nations, the IOC included the following words on the stadium messageboard during the opening ceremonies: "Classification by points on a national basis is not recognized." Apparently no one noticed.

At the end of the first day's competitions, newspapers throughout the world carried the news that the Soviet Union had a 43-35 lead over the United States in the Olympic Games team standings.

As the Olympics progressed, the media in both the USA and the USSR became so obsessed with the daily point totals that the Games had again become a dual meet between the two greatest of all sporting nations, with other countries merely along for the ride. Even when Ron Delany of Ireland won the 1500 meters, one U.S. journalist wrote it was "a left-handed victory for the United States because the points the American-trained collegian made went to Ireland."

FROM SILVER TO GOLD

When the great Emil Zátopek won his first Olympic gold medal in the 10,000 meters in 1948, trailing him to the tape was his friend, Alain Mimoun of France, who won the silver medal. Four years later, when Zátopek won gold medals in the 5,000 meters, 10,000 meters, and marathon, he was followed to the tape in the two shorter races by Mimoun again, who won two more silver medals.

In 1956, Mimoun had one last chance for a gold. Both Zátopek and Mimoun were entered in the marathon, but the 34-year-old Zátopek was at the end of his running career. Mimoun, who built up a large lead over the 26 miles and won easily, waited at the finish line for his old friend. Zátopek entered the stadium in sixth place, exhausted and struggling. As soon as he crossed the finish line, Mimoun gave him a big hug.

OUTLEANED AGAIN

The world record holder in the 110-meter high hurdles, Jack Davis of the United States, who was "outleaned" by a teammate in a tight finish in Helsinki, was outleaned by a teammate again in Melbourne.

In 1952, Davis and Harrison Dillard were both clocked in an Olympic record 13.7 seconds as Dillard's more extreme lean nipped Davis at the tape. In 1956, Davis lost by an eyelash again, this time to Lee Calhoun, although it took the officials 25 minutes to decide who had won. Both were clocked in 13.5, a new Olympic record.

Jack Davis thus had the rare distinction of sharing Olympic records twice without ever winning a gold medal.

TRUE SPORTSMEN

In the 3000-meter steeplechase, Great Britain's Chris Brasher was a clear winner over Hungary's Sándor Rozsnyói and Norway's Ernst Larsen. But after the race it was announced that Brasher had fouled Larsen while clearing a barrier during the last lap and was disqualified. The Aussie fans howled in protest.

Brasher appealed and was immediately supported in his appeal by Rozsnyói, Larsen, and the fourth place finisher, Heinz Laufer of Germany. All three said there had been no foul. Larsen said he had felt a bump while clearing a barrier, but it didn't affect the outcome of the race. Three hours later, Brasher's appeal was upheld and Britain had its first track and field gold medal in 24 years.

A FALSE START MAKES HISTORY

It was a first and maybe an "only." The starter for the marathon saw one of the runners move before the gun was fired and he fired the recall gun. All of the 46 runners had to return to the starting line because of the first-ever false start in an Olympic marathon race.

AN ENDURING CHAMPION

America's world record holder in the discus throw, Fortune Gordien, who had finished third in the 1948 Games and fourth in 1952, was one of the favorites to win in 1956. Another favorite was Adolfo Consolini of Italy, who had won in 1948 and taken silver in 1952. But it was an unseasoned 20-year-old from the U.S., Al Oerter, who surprised the favorites—and himself—by winning the gold medal in Melbourne. Oerter, who had the three longest throws in the competition, won the title by more than five feet, setting a new Olympic record.

This was just the start of an amazing Olympic career. In 1960, Al Oerter was slightly favored to win his second discus title, but after four of the six rounds had been completed, he

1956 discus gold medal winner Al Oerter, flanked by bronze medalist Des Koch (L) and silver medalist Fortune Gordien (R).

was in second place, behind countryman Rink Babka. He then changed his technique slightly and his fifth throw landed beyond his own Olympic record, earning him his second gold medal.

It appeared in 1964 that Oerter had little chance of winning his third crown in a row. During a practice session in Tokyo, he slipped and fell, tearing cartilage in his rib cage. He was in so much pain during the Games that when he got off his best throw of the day, he doubled over, unable to watch the implement land. Only the roar of the crowd let him know he had won another gold medal. It was also another Olympic record.

When Al Oerter made his fourth Olympic team in 1968 at the age of 32, not many gave him a chance to win again. For one thing, he was suffering from a cervical disc injury which required that he wear a neck brace much of the time. But a bigger problem was the formidable competition, led by his U.S. teammate Jay Silvester. Silvester had recently set a world record that was 17 feet beyond Oerter's best-ever mark.

In the finals, Oerter trailed in fourth place after two rounds, but on his third throw he again surprised everyone, surpassing his own Olympic record to take the gold once again. Oerter's typical come-from-behind win completed an unprecedented string of four gold medals at successive Olympics in the same event, a feat unmatched in track and field throughout the first century of Olympic competition. And he had set an Olympic record each time.

"I guess I'm a little jealous of my gold medal," Oerter said after the Mexico competition. "I don't want to give it up."

A FAIRYTALE ROMANCE

The biggest story of the Melbourne Olympics was the Olympic village romance of two gold medal winners, hammer thrower Harold Connolly of the United States and discus thrower Olga Fikotová of Czechoslovakia. They met in the Olympic village, fell in love, and decided 18 days later they wanted to be married.

Hal Connolly, a high school English teacher in Massachusetts, won the hammer throw and set a new Olympic record in Melbourne, edging out his Soviet rival, Mikhail Krivonosov, by a mere six inches.

Connolly's performance was particularly impressive because of the lifelong physical handicap he had overcome to become the world's best. His left arm was broken and his left brachial plexus was crushed at birth.

He underwent an operation three months later and wore a brace on his arm until he was eight. "I hated the brace," Connolly said later. "When I was told I'd never have to wear it again, I went to the cellar and threw it in the furnace." When Connolly began throwing the hammer, at age 22, his left arm was four inches shorter and was much weaker than his right arm.

Fikotová, a medical student studying to be a surgeon in Prague, won the women's discus throw and set a new Olympic record in Melbourne, soundly defeating two Soviet rivals. Fikotová was a standout basketball and handball player. She switched to discus throwing because it didn't take as much time away from her studies.

Because they were from opposite sides of the Iron Curtain and from different religions, the young couple had to overcome countless obstacles before they finally were allowed to marry. Connolly was even excommunicated from the Catholic church, but he was reinstated three days later.

Before it was over, Czech president Zapotocky, U.S. Secretary of State John Foster Dulles, and Archbishop Richard Cushing of Boston (later Cardinal Cushing) were all involved. The romance that the Czech government did not want publicized was making headlines throughout the world. The final "persuader" that forced the Czech government to allow the marriage was world opinion.

Several books describe the courtship as "long and difficult." There is no doubt it was difficult, but from the time Hal and Olga first met until they were married was less than 4½ months.

The wedding was held in Prague, with fellow Olympic champions Dana and Emil Zátopek serving as witnesses. There was first a civil service in Prague's Town Hall, followed by services in two churches—one Catholic and one Protestant. There were more than 20,000 people outside the Town Hall, waiting to greet the happy couple after the civil ceremony.

Hal Connolly went on to participate in three more Olympics. Olga, competing for the United States, participated in four more. The couple was divorced in 1973.

HOMEMADE SHOES

Many of the Olympic books say that Hal Connolly won his Olympic gold medal in the hammer throw while wearing ballet slippers. Connolly himself said, after the event, "I changed to ballet slippers, white ones like the gymnasts use, and I had much better footing." However, they were actually gymnastics slippers with a special sole that Connolly and a Boston cobbler had designed.

Connolly had found that the usual shoes used in hammer throwing were "stiff and cumbersome." By cementing a quarter-inch thick composition sole to the bottoms, the slippers were perfect for hammer throwing. "However," Connolly explained, "because there were no laces, I had to tape them to my feet."

Later, the cobbler made further improvements in the shoes, even adding laces. These new shoes became so popular with distance runners they soon became the New Balance Company's line of sports shoes.

ROUGH PLAY AMONG ENEMIES

Enemies on the field of battle, Hungary and the Soviet Union were pitted against each other in a bitterly-fought water polo competition. The Soviets were jeered throughout the competition by fans who were supportive of Hungary's bid for independence, many of them Hungarian immigrants. The Soviets, disturbed by their inability to score goals and by the attitude of the fans, began to play progressively rougher, until Hungary's Ervin Zádor was butted by Valentin Prokopov of the Soviet team and had to leave the game with a split eyebrow.

The Hungarian expatriates among the spectators were about to intervene when the police restored order. Hungary won the match, 4-0, and went on to win the gold medal.

An Olympic history book written during the Cold War by Hungarian Sándor Barcs, which presents a very detailed account of each of the Olympic Games, does not mention the 1956 water polo match. There isn't even a mention of the 13-day Hungarian revolution, the Soviet intervention in Hungary, or the problems of the Hungarian athletes.

Olga Fikotová Connolly

Hal Connolly

THE BATTLE OF THE TITANS

In the weight lifting competition, Paul Anderson, advertised as "the strongest man in the world," was the entry for the United States in the heavyweight division. Anderson's reputation was so well known, the Soviets didn't even bother to enter anyone against him.

But Paul Anderson didn't scare Humberto Selvetti of Argentina. The two giants were evenly matched, right up to Anderson's final lift. Finally, when both competitors had reached their limit of 1,100 pounds for the total weight for three different lifts—the judges declared a tie.

However, in weight lifting, ties are broken by awarding the championship to the lighter man. Surprisingly, Anderson, at 304 pounds, was lighter than the Argentine lifter, who tipped the scales at 316. Anderson won the gold medal.

VEGGIES ONLY

The Australians were dominant in the swimming pool, winning a total of eight gold medals and setting three world records and seven Olympic records. Leading the Aussie assault was Scotland-born Murray Rose, who won gold medals in three events. A strict vegetarian, Rose started a new food fad among swimmers when he announced that he enjoyed eating seaweed before competitions.

AN EXUBERANT CLOSE

The closing ceremonies were described in an Australian report on the Melbourne Games as "fittingly simple." However, one "inspired innovation" was mentioned as a model for future Olympics. For the first time, the athletes did not march into the stadium as national teams. "They walked in mixed and happy files, side by side with chosen friends from other countries." But they didn't stay in their "files" for long. They broke ranks, ran to embrace other newfound friends, joined hands in song, and danced.

Shirley Strickland (later, de la Hunty), who won three gold, one silver, and three bronze medals for Australia in three Olympics, described the closing ceremonies: "The intermingling of athletes in the parade typified the brotherhood of sport which the Olympic Games had developed. The flame died, the athletes departed, but the spirit and the memory of this Olympiad will stay with us for the rest of our lives."

Olympiad XVII
ROME, 1960

A MIXTURE OF OLD AND NEW

In 1955, the IOC voted to award the 1960 Olympic Games to Rome, the city where the order to abolish the ancient Olympic Games was decreed in the year 393. So, 1,567 years after the edict from Emperor Theodosius, the modern Games were staged in Rome, with classical ruins serving as a background for many of the events.

The wrestling venue was the 1,650-year-old Basilica of Maxentius, the Roman Forum, where Roman wrestlers had once participated in similar contests. The marathon finished at the ancient Arch of Constantine, the first Olympic marathon that did not finish at the site of the track events.

There were also modern structures, including the new 100,000-seat Olympic Stadium and the adjacent Olympic swimming pool. They were constructed in a sports complex near the 20-year-old Stadio dei Marmi, a smaller stadium ringed by forty marble statues of athletes.

Constructed under the direction of Italy's World War II dictator, Benito Mussolini, the Stadio dei Marmi was originally a part of Mussolini's dream that Rome would host the 1944 Olympics. To this day, at the entrance to the complex, there is a large marble monument engraved with MUSSOLINI DUX (Latin for Mussolini the Leader).

THE COLD WAR BEGINS TO THAW

The cool relationships between East and West that were experienced in recent Olympics warmed up a bit in Rome. The chairman of the Soviet Olympic Committee, Constantin Andrianov, said, "Politics is one thing; sports another. We are sportsmen." Athletes from the East and West mingled freely in the Olympic village. They talked, sang, joked, danced, and posed for pictures together.

A PERSONAL SURVEY

The athletes living in the Olympic village were encouraged, but not required, to participate in a "scientific" survey that was being conducted during the 1960 Games. Many of the athletes refused to fill out the survey questionnaires, objecting that they were far too personal. The survey asked questions regarding economic background, drinking habits, marital problems, and sexual "temperament."

A PIN WITH A MESSAGE

Ralph Boston, America's popular Olympic long jump champion, participated in the custom of Olympic pin-trading, as do most athletes and fans at the Olympics. Boston traded one of his U.S. pins for an Italian one, which he pinned to his shirt. Only after several people stood up on buses to offer him a seat did he realize that the Italian pin indicated he was handicapped.

THE FIRST TV CONTRACTS

CBS-TV received the U.S. rights to televise both the winter and the summer Olympics in 1960. According to recent Associated Press figures, the network paid $50,000 for the winter Games in Squaw Valley, and $394,000 for the summer Games in Rome.

Those figures, which seemed high at the time, are paltry in comparison with the high-stakes bidding that has taken place since. NBC-TV's contract for the U.S. rights to televise the 1996 Olympics cost the network $456 million.

AN AUDIENCE WITH THE POPE

Pope John XXIII held an audience for the athletes on the day before the opening ceremonies. There were 3,500 athletes in attendance, including 10 Russians. During the Olympics, the Pope watched some of the events on television, but not boxing events or any events with women who were not fully clothed.

A BRIEF PROTEST

During the opening ceremonies, everything went by the book, with only a single surprise. During the march-by of the athletes, representatives of Nationalist China participated in a brief protest. The IOC had said they would have to participate under the name Formosa, not China or Taiwan.

When the "Formosans" reached the reviewing stand, one of the team leaders held up a sign that read, "Under Protest," and then he put the sign away as quickly as it had appeared.

HEADING FOR HOME?

At one point in the opening ceremonies, a cannon fired and 5,000 pigeons were released. The pigeons circled the stadium once, appearing to try to get their bearings, and then, as one journalist cracked, "they headed straight for St. Mark's Square in Venice."

SKEETER

The star of the women's events at the Rome Olympics was a tall, graceful, 20-year-old Tennessean named Wilma "Skeeter" Rudolph, who won the 100 and 200 meters, and anchored the winning 400-meter relay team. Rudolph was the first American women to come home with three Olympic gold medals.

Rudolph, from a family of 19 children, suffered scarlet fever and pneumonia at the age of four and could not walk until she was seven. She wore an orthopedic shoe until she was 12.

After exercising regularly for several years, Rudolph developed into the fastest woman in the world. When asked by a reporter why she was so fast, she responded, "I am number 17 out of 19 children. I had to be fast to get anything to eat."

REVERSE PSYCHOLOGY

America's John Thomas was the best high jumper in the world in 1960, jumping consistently over 7 feet. In the U.S. Olympic Trials, he had jumped 7 feet 3 3/4 inches to set a new world record.

His strategy for winning the Olympic title in Rome was to "psych out" his opponents by doing several warmup jumps at 7 feet. However, in the competition he could manage only 7 feet 1/4 inch, while two unheralded Soviet jumpers, Robert Shavlakadze and Valeriy Brumel, cleared 7 feet 1

Wilma Rudolph

to win the gold and silver medals. Thomas received the bronze.

PRESSURE TO WIN

Hal and Olga Connolly, both gold medal winners in 1956, and the players in the storybook romance that shook the East and thrilled the West, were expected to win again in 1960, "to keep the story going." Both were under great emotional strain because it appeared to many non-experts to be a foregone conclusion that they would again be Olympic champions—this time as husband and wife.

Someone showed the Connollys a mockup of a cover of *Life* magazine with their picture on it. The cover would run, they were told, if they both won. As it turned out, the emotional drain from all the hype took its toll. Hal finished eighth in the hammer, Olga seventh in the discus.

GO FOR THE GOLD

U.S. army lieutenant Bill Nieder, who was stationed at the Presidio in San Francisco, was one of the favorites in the Olympic shot putting competition. As a challenge and incentive, Nieder's fellow officers said they would present him with a regulation-size gold shot if he won the Olympic gold medal.

When Nieder won, the officers decided a solid gold shot would be too expensive, so they presented him with a gold-plated one instead. The solid gold shot, with the price of gold at $35 an ounce, would have weighed 20 pounds and cost $11,000. If the officers had made the investment, the shot would have been worth about $272,000 when gold prices peaked 20 years later.

A TEMPORARY SUSPENSION

Lee Calhoun repeated as the gold medal winner in the 110-meter hurdles with another of his famous leaning photo finishes. He had outleaned Jack Davis to win the gold medal in 1956, and this time he outleaned Willie May.

During the time between Calhoun's two victories, there were some doubts that he would even be able to compete in 1960. Calhoun and his new wife had received gifts for appearing on the TV program *Bride and Groom* in 1958, and this made Calhoun a professional in the eyes of the U.S. Amateur Athletic Union. Calhoun was suspended from competition, but after one year, the suspension was lifted.

A SELF-PROCLAIMED TARZAN

Don "Tarzan" Bragg was a stocky, muscular pole vaulter who had set a world record in the Olympic trials and was favored to win in Rome. Bragg was known as Tarzan because he let it be known, whenever he had the opportunity, that his sole ambition, besides winning the gold medal, was to play the role of Tarzan in the movies.

In the pole vault competition, Bragg cleared 15 feet 5⅛ inches to win the gold medal, defeating his more reserved teammate, Ron Morris, and breaking the Olympic record by nearly six inches. After Bragg received the gold medal and the awards ceremony was over, he cupped his hands to his mouth and let go with an ear-shattering Tarzan yell. Bragg said later, "It echoed all over the stadium. The crowd went wild." But he never did get to play Tarzan in the movies.

A LONG JOURNEY FOR NOTHING

Wim Essayas, Surinam's only Olympic competitior, was probably the most disappointed athlete in Rome. Essayas was scheduled to run in the heats of the 800 meters one afternoon, so he slept late that morning. When he got up, he saw his race being run on television. Olympic organizers had switched the 800 heats to the morning and Essayas hadn't been told. "It's a disaster," he said. "What will the folks back home say?"

Later, Essayas' disappointment turned to anger. He announced he was filing a lawsuit against Freddy Glanz, his team leader. Essayas said Glanz failed to notify him the 800 heats had been changed.

AN UNNECESSARY TRIP TO THE HOSPITAL

Great Britain's Stan Vickers, after finishing third in the 20-kilometer walk, sat down by the track to rest. Two non-English-speaking Italian paramedics, thinking Vickers was ill, grabbed the protesting Vickers and rushed him to a hospital in an ambulance. Several hours later, British officials located Vickers and obtained his release.

BAREFOOT IN THE DARK

The winner of the marathon, which started at twilight to avoid the heat and finished long after dark, was Abebe Bikila of Ethiopia, a member of Emperor Haile Selassie's personal guard. Bikila ran the entire race barefoot, finishing by moonlight and torchlight on the cobblestones of the ancient Appian Way.

Bikila, who ran the best marathon time in history, was Ethiopia's first Olympic champion. He thought it was fitting that Rome was the site of his victory, since his father had fought against Benito Mussolini's invading troops in Ethiopia 25 years earlier, when Abebe was only three years old.

A DRUG DEATH

One of Denmark's cyclists, Knud Enemark Jensen, was peddling madly near the end of the

88

cycling road race when he suddenly collapsed. Because of the 92-degree heat, a doctor treated Jensen for sunstroke and then had him rushed to a hospital, where he died.

The Danish team trainer admitted later that he had administered a stimulant drug designed to increase blood circulation to the entire Danish cycling team. Two other Danish riders also collapsed during the race, but they recovered.

A PHOTO FINISH IN THE POOL

The swimming and diving events, which were conducted at night in the outdoor Olympic pool, included one international controversy. In the 100- meter freestyle, American Lance Larson came from behind and touched first, barely ahead of Australia's John Devitt. The judges and timers couldn't decide who had won, even though the stopwatches indicated Larson had touched first.

Finally, Devitt was awarded the gold medal, even though a replay of slow motion movies showed that Larson had won. There was an immediate protest from American Max Ritter, a member of the executive board of the International Swimming Federation, but the decision stood. An Australian member of the Swimming Federation, responding to Ritter's protest, was quoted as saying: "We rubbed your noses in it and we'll show you some more before we're through."

LONGEVITY

Hungary's Aladár Gerevich, at age 50, won his sixth consecutive gold medal as a member of the Hungarian saber team. He had previously won golds at Los Angeles in 1932, Berlin in 1936, London in 1948, Helsinki in 1952, and Melbourne in 1956. He also won a gold medal in the individual saber event in 1948.

FIRE UP

While watching the boxing events in the Palazzo dello Sport, the Italian spectators rolled up newspapers and burned them as torches to demonstrate their approval of performances and decisions. When their countryman Franco de Piccoli knocked out the Soviet European champion, Andrey Abramov, shortly after the heavyweight fight began, the fans began a wild demonstration. There were so many torches burning, the arena appeared to be ablaze. There were concerns for the safety of the spectators and the building, but everyone survived.

A WATERY GRAVE FOR CLAY'S GOLD?

In the light heavyweight boxing competition, a brash, gregarious, outspoken 18-year-old from Kentucky named Cassius Clay won the gold medal easily. At ringside, encouraging the young fighter, was singer-actor Bing Crosby. Later known affectionately as "The Louisville Lip," Clay turned professional, changed his name to Muhammad Ali, and became the heavyweight champion, and at the time the most famous athlete in the world.

When young Cassius Clay returned to Louisville after the Olympics, he and his gold medal

Cassius Clay (Center)

were inseparable. He even slept with it. But one night, according to Ali's autobiography, *The Greatest,* he was involved in a racial confrontation that turned into a bloody fight.

Following the fight, Ali went to the center of the long bridge that separates Louisville from Jeffersonville, Indiana, and without hesitating, he threw the gold medal into the Ohio River.* He wrote: "I wanted something that meant more than that. Something that was as proud of me as I would be of it."

A DIFFERENCE OF OPINION

Judging was again a problem in the boxing events. There were matches in which one of the five judges awarded all three rounds to one fighter, while another judge awarded those same three rounds to the other fighter. There were so many complaints about the officiating that the International Boxing Federation dismissed 15 of the 30 referees and judges for incompetence.

LOPSIDED VICTORIES

The U.S. basketball team, always a winner in the Olympics, was unbeatable in Rome. They won eight consecutive games, averaging 102 points to their opponents' 60. The closest game was an 81-57 rout of the Soviet Union. In that game, the Soviets 7-foot, 3-inch star, Yan Kruminsh, did not score a point.

HOT MATS

The wrestling events were held virtually outdoors in the ancient Basilica of Maxentius, where the wrestling mat was under a huge arch of ancient bricks, but the spectators sat in the hot sun. At times during the competitions, the sun was shining on more than half the mat, causing the wrestlers to scream out in pain whenever their skin touched the sunny portion of the mat.

A SOMBER CLOSING

The closing ceremonies, unlike most, saw only the flagbearers from each nation walking slowly around the track and onto the infield. There were no other athletes. It was a solemn, rather than a joyous, celebration.

The flags of Greece, Japan, and Italy were raised as the choir sang the anthems of each of the three nations. The Italian spectators sang along heartily when it was their turn. The Olympic flag was lowered, the flame went out, and fireworks began to explode overhead.

Thousands of Italians again added their light to the show by setting fire to rolled up newspapers and holding them high. The stadium seemed ablaze as the 1960 Games came to an unrehearsed close.

A FIERY FINISH

The spectacular fireworks display during the closing ceremonies got out of hand suddenly and became even more spectacular. Falling fragments of sky rockets began setting fires in and around the wooded hillsides to the west of the stadium. Firemen fought blazes in the gardens of private villas and in the wooded area surrounding the Villa Madama, where the Italian government entertained official guests. A number of cars parked in the area were also set ablaze as the Rome Olympics came to a fiery end.

This story, which is part of the Olympic lore and was included in a 1996 edition of Sixty Minutes *on CBS television, appears to be a fabrication. Ali has told close friends he still has the gold medal. They said he just couldn't resist a good story.*

OLYMPIAD XVIII
TOKYO, 1964

TOKYO SELECTED

In 1936, Tokyo had been awarded the 1940 Olympics, the first city in Asia to be selected to host the Games. But Japan's expansion of the Sino-Japanese War forced them to give up the project in 1938.

In 1959, with the horrors of World War II and the struggles of postwar reconstruction behind them, Tokyo bid to host the 1964 Olympics. Also bidding were Brussels, Detroit, and Vienna, but Tokyo was selected by a wide margin on the first ballot.

As soon as the selection was announced, it became clear that the Japanese planned to host the best organized, most joyous, least troubled (and as it turned out, most expensive) Olympic Games ever. And, according to those who participated and attended, they were successful beyond even their own wildest dreams. Dubbed "the happy games," the huge Tokyo success can be credited to the eager-to-please and unflappable Japanese, who were determined to erase their World War II image.

CLEANING UP THE CITY

One of the concerns of the Japanese organizers was that stray dogs—common in Tokyo at the time—might interfere with the marathon runners as they ran the 26-mile, 385-yard route through the city. So they organized a massive dogcatching effort and hauled the dogs out of the city. While they were at it, they also picked up and detained known pickpockets, scantily-clothed bath attendants, and "professional hostesses."

One athlete wrote later that the Japanese did everything they could to make a good impression on their visitors. "They told the locals not to urinate in the streets during the Olympics," he wrote, "and not to go out in public in their underwear." (It should be noted that there was a great shortage of public toilets in Tokyo in 1964—only one for every 12,000 people—which prompted officials to begin

placing portable toilets around the city. Signs were posted, saying: "Let's stop urinating in public. The Olympics are near.")

FLAWLESS OPENING CEREMONIES

The opening ceremonies, which featured the parade of the athletes past Emperor Hirohito and a replaying of the gramophone recording made by Pierre de Coubertin for the 1936 Olympics, were brief and flawless.

The Olympic flag was raised on a flag pole commemorating the first Japanese athlete to win an Olympic gold medal, triple jumper Mikio Oda. The pole was exactly 15.21 meters high—Oda's winning distance in 1928.

The most moving moment of these impressive ceremonies was the appearance of the Olympic torchbearer on the last leg of the long journey from Olympia. He was 19-year-old Oshinoro Sakai, who was born near Hiroshima on August 6, 1945, one hour before the atomic bomb was dropped on his city.

CLASHING OUTFITS

One minor flaw in the opening ceremonies, according to British athlete and writer Chris Brasher, was that the teams from Great Britain and Germany were lined up next to each other on the infield "all dressed in exactly the same shade of pink. It was as if the Queen and America's First Lady turned up at the same party in the same dresses." If that was the biggest gaffe of the day, the opening ceremonies must have been perfect indeed.

DELAYED TV COVERAGE

NBC-TV provided television coverage for the United States via a Telstar communications satellite, but because of time differences, some of the events were tape-delayed. However, the delays were sometimes longer than they needed to be. West coast viewers, for instance, had to wait until 1:00 A.M. to see the opening ceremonies because NBC wanted to avoid a conflict with Johnny Carson's *Tonight* show.

WINNING IS EVERYTHING

The Tokyo Olympics, although wonderfully organized and beautifully staged, have been described by many as the first Olympics completely devoid of the Olympic spirit. Valeriy Brumel, the Soviet Union's Olympic champion high jumper, updating the words of Pierre de Coubertin, said, "The important thing in the Olympic Games is to take first place."

Before the final of the 100-meter freestyle, British swimmer Bobby McGregor said, "No one remembers you if you finish fourth, third, or second in the Games." (McGregor finished second to America's Don Schollander.)

Spanish featherweight boxer Valenin Loren, who was disqualified by the referee for hitting with open gloves and repeated holding, quickly responded by hitting the referee with two lefts and trying to punch a judge. When Loren was told he would be banned for life as an amateur, he responded, "I want to be a pro, so I don't care."

Soviet javelin thrower Elvira Ozolina, who was the defending Olympic champion and former world record holder, fouled on her final four throws and finished only fifth. To demonstrate her shame, she went to the hair styling shop in the Olympic village and had her head shaved completely bald.

The most extreme case of the presumed importance of winning was demonstrated by Japanese marathoner Kokichi Tsuburaya, who had hoped desperately to win the Olympic marathon. After finishing only third, he became increasingly despondent. Two years later he wrote a note of apology to his country and committed suicide.

SOUTH AFRICA IS OUT

The problem of South Africa's apartheid policy, which explicitly discriminated against their black athletes and was thus a breach of Olympic rules, had been avoided by the IOC for several years. The South African Olympic Committee had contended there was no discrimination; it just happened that all their best athletes were white. As soon as black athletes reached Olympic caliber, they said, the Olympic team would welcome them.

In January of 1964, the IOC voted to suspend the South African Olympic Committee. South Africa would not be invited to participate in the 1964 Olympics, or in any future Olympics until their apartheid policy was changed. It would be 28 years before South Africa would participate in the Olympics again.

THE SHOE WAR BEGINS

In the 1960s, the code of Olympic amateurism began to erode when two warring German shoe companies began paying athletes—under the table—to wear their shoes. The companies were owned by two brothers, Adolf (nicknamed Adi) and Rudolf Dassler. The shoes were called Adidas and Puma.

The Dassler brothers had been partners manufacturing Adidas sports shoes before World War II, but after the war they had a major disagreement and Rudolf left Adidas to start the Puma company. Since then, they only communicated through lawyers.

At the Tokyo Olympics, representatives of the two companies—Horst Dassler (Adi's son) for Adidas, and Armin Hary (the 1960 Olympic 100 meters winner) for Puma, began a bidding war to convince the top Olympic athletes to wear their shoes.

One of the few athletes who later admitted receiving payment was American sprinter Bob Hayes, the favorite in the 100 meters in Tokyo. Hayes worked Dassler and Hary, back and forth, until he was able to get a bid of $8,900 from Dassler to wear Adidas in the 100 meters and the relay. It was merely a warmup for the series of bizarre events that would involve the two shoe companies four years later in Mexico.

AN AMAZING REPEAT WINNER

Five weeks before the marathon was to be run, it appeared there would not be a repeat winner. Ethiopia's Abebe Bikila, who had won with ease while running barefoot four years earlier, was stricken with appendicitis and had to have his appendix removed.

But two weeks later, Bikila was back on the track, training as hard as ever, and by the time the marathon was run, he was in top form. He again won the marathon easily, this time wearing shoes.

Avery Brundage awards medals to the victorious U.S. 4x100 team. Note Paul Drayton and Gerry Ashworth in Puma shoes and Richard Stebbins and Bob Hayes (far right) in Adidas.

THE IMPERFECT SPRINTER

American sprint champion Bob Hayes outclassed his rivals throughout the early rounds of the 100 meters, even though sports technicians criticized what one described as his "rolling, lumbering stride." One writer said, "His mid-race gait is painful for the purist to watch."

Another said, "It was a bison in the middle of a horse race." Another said, "He looks more like a heavyweight boxer than a sprinter." And another decried his "pigeon-toed ungainly gait."

In the 100-meter final, Hayes suffered a slow start and had to come from behind, but he won the race in world record-equaling time. After the race Hayes was approached by a French reporter, who said, "You have a bad start. You have terrible form. You're just faster than anyone else." Hayes' reply was, "Man, that's what it's all about."

RUNNING BRAVE

Australia's Ron Clarke, who had made his first Olympic appearance as the final torchbearer at the 1956 Olympics in Melbourne, was the favorite to win the 10,000-meter run in Tokyo. Clarke had set the 10,000 world record of 28:15.6 eleven months earlier and was running consistently well in 1964.

As the race progressed on the slow, rain-soaked track, Clarke wore down many of the other top runners, who lost contact with the leaders and were out of the running. In the closing stages of the race, there were only three other runners besides Clarke in contention for the three medals—Mohamed Gammoudi of Tunisia, Mamo Wolde of Ethiopia, and Billy Mills of the United States. Soon, Wolde also faded, leaving only Clarke, Gammoudi, and Mills to fight for the medals.

In the final lap of what has been described by some journalists as the most exciting distance race ever run, Clarke appeared to be in the best position to win. His only two challengers were a Tunisian who had never broken 29 minutes and an American who was such an unknown in Tokyo that no journalists had even bothered to talk to him in the days leading up to the race.

Clarke and Mills were running side-by-side, with Gammoudi just behind. On the backstretch, Clarke tried to get Mills to move out so he could pass a runner who was being lapped. When Mills didn't move, Clarke shoved him, causing Mills to break his stride and run wide.

Gammoudi, seeing the opening, ran between the two front runners and opened up a lead. Clarke chased Gammoudi and passed him at the beginning of the final stretch. But Gammoudi hung on, pulling back up beside Clarke.

But then the impossible happened. As Clarke and Gammoudi were racing down the straightaway for the gold medal, Mills sprinted past them to win the race by three meters, beating his own personal best time by 50 seconds.

Clarke, who had never heard of Mills before the race, was told later that Mills was seven-sixteenths Sioux Indian. "Crikey," Clarke said, "I burn off all the regular distance runners and what am I left with? An Ethiopian, a Tunisian, and a half-Sioux Indian."

SHORTENED ANTHEMS

Because of the length of *The Star Spangled Banner*, it has been customary over the years for host countries to play a shortened version of the anthem whenever there was an American winner on the victory stand. The shortened version concluded with: " . . . were so gallantly streaming." Until 1964, the last time the entire anthem had been played was in 1956 when hammer thrower Harold Connolly was presented his gold medal.

But in 1964, the tradition of playing the condensed version of the anthem was broken on the final day of the track and field events, during the awards ceremonies for the 400- and 1600-meter relays. Each time when *The Star Spangled Banner* came to an abrupt halt, two trumpet players in the stands finished the anthem, to the delight of the 75,000 spectators. The trumpeters were track fans Uan Rasey and Mannie Klein, who were

Jostling on the final lap of the historic 10,000 meters. L to R, Mills, Gammoudi, Clarke.

studio musicians in Hollywood.

Strangely, one of the U.S. news agencies reported that the anthem was completed by Bob Crosby and his Bobcats, a popular jazz group led by singer Bing Crosby's younger brother. It is true that Rasey and Klein played with the Bobcats in various Tokyo nightclubs, but the only players in the Olympic stadium that day were the two trumpeters.

"LONG IN THE TOOTH"

The shot put gold medal was won by Dallas Long, a dentistry student who was anxious to get back to his studies in California. "It's time to stop

94

putting and start pulling," he commented as he said his goodbyes.

A NEW ANTHEM?

The Americans completely overshadowed the rest of the world in the swimming events, winning 16 of the 22 gold medals. One British Olympic author, writing about the number of times *The Star Spangled Banner* was played in the swimming hall, commented on the significance of the U.S. anthem's line: "Then conquer we must, for our cause it is just."

If you don't immediately recognize that line from *The Star Spangled Banner*, you are not alone. However, it can be located in the anthem's fourth verse, which appears to be even less singable than the ever-popular first verse.

A LONE PROTEST

Flyweight boxer Choh Dong-Kiu of South Korea sat on a stool in the middle of the ring for almost an hour to protest his disqualification for hitting his opponent after the referee had told him to stop.

Officials were afraid to remove Choh forcibly because of the large number of Korean fans in the arena who also disagreed with the referee's decision. Finally, after more than 50 minutes, Choh's own second dragged him out of the ring after assuring him there would be a full inquiry the next morning.

THE AGE OF SWIMMING

After 15-year-old Sharon Stouder of the United States finished second in the 100-meter freestyle, she was asked, "What is middle-aged in girls' swimming these days?" After a moment's thought, Stouder answered, "Well, 13 is quite young and 17 is really old, so I guess at 15 I'm a middle-aged swimmer."

Another American swimmer, Kathie Ellis, after finishing third in the women's 100-meter butterfly, said, "I'm an old, old lady who's getting out of swimming with all the pressure coming from these kids." Ellis was 18.

THE DAWN OF TROUBLE

Australia's feisty swimmer, Dawn Fraser, who won gold medals in three consecutive Olympic Games, was out celebrating her win in the 100-meter freestyle with two teammates when they decided to steal a flag from the grounds of the Imperial Palace. Although her teammates managed to get away, the police arrived in time to arrest Fraser, who had the flag. She had jumped on a bicycle to try to escape, but was cornered by the police when she reached the moat surrounding the grounds.

At the time, there were many stories circulating about the incident, some of which are still included in Olympic history books. One story was that Fraser swam across the moat to get to the Palace grounds. Another was that she swam the moat in the nude. "Have you seen the moat?" Fraser asked when being interviewed later. "Ugh. It's full of green slime. None of the things they said were true."

The police were about to haul Fraser off to jail when they realized who she was. They released her and let her keep the flag. However, the Australian officials, who were not amused by the incident, slapped a ten-year suspension on her. "I finally sued on the grounds of defamation," Fraser said, "and they had to apologize and lift my suspension."

THE WILL TO WIN

Women's volleyball was a new Olympic sport in 1964 and the Japanese were determined to be the first Olympic champions. They underwent long, hard, sometimes near-inhumane practice sessions for more than a year to prepare for the Olympics.

They worked at their normal jobs until 3:30 p.m. each work day, and then went to the gymnasium for eight straight hours of what one writer described as "sadistic training." On Sundays they worked out for 12 straight grueling hours. "The preparation for winning is a personal challenge," their coach explained. "It is accepted without question."

But the night before the Games were to open, the North Korean team withdrew from the Olympics and went home, leaving the volleyball competition with only five teams. Since Olympic rules require that a minimum of six nations be entered before a sport can be contested, it began to appear that all of the Japanese volleyball players' work had been for naught.

In desperation, the Japanese offered nearby

South Korea one million yen (about $3,000) to organize and outfit a team, and to send the team to Tokyo. The South Koreans agreed. The Japanese women, as expected, took every match and won the gold medals easily. The South Koreans, as might be expected, lost every match and finished last.

A NEW DRUG EMERGES

The 1964 Olympic Games ushered in a new phase of Olympic history that would change the future complexion of the Olympic Game. For the first time, many Olympic athletes were taking anabolic-androgenic steroids, the synthetic drugs that are now known simply as steroids. But the athletes who used them were not Russians, as has often been alleged. An American doctor initiated the development of the first commercially-produced steroid products, and it was American athletes who used them in Tokyo.

Anabolic (growth and strength increasing)-Androgenic (masculinizing) steroids are synthetic modifications of testosterone, the male sex hormone.

Combined with intense training, anabolic steroids increase lean muscle mass and work capacity, providing athletes with increased strength, power, and speed. In 1964, they could be taken by injection with a syringe or orally in pill form. The injections provided a more effective action of the drug, but the pills provided a higher level of secrecy.

It is known that American weight lifters in the 1948 Olympics and Soviet weight lifters in the 1952 Olympics began experimenting with pure testosterone as an anabolic agent. But the side effects were so extreme that only the most obsessive competitors took testosterone and faced the accompanying physical risks.

In 1956 at the World Games in Moscow, an American physician, John B. Ziegler, observed testosterone being administered to some of the Soviet weight lifters. Noting the potential side effects associated with taking pure testosterone and realizing the great advantage the Soviet athletes were gaining over U.S. athletes, Dr. Ziegler decided America needed to develop a synthetic form of testosterone. His idea was to develop a drug that would provide the desired anabolic effects while eliminating the harmful side effects.

Dr. Ziegler worked with the CIBA Pharmaceutical Company during the late 1950s to develop Dianabol, the U.S. alternative to testosterone. By 1964, Dianabol was available, supposedly only by prescription, throughout the American sports scene.

Four-time U.S. Olympian Hal Connolly, testifying during U.S. Senate hearings in 1973, said: "Just prior to the 1964 Olympic Games in Tokyo, all around me it seemed that more and more athletes were using steroids . . . An athlete who did not use steroids was placing himself at a decided disadvantage if he did not also get on the sports medicine bandwagon."

One 1964 U.S. gold medal winner, who did not want his name used, said he had witnessed a team physician injecting his Olympic village roommate with anabolic steroids before his race at Tokyo. Connolly, confirming this was not an uncommon practice, said his own roommate in Tokyo provided the Olympic team physicians with vials containing drugs prescribed by the roommate's doctor.

"If an athlete's personal physician prescribed a medication as part of the athlete's training," Connolly explained, "the Olympic doctors had a professional obligation to provide the athlete with whatever had been prescribed."

To be fair to the athletes and the doctors who were involved, the use of anabolic steroids to improve sports performance was not illegal and was not considered unethical in 1964. Steroids were considered by many of those involved as merely a means for strengthening the body, the same as using tape on weak ankles. The use of anabolic steroids would not be ruled illegal by the IOC until 1975.

Steroid use by Olympic athletes was a closely-guarded secret in 1964. Apparently the involved athletes, coaches, doctors, and trainers either (1) had a feeling that the use of such drugs might appear unethical, even if they were not illegal, or (2) their use provided an advantage that should not be shared with the public, or perhaps more importantly, with the competition.

It was almost three years later that the first published article on the use of steroids by athletes appeared in a United States publication. The article was originally scheduled to appear in *The Saturday Evening Post* in 1966, but when one of the U.S. Olympic team doctors told the *Post* editors that such drugs did not exist, the *Post* rejected the project. The article was finally published, with little fanfare and even less public response, in *True* magazine in April of 1967.*

AN OLD DRUG BECOMES MORE POPULAR

Amphetamine use by Olympic athletes appears to have begun in 1952, when several speed skaters in the winter Games overdosed and had to receive medical attention. It didn't take long for word to spread in the sports community, and by 1956 and 1960 the use of stimulants was becoming more widespread in most of the Olympic sports. The death of Danish cyclist Knud Jensen in 1960, which was at least partially attributed to a stimulant drug, brought world attention to what had been a closely-guarded secret.

Amphetamines can have enormous positive effects on an athlete's performance. They act as a stimulant of the central nervous system, increasing heart rate, blood pressure, and metabolism. Researchers and athletes have reported that amphetamines increase speed, increase energy, delay fatigue, and mask pain.

By 1964, amphetamines had become very popular among Olympic athletes from many

---

*"The Pill That Could Kill Sport" by Tom Ecker, True, *April, 1967.*

countries. "It was quite common for athletes to take oral stimulants—amphetamines—in the 1964 Olympics," said Hal Connolly, one of the few athletes willing to go on the record about the use of drugs in sports. "They were very easy to get."

One American track and field gold medal winner in Tokyo, when asked if he had used anabolic steroids before his race, said he had not. Not realizing what he was admitting, he then said he had only taken "some of the pills that were going around." The pills, it turned out, were amphetamines.

THE GAMES COME TO A CLOSE

The Olympic flame, which two months earlier had been lit by rays from the sun on the other side of the earth, was extinguished at the closing ceremonies. The Olympic flag was lowered and carried from the stadium.

And some 5,000 athletes entered the stadium, not marching "eight by eight," as the public address announcer was pleading, but running, skipping, laughing, and alternately snapping photos and posing for photos. Only the Japanese team, the last to enter and organized to the very end, marched solemnly in eight-by-eight ranks.

With fireworks exploding above, the athletes congregated on the infield, where they were surrounded by hundreds of Japanese girls carrying torches. The massed bands played *Auld Lang Syne* and the electronic scoreboard flashed its final message: *Sayonara, Sayonara, Sayonara—we meet again in Mexico City in 1968.*

Olympiad XIX
MEXICO CITY, 1968

THE MOST CONTROVERSIAL OLYMPIC SITE

In October of 1963, the IOC awarded the 1968 Olympic Games to Mexico City, a decision which brought immediate criticism from around the world. Coaches, athletes, sports scientists, and doctors were agreed that the rarefied air in a city that lies 7,573 feet above sea level would restrict performances in all endurance events, leaving even the best sea level athletes gasping for air.

Pointing out that the highest previous Olympic city was only 658 feet above sea level, the critics said the altitude would favor athletes who lived at altitude, or sea level athletes who could afford to train at altitude, but would condemn to automatic defeat those who lived and trained at or near sea level. Onni Niskanen, the Finnish coach of Ethiopia's Abebe Bikila, even predicted: "There will be those who will die."

As it turned out, those concerns were dwarfed by the other problems that plagued the Mexico Olympics. With the world in turmoil in 1968, it should not have been surprising that the Mexico Olympics would later be described as even more politicized than the 1936 Games of Nazi Germany.

THE TRAINING RULES ARE TIGHTENED

The problem of preparing for altitude competitions was further complicated when the IOC, in an attempt to prevent the widespread migration of athletes to high altitude countries to train, ruled that competitors would be allowed to train at high altitudes for only four weeks during the three months preceding the Olympics. As it turned out, the rule proved to be unenforceable.

The Americans constructed a "medical and testing facility" at South Lake Tahoe, Nevada, where U.S. athletes could train at altitude on a year-round basis. The French and the Swiss followed suit by constructing high-altitude sports training centers in the towns of Font Romeu, in the Pyrenees mountains, and St. Moritz, high in the Swiss Alps.

In a clever move to circumvent the IOC's rule, Olympic athletes from several low altitude countries enrolled at high-altitude American universities to study (and, incidentally, to train for the Olympics). The athletes' expenses were paid by special "scholarships" provided by their national sports federations.

THE OLYMPIC PROJECT FOR HUMAN RIGHTS

A series of events that began in the fall of 1967 were to become of much greater concern to the Mexican organizers than the problems of altitude. They began in Japan when U.S. sprint star Tommie Smith was asked in a radio interview if there was any truth to the rumors that black athletes from the U.S. planned to boycott the 1968 Olympics to protest racial injustice in the United States. Not expecting the question, Smith did not deny it, replying that anything was possible.

The media response and the opinions on both sides of the issue were immediate and extreme. So were the personal attacks suffered by Smith, who began receiving hate letters and telephoned death threats. People would call Smith, yell out "Bang!" when he answered, and then hang up.

At San Jose State, where Smith was a student, sociology instructor and black activist Harry Edwards had been organizing a "black athlete revolt." As a part of the revolt, Edwards suggested activities that would draw attention to the cause, including boycotting the Olympics. Among those involved in the initial meetings, besides Tommie Smith, were other San Jose track stars, John Carlos and Lee Evans.

On October 7, 1967, Edwards announced the formation of the Olympic Committee for Human Rights. The segment of the committee dealing specifically with an Olympic boycott was called the Olympic Project for Human Rights. On November 23, Edwards announced there would definitely be a boycott of the 1968 Olympics.

SOVIET SUPPORT

Yuriy Mashim, head of the Soviet Union's Olympic committee, announced that he supported the idea of the proposed boycott. Mashim, whose motives might be questioned, said, "I think the proposed boycott of the Olympics by U.S. Negro athletes is a good idea."

SOUTH AFRICA CONSIDERED AGAIN

Early in 1968, the plans for a U.S. black boycott became even more complicated when the IOC met to consider allowing South Africa back into the Olympics. The South Africans, whose apartheid policies had kept them out of the previous Games, had guaranteed they would have racially integrated teams in Mexico City. By a narrow margin, the IOC decided to invite South Africa—if its teams were multiracial and all competitors were treated equally.

Jean Ganga, leader of the Supreme Council of Sports in Africa, responded that if South Africa were allowed to participate, the 33 African countries would boycott the Olympics. He also said he would ask "the Negroes of the United States" to join them in their boycott.

By April, 40 countries, all of them from Africa and Eastern Europe, including the Soviet Union, said they would boycott the Games if South Africa participated. Worried that their Olympics would be severely damaged by a boycott of that size, the organizers pleaded with the IOC to reconsider South Africa's invitation.

In May, Avery Brundage called a meeting of the IOC executive board to reconsider their previous action. After two days of debate, the invitation to South Africa was withdrawn, to the great relief of the Mexican organizers.

The reversal was a bitter blow to Brundage, who had always maintained that racial segregation in South Africa was not a question of sports, but of politics. He felt South Africa's agreement to send an integrated team was a step forward.

Because of Brundage's "conciliatory attitude about South Africa," black athletes from the U.S.

Tommie Smith (L) and John Carlos interviewed by Jim McKay at the Olympic Trials.

announced they would not accept medals from him during any awards ceremonies. A bedsheet with "DOWN WITH BRUNDAGE" lettered on it hung from one of the windows of the American quarters in the Olympic village.

SOUTH AFRICAN ATHLETES PROTEST

Ironically, the decision to bar South Africa was met with loud protests from the black members of the South African team, who wanted to participate. Fred Thabede, the leader of South Africa's black athletes, even proposed a meeting with representatives of the other black nations to point out that their decision, in fact, discriminated against nonwhites. "We want to compete," Thabede said, "and it is the black African nations that are keeping the blacks of South Africa out of the Olympics."

THE BOYCOTT IS CANCELED

The U.S. black boycott, which had been announced by Harry Edwards the previous year, was called off in September, a month before the opening of the Games. But there were ongoing rumors that there would still be demonstrations of some sort. Worried USOC officials issued various warnings to the black athletes, which only fueled the flames.

THE STUDENT REBELLION

Mexican students, outraged by the amount of money being spent on the Olympics when there was so much poverty and suffering in Mexico, began organizing protest rallies around the city and on the university campus, which was across the street from the Olympic stadium.

Amid rumors that the students were planning to sabotage the Olympics, IOC president Avery Brundage warned Mexico's president, Gustavo Diaz Ordaz, that the Olympics would be canceled if there were student demonstrations at any of the Olympic sites.

The government's response to the Brundage warning was to extinguish the flickering "revolution." In a show of force, tanks and soldiers appeared along the roads around the university and the Olympic stadium. Mexico's defense secretary, General Marcelino Garcia Barragan, was given orders to crush the revolution at any cost.

Ten days before the Olympics were to begin, the students and their supporters—10,000 strong—staged a rally in the Plaza of the Three Cultures in central Mexico City. As the rally progressed, the Mexican army surrounded the plaza.

In what was later described by some journalists as a massacre, the army opened fire on the students, first with tear gas, and then with rifles, machine guns, and bazookas, killing at least 260 and wounding an estimated 1,200 during the brutal and bloody confrontation. Some estimates of the dead ran as high as 400.

John Rodda, a veteran British sports journalist who had spent the previous week investigating the causes of the student unrest, was held at gunpoint on the floor of an adjacent balcony throughout the battle so he could not see what was happening. Rodda, in an understandable state of shock, later contacted British and Olympic officials, urging that the Olympics be canceled.

RESPONSE TO THE MASSACRE

At an emergency meeting of the IOC the morning after the incident, Mexico's IOC member, General Jose Clark Flores, remarked that more people are killed in traffic accidents every day than were shot in the Plaza. He didn't think it was an important matter for discussion.

It was later reported that many of the dead were buried in an unmarked mass grave, making it difficult to determine the exact number of dead or the nationalities of some of the victims. In an attempt to calm U.S. critics, the Mexican government announced that many of those killed were Cubans who had been sent to Mexico by Fidel Castro to disrupt the Olympics.

The massacre at the Plaza of the Three Cultures was by far the bloodiest Olympic Games-related event of the century, and, considering its magnitude and severity, it was also the least publicized. The Associated Press reported that "25 were killed during a student rebellion." In the AP report, the government's press secretary was quoted as saying the trouble started when the students started shooting at each other.

In one of the more widely-distributed books on Olympic history, the massacre is described as "a wave of arrests a few days prior to opening ceremonies . . . to prevent any outbreaks during the Games." There is no mention of shootings, brutality, or deaths.

PEACE IN THE VILLAGE

At the time of the shootings in the Plaza of Three Cultures, most of the Olympic athletes had not yet arrived in Mexico. The military crack-down on the student rebellion was certainly effective. By the time the athletes arrived, the mood around Mexico City, and particularly around the Olympic village, had become festive and full of anticipation.

The village was made up of 29 apartment buildings, each six to ten stories high, containing 904 apartments which would be sold as condominiums after the Games.

Security was generally loose throughout the village, and there was a mood of international friendliness and companionship throughout. But security was tight at the entrances to the side-by-side buildings which housed the teams from the Soviet Union and the United States. Soviet officials, and perhaps even officials from the U.S., did not want athletes from the two nations mingling.

Yet on the rooftop, the Russians and the Americans were having daily parties together. When the athletes discovered passageways to the roof where they could meet without the knowledge of their team officials, the athletes spread out blankets, shared food and drink, listened to music, and talked about the Olympics.

THE CONSULTANT'S COMMITTEE

Jesse Owens, 55 years old and still an international Olympic hero, went to Mexico City as a guest of the Mexican government. He also served as chairman of the USOC's Consultant's Committee, an *ad hoc* group of former Olympians who were brought to Mexico City to help resolve athletes' "personal and political problems." Other members of the committee were Nell Jackson, Rafer Johnson, Hayes Jones, Bob Mathias, and John Sayre.

Since four of the six committee members were black, it was evident that the committee was created to try to keep the black athletes, as one journalist put it, "subdued and out of trouble." When asked his opinion of the boycott announcement by Harry Edwards, Owens said he was sympathetic with the motives of the athletes, but thought a boycott would be "the wrong approach to the problem."

THE SHOE WAR ESCALATES

The battle between the two German shoe companies, Adidas and Puma, each brand with its distinctive markings, reached new heights during the Mexico Olympics. For several years, the two companies had tried to entice the more famous athletes to wear (and thus to publicize) their shoes.

At first the companies merely provided free shoes to the athletes. By 1964 a few athletes received cash payments for wearing particular shoes. But by 1968 the stakes had been raised and many, many athletes were receiving their free shoes with traveler's checks or currency tucked into the toes.

The payment of athletes by the shoe companies was perhaps the decade's worst-kept secret. Several U.S. athletes cashed traveler's checks (issued by a German bank) at the Olympic village bank for amounts ranging up to $7,500. According to a representative of one of the shoe companies, the top price paid was $10,000 per race—but only to athletes who had a good chance of winning a gold medal.

It was not unusual for even the lesser-known athletes to find ten $50 bills in the toes of their new shoes when they unboxed them. "You might think there are a lot of injured athletes in the village," one journalist joked, "but they are probably limping because of all the money stuffed in their shoes."

OFF TO JAIL

The Adidas company outmaneuvered Puma early in the 1968 Olympic shoe war by signing an exclusive (and probably expensive) contract with the Mexican organizing committee. This gave Adidas the exclusive right to have a shoe store in the Olympic village, to import as many Adidas shoes as they wanted, and to keep Puma shoes from entering the country.

When 3,000 pairs of Puma shoes arrived at the Mexico City airport a few weeks before the Games, they were immediately confiscated by customs authorities. Puma did manage to bring in a few hundred pairs into the country, smuggled in by members of the British Olympic team, but the 3,000 pairs remained locked up at the airport.

A Puma representative from California, Art Simburg, decided to fight back. He went to several different sports delegations, asking for signatures on a petition to allow Puma shoes to be imported for the Olympics. Simburg was in the process of collecting signatures when two security agents asked him to come with them.

Simburg was whisked off to a so-called immigration station, a fancy name for a prison, where he was incarcerated for the next five days and nights. To people around the Olympic scene who knew Simburg, he had simply disappeared.

Simburg had no contact with the outside world. He had no opportunity to wash up or change clothes. He said, "The bread and water diet you associate with jails was supplemented in my case. I had bread and beans and water."

Simburg's "escape" was as unusual as his incarceration. He had explained his plight to an Ecuadorian inmate who understood some English, who passed it along to a sympathetic official who understood only Spanish. The official contacted the Puma representatives in Mexico City, who contacted Avery Brundage and the U.S. State Department, who applied enough pressure on the Mexican authorities to obtain Simburg's release.

When he returned to his hotel, his first shower in five days was a long one. "It was a celebration," Simburg said. Simburg would later marry two-time 100 champion Wyomia Tyus.

TIGHT SECURITY

On October 12, the opening ceremonies were conducted under the tightest of security. Mexican soldiers with loaded rifles lined the streets in full battle gear. Surrounding the stadium's parking lots were camouflaged tanks and antiaircraft guns. The camouflage was probably in place as much for the foreign visitors as it was for potential terrorists.

Inside the stadium was a different scene. There was no sign of the military anywhere. The ceremonies were conducted without a flaw in a festive atmosphere, as though they had never been threatened.

One problem the police handled during the opening ceremonies was keeping unticketed Mexicans out of the packed stadium. One American eyewitness reported, "All along the back wall, where we sat, were policemen. When a hand appeared on the top of the wall, already lined with glass shards, the policemen would bash the hand with a nightstick, sending the intruder off to what had to be a long fall. There weren't many successful gate crashers, although they continued to try all afternoon."

TO DIP OR NOT TO DIP

American hammer thrower Harold Connolly, in his fourth Olympic Games, was called to the office of the U.S. Olympic Committee and told he had been selected to carry the U.S. flag in the opening ceremonies. Connolly was both surprised and honored.

"I started to go out the door," Connolly recalled later, "and I thought, if I carry the flag, I really want to dip it. I was embarrassed that the United States was the only country that refused to dip the flag when passing the reviewing stand. It seemed arrogant to me."

When Connolly told the committee members he was going to break the 60-year tradition and dip the flag, they told him he couldn't. He'd be breaking a federal law. "They said they'd send me home and have me arrested," Connolly said.

After reiterating that he could not, in good conscience, carry the flag without dipping it, Connolly was replaced as flagbearer by six-time Olympic fencer Janice Romary. (To show how stories can be remembered differently, Jesse Owens wrote in 1970 that Connolly wanted to dip the flag

in 1968 "to dramatize the Negro's plight in America" but Owens talked him out of it.)

If Connolly had carried the flag and had dipped it, he would have been in violation of an act signed into law on December 22, 1942. Under the heading "Respect for the Flag" it states: "The flag should not be dipped to any person or thing." However, there is no provision in the law for punishing an offender, so Connolly almost certainly would not have been arrested.

THE SOVIET UNION VS. CZECHOSLOVAKIA

The spectators at the opening ceremonies were prepared to greet the athletes from Czechoslovakia and the Soviet Union in opposite ways as they marched into the stadium. Just two months earlier, Czechoslovakia had been invaded by the Soviets in an effort to suppress the liberal Alexander Dubček regime. World opinion was on the side of Czechoslovakia, of course, and so the stage was set for a public response to the Soviet aggression during the opening ceremonies.

When the Czech athletes marched into the stadium, they were greeted with a huge ovation from the crowd. The cheers continued until the Czechs reached the infield. When the Soviet athletes entered the stadium, just as the booing and jeering began, each of the Soviet athletes held high a small Mexican flag to go with the small Soviet flags they were carrying. The response from the largely Mexican crowd was a roar of cheers and applause. With their clever maneuver, the Soviets had elicited almost as much vocal support from the crowd as the Czechs had.

THE FIRST DRUG TESTS

Drug tests were administered to the first six finishers in every event, plus another four randomly selected from the other competitors. The tests were designed to determine the illegal use of stimulant drugs, including amphetamines and other chemical agents recognized with a broad-spectrum urinalysis.

In a rare disqualification for drug use, Hans-Gunnar Liljenvall, a member of Sweden's modern pentathlon team, was tested after the event and a banned substance was found in his system. It was alcohol—specifically prohibited in this event. Liljenvall claimed he had consumed only two bottles of beer before the competition, but the Swedish team was disqualified anyway.

NOT IN ATTENDANCE

Mexico's first Olympic champion, General Humberto Mariles, who won the equestrian show jumping competition in 1948, was not on hand for the 1968 Olympics. He was in prison, charged with the murder of a man who rammed into his car and refused to apologize.

ALTITUDE AFFECTS THE RESULTS

The altitude took its toll in the endurance events. Ron Clarke of Australia, who held several world records in distance running events and was again a favorite in the 10,000 meters, tried to stay with the "high altitude" runners throughout the race, but with two laps to go he faded badly. Clarke finished sixth and had to be given oxygen after collapsing at the finish. Later Clarke said, "It was an Olympics for the men of the mountains." The winner was Naftali Temu of Kenya, whose winning time was almost two minutes slower than Clarke's world record. This was hardly a fluke victory, however, as Temu had handily defeated Clarke at the Commonwealth Games in 1966.

The other endurance events produced about the same results, with Africans winning every race from 1500 meters through the marathon, with each of the winning times well off the world record. The longer the race, the greater the time difference. Mamo Wolde of Ethiopia scored a convincing win in the marathon, finishing more than three minutes ahead of the second place finisher, yet his time was almost 11 minutes slower than the fastest-ever marathon.

The thin air, which slowed all of the times in the endurance events, also provided 23 percent less air density. This meant that athletes in the "explosive" events, such as the sprints, hurdles, relay races, and the horizontal jumps, faced less air resistance and thus were able to achieve record performances. In the men's track and field events, world records were set in every race from the 100 meters through the 800 meters, including both hurdle races and both relay races, plus the long jump and triple jump. In the women's events, world records were set in the 100, the 200, long jump and the relay.

CLARKE GETS A GOLD MEDAL

Australian Ron Clarke, who had dominated distance running in the decade with 18 world records between 1961 and 1968, was heralded as the greatest distance runner since Emil Zátopek. Zátopek, winner of four gold medals in the 1948 and 1952 Games, had been Clarke's idol since Ron began running as a teenager.

In a visit to Prague, Czechoslovakia, after his competitive career was over, Clarke met with the great Zátopek. At the end of the visit Zátopek presented him with a small gift wrapped in brown paper. When Clarke opened the package later, he discovered that Zátopek had given him one of his Olympic gold medals from 1952. "It was a gesture of the man, recognizing the bad luck I'd had [in the Olympics] and paying tribute to me," Clarke said later. "It's something I value more than any other possession."

THE FOSBURY FLOP

A new back-dive high jump technique made its Olympic debut in 1968, thanks to Dick Fosbury of Oregon State University. The technique, which became known as the Fosbury Flop, was developed by Fosbury while he was still in high school, where he had cleared 6 feet 7 inches. As a freshman at Oregon State he was asked to try the conventional roll technique, but Fosbury was not nearly as successful using the roll.

After six months he went back to the flop and jumped 6 feet 10³/₄ inches as a university sophomore. The next year he was the Olympic champion and record holder at 7 feet 4¹/₄ inches. The quiet, unassuming Fosbury seemed to be as amazed by the unorthodox technique as the spectators. "Sometimes I see movies and I really wonder how I do it," he commented.

A SNIPER'S BULLET?

Tommie Smith and John Carlos, two of the principal players in the threats to boycott the Olympics, were also the two favorites in the 200 meters. Smith seemed to have the edge early in the competition. He equalled the Olympic record of 20.3 in the first round, ran 20.2 in the second round, and ran 20.1 in the semifinal round. But when he crossed the finish line in the semifinal and began slowing down, he let out a scream of pain. He had pulled an abductor muscle in his right groin.

Smith's immediate thought was that he had been shot by a sniper. He had received so many death threats prior to the Olympics, it was not surprising that he thought the sudden pain in his groin was from a bullet. "It was a piercing pain like I thought a bullet would feel," he said later. "I really thought I'd been shot."

A WHITE PHYSICIAN NAMED COOPER

Jesse Owens, who obviously did not approve of the militant agenda of Smith and Carlos, wrote later about Tommie Smith's abductor injury: "In the beginning, it didn't seem as though he'd be running the finals at all a few hours later. But a white physician from Oklahoma named Cooper worked on him and Tommie ran. And broke not only the Olympic record but the world mark."

The physician from Oklahoma was Donald L. Cooper, one of the Olympic team doctors. "Tommie had a little over two hours to the final," Cooper recollected years later. "We put an ice pack on him for 20 minutes. Then we walked over to the practice track. We did three sets of ice massage, each lasting 10 to 12 minutes. I gave him three aspirin and applied a final ice massage in the stadium tunnel just before the race."

"I called him the cold man," Smith told the author. "I never knew his name until now. If you see him, please thank him for me."

THE SMITH-CARLOS DEMONSTRATION

Long before the 200 meters was run, Tommie Smith had planned what he and John Carlos were going to do to demonstrate against racial injustice in the U.S. As *The Star Spangled Banner* was played, they lowered their heads and raised their clenched fists in a black power salute. They had obviously split a pair of black gloves so each could wear one. Smith wore the right glove, Carlos the left. There was a light mixture of cheering and booing from the spectators, but many unsympathetic American fans in attendance were infuriated.

"My wife Denise brought the gloves," Smith commented later. "There was only the one pair, and since they were mine, Carlos got the left one. I intended to use my right hand."

The two athletes had their pant legs rolled up, showing they were wearing long black socks.

Also, each was wearing an "Olympic Project for Human Rights" button. Silver medalist Peter Norman of Australia, who supported Smith and Carlos "for showing the courage of their convictions," also wore one of the buttons on the victory stand. Norman, who was later reprimanded by the Australian Olympic Committee, became a close and lasting friend of Smith.

There was one other part of the demonstration that has never been completely explained in the literature. When Smith and Carlos stood on the victory podium, they each held high a black and white Puma shoe. There were many interpretations of this bit of symbolism in the press, including a British journalist's explanation that the black and white shoes represented black and white brotherhood. The real reason was offered later by Tommie Smith himself: "We held up Puma shoes because it was Puma that supported us financially. It just happened they were black and white."

THE USOC RESPONDS

The next day, the USOC, pressured by the IOC, expelled Smith and Carlos from the U.S. team. Most accounts say they were also expelled from the Olympic village, but neither of them was living in the village at the time. They were living in a downtown hotel with their wives.

Most accounts also say their passports (or visas) were canceled and they were forced to leave the country immediately. But Olympic athletes did not have to have passports or visas to be in Mexico, and it was obvious that John Carlos did not leave. He was in the stadium two days later, cheering for women's 800-meter winner Madeline Manning.

Rumors circulated that other athletes would refuse to compete because of the USOC's treatment of Smith and Carlos, but everyone else did compete. However, there still were occasional signs of protest, although they were less obvious after that. The most obvious were the black knee-length socks and black berets that became a part of the uniform for some of the black Americans athletes.

When Smith and Carlos returned to the U.S., they were faced with many unpleasant situations that had long-lasting, devastating effects on their lives. They had trouble making a living and their marriages began to fail. "There was so much turmoil," Smith recalled. "There was constant moving and we were always living in fear. It was terrible for all of us, especially the wives."

According to Smith, the stress took its toll. First, both marriages ended in divorce. Later on Denise Smith suffered a mental breakdown and Kim Carlos eventually committed suicide.

A RUNNING WALKER

In the final lap of the 20-kilometer walk, a Mexican walker, Jose Pedraza, entered the stadium in third place, but his walking technique was different from the others. Walking requires that one foot touch the ground before the other foot leaves the ground, but that was not happening with Pedraza. It was obvious that Pedraza was airborne between steps. He was running.

He was also gaining on the two Russians who were ahead of him, to the great delight of the Mexican fans, who were shouting "Meh-hee-co, Meh-hee-co." There was near pandemonium in the stadium as Pedraza streaked past one of the Russians and finished second, barely missing the gold medal. A disqualification seemed inevitable, but a riot in the stadium would certainly have ensued. Apparently the judges agreed. Pedraza received the silver medal.

IT WAS A GOOD JUMP

Most noteworthy of the records set in the rarefied air was the long jump mark of 29 feet 2½ inches by U.S. jumper Bob Beamon. Beamon's mark has been acclaimed by many as the greatest sports achievement of all time, but when the effects of the thin air and the trailing wind are taken into consideration, that judgment must be tempered.

As the long jump competition began, a rainstorm was approaching behind the jumpers from the north, the temperature was dropping rapidly, the Tartan synthetic runway was firm and fast, and the wind was blowing hard along the runway, with intermittent gusts behind the jumpers.

The first three jumpers, Yamada of Japan, Brooks of Jamaica, and Boschert of West Germany, all fouled. According to coaches and athletes in attendance, their fouls resulted from the very fast runway and a strong trailing wind, both of which increase an athlete's speed and stride length.

Beamon, whose step pattern was so erratic that he occasionally took off from the wrong foot and often fouled, even under the best of conditions, was up next. He had fouled twice in the qualifying round the previous day and had almost failed to qualify for the final. But on this day, the stride-lengthening trailing wind which served as a disadvantage for the preceding jumpers would turn out to be an advantage for Beamon. In a classic example of two wrongs making a right, he hit the board perfectly on his first jump.

Nearby observers, who thought it suspicious that all of the first four jumps were recorded as having exactly the maximum allowable wind velocity—2.0 meters per second—noted that the official appeared to be more interested in world records than in accurate wind readings. Ron Pickering, the British coach of one of the long jump favorites, Lynn Davies, said that Davies and America's Ralph Boston estimated that the wind velocity was at least 5 meters per second at the time of Beamon's jump. Other nearby spectators agreed.

As soon as Beamon landed in the sand, there followed a comedy of errors on the part of the Mexican officials. Beamon had jumped beyond the sighting device being used to measure each jump, so, not knowing what to do next, the officials began running around looking for a tape measure. The competition was held up for several minutes until an "official" tape measure was finally located and the jump was measured.

By the time the other competitors could take their first jumps, the wind had changed direction, the rains came, and the runway became slippery.

Beamon was the only jumper who got off a fair jump under the most favorable of conditions. His second jump, which was made under the same conditions as the other jumpers, was only 26 feet 4½ inches, which, would have been good enough for sixth place in the competition. Wisely, Beamon quit jumping at that point, even though he had four jumps left.

It is a good thing that Beamon did take a second jump, to allow photographers to take pictures of "the world's longest jump." Many of the photographs of Beamon's jump that have been published were actually his "mediocre" second jump, or were taken the day before during the qualifying round. His record jump was the only one in which he was wearing the three-striped Adidas shoes and was not wearing long black socks. (There is one widely-circulated color photograph of the record jump, however, on which a touch-up artist has changed Beamon's shoes from Adidas to Puma.)

Announcing he might someday jump 30 feet, Beamon continued long jumping, off and on, for eight years after Mexico City. He did jump as far as 26 feet 11 inches once, but he never came close to his world record again.

There have been a great number of published analyses of Beamon's 1968 record jump, all of them reaching conclusions based on limited information. No one will ever know, for example, the exact wind velocity during Beamon's jump. It is calculated that if the wind was the estimated 5 mps, or even if it were blowing at only 4 mps, then Beamon's jump was good, but not earthshaking. However, if the official wind velocity of 2 mps was accurate, then the jump was truly spectacular—even at Mexico City's altitude.

A PATRIOTIC WINNER

A popular winner for the United States was heavyweight George Foreman, who waved a small American flag when he took the victory stand. Journalists were quick to point out the contrast between Foreman's conduct and that of some of the black medal winners in the track events. Foreman said, "That stuff's for college kids. They live in a different world."

A FAVORITE WITH THE FANS

Czechoslovakian gymnast Vera Čáslavská, who won seven gold and four silver medals in

Bob Beamon—the world record jump.

three Olympics, was a favorite with the Mexican spectators. At one point, after she had been given a score of 9.6 in the balance beam competition, the crowd roared its disapproval for so long that the competition was delayed until the judges raised her score to 9.8. She completed her performance with a free exercise routine to the tune of *The Mexican Hat Dance*, to the delight of the cheering crowd.

A HAPPY CLOSING

To be certain the closing ceremonies would be orderly, the Mexican officials limited the number of athletes that would be allowed to march in the parade of nations. The other athletes were seated in a corner of the stadium where they could watch the proceedings. But as the small groups of athletes marched into the stadium, first one at a time, then in groups, the seated athletes left their seats, and climbed over the low wall to join those who were parading officially. To the cheers of the spectators, the athletes hugged each other, danced, waved to the crowd, and exchanged hats, pins, shirts, and jackets.

Hundreds of mariachi musicians were massed on the infield, playing Mexican tunes as fireworks exploded overhead. Even the staid Avery Brundage, who didn't have a great deal to be happy about, said afterwards, "The spontaneous demonstration of international goodwill during the emotion-charged closing ceremony left hardly a dry eye in the stadium."

Olympiad XX
MUNICH, 1972

ALWAYS A BRIDESMAID

Detroit had been the USOC's choice to be the U.S. candidate to host the Olympic Games in 1960, 1964, and 1968. All three times, the Michigan city lost out in the final balloting.

When the IOC met in 1966 to select the host city for the 1972 Games, Detroit was again the U.S. choice, but once more Detroit lost out, this time to Munich, a city that was anxious to show the world a different side of Germany than the Nazis had presented in 1936.

THE 2,000-YEAR-OLD MONK

At the close of World War II, an eccentric "Russian monk" named Timofey Pokorov, decided to build a home and church in the middle of an open field near Munich. A portion of the field was being used as a dumping ground for the tons of bomb rubble from downtown Munich, so no one seemed to care if a Russian monk lived on the land or not.

Pokorov, who had flowing white hair and a long, full beard, announced to anyone who would listen that he was 2,000 years old. He and his younger sister (who didn't look a day over 1,500), scavenged items from nearby junk piles and built a "modest" home (no heat, no electricity, no water, no plumbing) and a small chapel. It was not a pretty sight.

When the German Olympic Committee decided the open field would make an ideal site for the 1972 Olympic Games, Pokorov was told he would have to move. The monk refused, not knowing that he was soon to become the subject of the human interest story of the year. As the Munich newspapers began running articles about the threatened eviction of a 2,000-year-old monk, the German people rallied behind the underdog. Thousands of letters poured into the offices of the Olympic committee from people who had never heard of Pokorov before, insisting the monk be allowed to stay.

Finally, much to the regret of the Olympic committee, it was decided the Olympic grounds would have to be built around Pokorov's land. Like thorns among the roses, the monk and his sister, appearing to relish their new-found fame, remained on the Olympic grounds, offering tours of their shack-like chapel to passersby.

RHODESIA IS IN, THEN OUT

Before white-ruled Rhodesia was issued an invitation to participate at Munich, Rhodesian officials had to agree to eliminate their apartheid policies and provide a racially-mixed team. The Supreme Council for Sport in Africa said the other black nations of Africa would compete against Rhodesia if those conditions were met.

The Rhodesians did come to Germany with a racially-mixed team of 46 athletes, but apartheid practices obviously still prevailed at home. In protest, 21 African nations threatened to withdraw from the Games. Further pressure was applied when Lee Evans, 1968 Olympic champion and world record holder in the 400 meters, distributed a statement threatening a boycott by U.S. black athletes to "stand by our black brothers."

Four days before the opening ceremonies, the IOC voted 36-31 to withdraw Rhodesia's invitation. It was said that Avery Brundage, who had been insistent that Rhodesia be allowed to participate, was both outvoted and outraged.

OLGA CARRIES THE FLAG

In all of the previous Olympic Games, the American flagbearer for the opening ceremonies parade had been selected by the U.S. Olympic Committee. But in 1972, in a move to help appease the athletes who complained of the USOC's dictatorial ways, it was decided to make the choice by conducting an election among the athletes. It was a decision the USOC was soon to regret.

The election winner, by a two-vote margin, was discus thrower Olga Connolly. Connolly, who had won an Olympic gold medal for Czechoslovakia in 1956 and then married American hammer thrower Hal Connolly, was competing in her fifth Olympic Games, her fourth for the United States.

It was no secret that the USOC considered Connolly to be a rebellious promoter of liberal causes, which made her far less popular with them than she was with her teammates. During the previous days, she had even circulated petitions demanding the U.S. halt the Vietnam war during the two weeks the Olympics would be in session.

But the USOC's immediate worry was that Connolly would break the 64-year-old tradition and dip the flag as she marched before Germany's president, Gustav Heinemann. Husband Hal of course had been replaced as Mexico '68 flagbearer when he said he would dip the flag. The USOC couldn't replace Olga; she had won the election.

"Philosophically, Olga agreed with me," Hal recalled later. "She was European and thought it was arrogant for the United States to be the only country that refused to dip its flag. I didn't know until she marched out on the field what she was going to do."

The USOC held its collective breath as Olga led the U.S. athletes into the stadium. Surprising many, she did not dip the flag when she passed before the reviewing stand. She had struck a compromise with her teammates, agreeing to forego dipping the flag before the German president, but instead lowering it later as the Olympic oath was recited.

AN AMAZING RECOVERY

Finland's Lasse Viren, following in the footsteps of the Finnish distance legends of the past, won both the 10,000- and 5,000-meter runs. In the 10,000, Viren was running with the leaders at the halfway point, in fifth place, when he tripped and fell, causing Mohamed Gammoudi of Tunisia to tumble over him.

Viren rose to his feet and began running again. Slowly he gained on the leaders, Mariano Haro of Spain and Emiel Puttemans of Belgium. He

Lasse Viren, in fourth place above, has caught the front runners in the 10,000m and is preparing for his kick with 1½ laps to go. USA's Frank Shorter, at left, finished fifth.

passed them and reached the finish line six meters ahead of the field, setting a new world record.

UGANDA'S FIRST WINNER

John Akii-Bua of Uganda held off the defending champion, David Hemery of Great Britain, to win the 400-meter hurdle race, set the world record, and collect Uganda's first-ever gold medal. Akii-Bua had many siblings cheering for him back in his homeland. He was one of 43 children. (His father had eight wives.)

THE MUNICH NIGHTMARE

In the early morning hours of September 5, eight Arab terrorists, using a duplicate key they had acquired, entered the Olympic village apartment of the Israeli athletes and coaches and began shooting. Two Israelis died as a result of the original attack in the three-story building at Connollystrasse 31, and nine more were held hostage.*

The terrorists, members of the Black September faction, demanded that the Olympic Games be canceled, that 200 political prisoners held by Israel be released, and that they be given passage to an Arab country, accompanied by the Israeli hostages. They said one hostage would be killed every hour, beginning at 1:00 that after-

---

Connollystrasse was not named for Hal and Olga Connolly, as some have reported, but for triple jumper James B. Connolly, the first Olympic champion of the modern era.

noon, if their demands were not met.

Avery Brundage learned of the crisis at 6:00 A.M. and was in the village by 6:30. Without consulting with any other IOC members, Brundage took control of the situation himself. He did not even bother to contact Lord Killanin, who would succeed Brundage as IOC president after these Games, before Killanin and two other IOC members left for the yachting events in Kiel.

Brundage told the German authorities that the IOC, which in this case was only Brundage, would not approve of a transfer of Olympic athletes out of the country. At that point, German sharpshooters were brought in.

When the terrorists' 1:00 P.M. deadline passed, they extended it to 5:00. At 4:00 P.M., Brundage and German Olympic leader Willi Daume issued a communiqué canceling the rest of the day's Olympic events "with deep respect for the victims and a sign of sympathy with the hostages not yet released." The communiqué also announced that "services in commemoration of the victims" would take place at 10:00 the next morning in the Olympic stadium.

The drama in the Olympic village lasted throughout the day and long into the evening as Olympic events were suspended and the world watched, nonstop, on television. Jim McKay, ABC's indomitable sports commentator, stayed on the air for 15 hours, reporting the events of that tragic day to the American public. (Under the clothing McKay was wearing on television was the yellow swimsuit he was wearing when he received the call to go on the air. Hurriedly, he had put on his TV clothes over the swimsuit, which he wore for 20 straight hours.)

After hours of uneasy negotiations, German officials agreed to allow the terrorists and their hostages to fly by helicopter to the nearby Fürstenfeldbruck military air base. There, a German airliner would fly them to Egypt. (In reality, the Germans were not going to allow the terrorists to leave the country. Their sharpshooters were going to see to that.)

At 9:20 P.M., three helicopters arrived at the Olympic village. At 10:20 they left, two of them carrying the hostages and their captors. The other carried German officials, including Munich's chief of police.

Shortly after the helicopters arrived at Fürstenfeldbruck, police sharpshooters opened fire. Five terrorists were killed in the shootout and three were captured, but not before a terrorist managed to throw a hand grenade into the helicopter where the nine Israelis were strapped in their seats.

The first reports from Fürstenfeldbruck said the hostages had been saved. But four hours later the awful truth was announced. All of the Israeli hostages were dead.

The three surviving terrorists received long prison sentences, but they were released just a short two months later in exchange for the passengers and crew of a German Lufthansa plane that had been hijacked by a Palestinian commando.

THE TERRORIST MYSTERY

When the hostage crisis began, initial reports said the terrorists, dressed as athletes in warmup suits, had entered the village at 4:00 A.M. by climbing over a 6 ft. 7 in. fence. Authorities assumed that the intruders then changed clothes (since they were not wearing warmup suits the rest of the day) before proceeding the 50 meters to the building housing the Israelis. The shooting began as soon as they arrived, at 4:25.

French journalist Serge Groussard, who describes himself as "a witness from the first negotiations in front of Building 31 to the final shots at the air base," has conducted exhaustive research on the events of that day. Although Groussard's probing was often blocked by German authorities, who "threw up a wall around the events of September 5-6, 1972," he did manage to compile a reasonable chronology of events. But even Groussard admits there are many unanswered questions.

Groussard tells of four athletes from Arab nations in warmup suits spotted climbing a fence. Groussard's source is two passers-by who were later interviewed, but who refused to give their names. Groussard mentions that it would have been easy for anyone to obtain warmup suits, since athletes from all nations were trading their spare suits for other souvenirs. The obvious question, then, is why would the terrorists have obtained Arab-nation warmup suits, which might attract attention, when suits from other nations could have been obtained as easily.

And then there are what Groussard describes as "strange contradictions." Why did it take the terrorists 25 minutes to get from the fence to the nearby Israeli quarters? Why did they bother to change from warmup suits into the clothing they wore throughout the day? What happened to the warmup suits, which were never found?

The answers become clear when you hear the testimony of three Swedish athletes who kept their innocent involvement in this story quiet for more than 20 years.

According to pole vaulter Hans Lagerqvist, most of the Swedish team had been out for dinner on the night of September 4 and had come back to the village well after midnight. They were all wearing their blue and yellow Swedish warmup suits.

When they arrived outside the village, some of the women athletes invited three of the men to join them for coffee in the women's portion of the village, where men were strictly forbidden. After entering the men's village, the three athletes walked along the two-meter fence separating the two villages until they found an unguarded portion. In near total darkness, they scaled the fence, and then proceeded to one of the women's bungalows, where they played cards with the women until almost 4:00 A.M.

When the three athletes left the bungalow to return to the men's village, they climbed the fence again. But this time only two of the athletes got over easily; the third got stuck on top of the fence, which broke under his weight. The two who had cleared the fence began teasing their less fortunate teammate.

A nearby guard, hearing the commotion, began yelling at the three athletes, who ran to the nearest building on the men's side of the fence—Connollystrasse 31—and hid in the crawl space under the building. After a brief pause, they proceeded to their own apartment on Nadistrasse, the next street.

The following morning, word of the terrorist attack reached the three Swedish athletes. Since they were not aware at the time that the terrorists had been identified as Arabs and that they were still in the village, the Swedes' immediate fear was that fingerprints on the fence might lead to them. There was also some concern, of course, that there might be repercussions if they admitted they had spent most of the night in the women's village, where men were not allowed.

"According to the news reports that morning," Lagerqvist relates, "the terrorists came over the fence at 4:00 A.M. dressed as athletes. We knew at the time it was us they'd seen and we still believe it."

How, then, did the terrorists get into the village? With a key to the padlock on gate 25A, a service gate which was locked every night at midnight and remained unguarded until morning. (The gates used by village residents, where identification was required, remained open all night.)

How did the terrorists get a key to the gate? The same way they got a key to the Israeli apartment: from an unnamed locksmith. According to Groussard's research, two of the eight terrorists were already working inside the village and were able to let the others in through the gate. One insider was a cook in the restaurant and one was a groundskeeper.

Groussard refers to a third conspirator, but it is not clear if he was an insider or not. He is identified only as a locksmith known as the "headman" or "the Munich craftsman." He is the man who made a duplicate key to the Israeli quarters. If the locksmith could make a duplicate key to the Israeli apartment, there is no reason to believe he could not also produce a key to a gate that was not considered particularly important to the security forces.

The entire truth about the events of those days will probably never be known, but it appears likely now that the often-told story of the terrorists scaling a fence to enter the village is not true.

THE MEMORIAL SERVICE

The morning after the tragedy, all flags were at half-staff as the Olympic stadium filled to capacity for the service for the 11 slain Israelis. The 80,000 seats were reserved for those who held tickets for that day's track and field events. There were additionals chairs set up on the infield for the thousands of athletes and officials who attended, including 11 seats in the front row that remained empty.

After the Munich Philharmonic Orchestra played the funeral march from Beethoven's Third Symphony (the "Eroica"), the service began simply, with a heartfelt and moving address by Willi Daume, president of the German organizing committee. Then followed an emotional speech by

Shmuel Lalkin, the Israeli team manager, who spoke of "the barbaric rape of the Olympic spirit." Lalkin finished by saying the Olympic Committee, the police, and the security forces "have earned our gratitude."

Unfortunately, Avery Brundage also spoke. In an inappropriate address that offended some in the audience and disgusted others, he treated the murders of the Israelis as just another intrusion on the Olympic movement. Brundage said, "Sadly, the greater and more important the Olympic Games become, the more they are open to commercial, political, and now criminal pressure." Then, attempting to equate the murders of the Israelis to the barring of Rhodesia from the Olympics, he said, "The Games of the 20th Olympiad have been subjected to two savage attacks. We lost the Rhodesian battle against naked political blackmail."

THE CALL TO CANCEL

From around the world came demands that the Games be halted. But Avery Brundage and the IOC, fearing cancellation would mean the end of the modern Olympic Games, were adamant in their stand: "We cannot allow a handful of terrorists to destroy this nucleus of international cooperation and goodwill we have in the Olympic movement," Brundage said. "The Games must go on."

Brundage did agree to a 24-hour period of mourning, but he made it retroactive to 4:00 P.M. the previous day. In other words, the Olympic events would begin again later that afternoon. The Israeli team withdrew from the Games and returned home, as did the teams from Norway, the Netherlands, and the Philippines. Apparently fearing reprisals, the teams from Egypt, Syria, and Kuwait also went home.

A HASTY DEPARTURE

Swimmer Mark Spitz, who had won two gold medals and a bronze four years earlier, won seven gold medals in Munich, prompting many to suggest the swimming program should be reduced because there were so many similar events. There was further controversy when the IOC accused Spitz of advertising a particular brand of shoes as he took the victory stand to receive one of his gold medals. He was later exonerated.

After the terrorist attack in the Olympic village, security around Spitz, who is Jewish, was extremely tight. There were five armed guards posted outside his room. After a press conference that was conducted with considerable nervousness, Spitz left Munich.

THE ELECTRONIC TIE-BREAKER

Swimmers Gunnar Larsson of Sweden and Tim McKee of the U.S. appeared to have finished in a dead heat for first in the 400-meter individual medley. In most competitions the race would have been called a tie. But the sophisticated electronic timer in Munich showed that Larsson had finished in 4 minutes 31.981 seconds, while McKee had finished in 4 minutes 31.983 seconds, a difference of two-thousandths of a second. Larsson received the gold medal.

MUNCHKIN IN MUNICH

Seventeen-year-old Olga Korbut was an alternate on the USSR gymnastics team in 1972. Had it not been for a teammate's injury, the world might never have known of or been captivated by the personable "munchkin."

The star of the Soviet team was the regal Lyudmila Tourischeva, who collected the all-around title. But it was the bubbly Olga who captured the hearts of the public, both in the arena and on international television. She added new and daring moves in the balance beam, floor exercises, and uneven bar competitions—changes that would create an entirely new standard for women's gymnastics. And she performed them with grace and an engaging smile.

Korbut's popularity in the West did not sit well with Soviet officialdom. She was accused of exploiting her personality at the expense of the team. But that didn't slow her down. She captured gold medals in the beam and floor exercise and was the gymnast people remembered after the Games were over.

Korbut made such an impression on young people in the United States that participation in women's gymnastics more than tripled. Even business was affected. The Nissen Corporation, then the largest manufacturer of gymnastics apparatus in the world, reported that their business doubled between 1972 and 1974, all because of Olga Korbut.

EMPTY STARTING BLOCKS

One of track and field's most bizarre and unsettling incidents occurred when two of the three American sprinters arrived late for the quarterfinal round of the 100 meters and were thus eliminated from the competition. Many have written that the late arrival was caused by a U.S. coach's misreading of the "European" starting time of 16:15 as 6:15 p.m., but the most reliable sources say the cause was an outdated time schedule.

The previous day, all three American sprinters—Eddie Hart, Rey Robinson, and Robert Taylor—had won their first round heats, qualifying for the quarterfinal round. As the time was approaching for their races, the three sprinters and their coach, Stan Wright, were casually waiting for a bus to the stadium. It was 4:15 p.m.—plenty of time to get to the stadium and prepare for races they thought were to begin at 7:00 p.m.

While the four were waiting, they wandered over to the doorway of the adjacent ABC-TV headquarters to look in at the television set in the reception area. When they saw sprinters on the TV, lining up for the 100 meters, they thought they were seeing a rerun of the previous day's first round heats. But then, to their horror, they realized the quarterfinal races were beginning.

ABC staffers quickly got the three sprinters and the coach into one of their cars, and a part-time employee, Bill Norris, drove them to the stadium at breakneck speed. Taylor, ranked as the third-best sprinter of the trio, managed to get to the track in time to qualify for the next round, but Hart and Robinson, who were co-holders of the world record, were too late.

Wright, for reasons that have never been fully explained, was working from a time schedule that was a year-and-a-half old. At first the U.S. Olympic officials tried to blame German officials for the mixup, but that charge was later abandoned when it was realized that the U.S. was the only country at the Olympics that had the wrong schedule. A *Sports Illustrated* reporter wrote: "It could have been worse. Stan Wright could have been coaching Mark Spitz."

Attracting more attention in the U.S. than the incident itself was the television interview of Wright by ABC's Howard Cossell. Because of the harsh and relentless questioning by Cossell and the apologetic demeanor of an obviously dis-

Wayne Collett and Vince Mathews during the anthem.

traught Stan Wright, public opinion sided with Wright. Cossell had come across as a badgering, brutalizing critic of a man who had made a human mistake.

ANOTHER AWARDS DEMONSTRATION

America's Vince Matthews and Wayne Collett created a brief stir on the victory stand when they received their gold and silver medals for the 400 meters. Sloppily attired, both Matthews and Collett climbed to the top step, normally reserved for the gold medal winner alone. Stating later they did not believe the words of *The Star-Spangled Banner* were true, they stood with their hands on their hips, not looking at the flag, fidgeting, and chatting with each other as the anthem was played. There was a chorus of booing and whistling from the spectators. In contrast, the third place finisher, Julius Sang of Kenya, stood at attention.

Matthews jumped down from the stand before the anthem was completed and twirled his medal on its ribbon as he walked off the field. Collett, walking behind, gave the black power

113

salute to the crowd.

Upset officials, already under a great strain because of the events of the past days, ordered the two to leave the Olympic village and banned them from participation in further Olympic competition. The ban resulted in the withdrawal of the U.S. 1600-meter relay team from competition three days later when enough healthy runners could not be found.

THE HONEYMOON WAS OVER

After Dave Wottle qualified for the U.S. Olympic team in the 800 meters, he announced he was going to be married. Much to the consternation of U.S. officials, he also said he and his bride would use the trip to Munich as a honeymoon. It was generally agreed that Wottle's concentration and training would be compromised, erasing any chance he might have for a medal. "He'll be lucky to get past the first round in the 800 meters," head coach Bill Bowerman said.

White-capped Dave Wottle nips the fallen Arzhanov.

Running in his distinctive white golf cap and always coming from well back, Wottle managed to get through each of the qualifying rounds. In the final, Wottle would be pitted against the favorite, Yevgeniy Arzhanov of the Soviet Union, who had not lost an 800-meter race in four years.

After the gun was fired, Wottle ran in the back of the pack, falling farther behind than usual. But with 300 meters to go, Wottle began to sprint, although it appeared to be much too late. In a miraculous finish, he passed Mike Boit of Kenya and at the tape edged a struggling and diving Arzhanov. Wottle won by three-hundredths of a second.

Wottle was so accustomed to wearing his white cap that he forgot to remove it as he stood at attention on the victory stand for the playing of the national anthem. Only later, when reporters asked him if he had been staging a protest did he realize what he had done. In tears, Wottle later apologized to the American public.

A MARATHON IMPOSTER

American marathoner Frank Shorter, who was born in Munich, returned to his birthplace to win the Olympic marathon in a most convincing manner. ABC-TV covered the race throughout, and as Shorter approached the stadium, he was leading the race by about 750 yards.

As the crowd awaited the runners, a 22-year-old German college student, Norbert Sudhaus, dressed as a runner and pretending to be the marathon winner, entered the stadium and ran around the track toward the finish line. The scene was described by an excited Erich Segal, who was ABC-TV's distance running analyst. U.S. viewers heard Segal's screaming voice: "That's not Frank. He's an imposter. He's an imposter. Get him off the track. Here comes Frank now. He doesn't know what's happening. My God, look at the anguish on his face. It's all right. You've won, Frank."

It wasn't anguish on Shorter's face; it was surprise. He had expected great cheering when he entered the stadium, but the crowd was booing the imposter as security guards were hustling him out of the stadium. After he crossed the finish line, Shorter took a well-deserved victory lap, as though nothing had happened.

114

THE GREAT BASKETBALL FLAP

Never has there been a finish to an Olympic basketball game like the one experienced by the United States and the Soviet Union in Munich. It was the final game—the one that would decide the gold and silver medals—and the United States had never lost a basketball game in Olympic history.

The Soviets were ahead 44-36 with five minutes to play, when the Americans began to close the gap. In the final seconds of the game, with the U.S. team behind by one point, Doug Collins was fouled. The clock was stopped with three seconds left. He made both free throws, putting the U.S. ahead by one.

Even though the game was witnessed by millions of people on television, there is still considerable disagreement concerning the game's final three seconds. Through the deafening noise of the crowd, the Soviet coach was frantically trying to get a timeout when time ran out and the Americans began to celebrate their 50-49 win.

By Olympic rules a coach may call a timeout from the bench, but it was decided the Soviet coach did not have the opportunity to do so. Some accounts say the timeout horn sounded with three seconds on the clock as Collins released his second free throw. Others say the timeout horn was mistaken for the final horn. One account says the game was stopped by the official when he thought a noise from the crowd was "the final whistle." Another says the umpire restarted the game, but two seconds later called a halt, with the Americans thinking they had won the game. Another says "an off-the-court" horn sounded.

R. William Jones, secretary general of the International Amateur Basketball Association explained it this way: "The whole trouble started when someone at the scorer's tabled sounded the buzzer too late for a timeout requested by the Russians." Then he added, "The Americans have to learn how to lose, even when they think they are right."

In any event, the officials ruled that three seconds were to be put back on the clock and the game was to be continued. When play resumed and the three seconds ran out without a score, the Americas began to celebrate again. But then it was ruled that the timing equipment had malfunctioned and the three seconds had to be played

again. This time, Ivan Edeshko hurled the ball the length of the court to Alexander Belov, who muscled his way past Jim Forbes and Kevin Joyce to score an easy layup. The Soviets won, 51-50.

The Americans protested, but after the appeals jury studied television film of the game's end, the appeal was denied. The Soviet Union had ended the long U.S. reign as basketball's only gold medal winners.

As one might expect, the reviews were mixed about the fairness of the game's outcome. Most Americans, who watched the game and ABC-TV's many replays of the incident, were convinced the U.S. had been cheated. Much of the rest of the world disagreed.

In what was described by one historian as "a sorry display of poor sportsmanship," the American team and coaches refused to appear at the awards ceremony or to accept the silver medals. U.S. Olympic basketball committee chairman Bill Summers explained, "We do not feel like accepting the silver because we feel we are worth the gold." To this day, the silver medals remain uncollected.

BLOOD BOOSTING (OR BLOOD DOPING)

Late in 1971, three Swedish researchers at GIH (Stockholm's well-known Sports and Physical Education Institute) announced they had been conducting experiments using a unique method for increasing athletes' endurance. The procedure, which became known as blood boosting, requires the removal of one liter (about two pints) of the athlete's blood, which is frozen and stored for later use. Then, after a wait of two weeks or more, when the athlete's body has rebuilt its blood supply to normal levels, the stored blood is thawed and then reinfused in the athlete just before a major competition.

The result is increased red blood cells, which transport oxygen and waste products in the blood stream and increase the athlete's endurance. The Swedish experiments reported physical performance levels that were 20-25 percent beyond previous maximums.

The effects of blood boosting are brief, with maximum results lasting no more than a few days at the most. This could explain why some distance runners are very good occasionally and only average the rest of the time.

Although the procedure is often called blood

doping, the term blood boosting seems to describe the procedure better, since only the athlete's own blood is involved, without the use of any drugs. The process was not against the rules at the time, since the athletes used their own blood, but there were many who felt it was unethical.

Early in 1972, a year after it was announced that Swedish researchers were conducting blood boosting experiments, it became known that some Finnish doctors and athletes had been aware of the procedure as early as 1968. Finland's reported knowledge about blood boosting, which had been kept secret for at least four years, immediately caused people to be suspicious about Lasse Viren and his seemingly superhuman performances in the Olympic 5,000- and 10,000-meter runs.

Four years later, in the Montreal Olympics, Viren repeated his "superhuman" feat, becoming the only Olympian in history to win the 5,000- and 10,000-meter double for a second time. After his startling performances in Montreal, journalists, who had become knowledgeable about blood boosting, asked Viren more questions about his blood than they did about his races. Viren not only didn't seem to understand what blood boosting was, he didn't seem to understand English, even though he had spent a year as a student at Brigham Young University in Utah.

Later, several other Finnish distance runners admitted they had been blood boosted for the Olympics, but Viren never admitted it. He said his secret for success was drinking reindeer milk.

BRUNDAGE STEPS DOWN

After 20 stormy years as IOC president, Avery Brundage finally gave up the presidency, but only because he believed the Olympic Games were finished. According to his successor, Lord Killanin, "He contented himself with telling me, with much relish, that the Montreal Games would never take place."

Elected IOC president in 1952, Brundage decided to make the Olympic Games "the greatest social force of our times." He immersed himself totally in his Olympic dream, often acting with unbending, dogged determination. He was a staunch conservative, and was described as independent, opinionated, tough, and sometimes close to fanatical.

Although there were those who had great respect for Brundage, there were also many who despised him. His list of detractors was long, with some calling him a fascist, a Nazi, or a racist, depending upon the occasion, and others saying he was unrealistic and unreasonable. Yet without Brundage and his strict, dogmatic ways, the Olympic movement might have collapsed somewhere along the way. Avery Brundage had made his mark on Olympic history.

At the conclusion of the closing ceremonies, the Munich organizing committee paid tribute to Brundage with a simple message flashed on the electronic messageboard. Typical of the many misfortunes of the Munich Olympics, the message read: "THANK YOU AVERY BRANDAGE."

A SECRET LIFE

In 1927, when Avery Brundage was 40 years old, he and singer-pianist Elizabeth Dunlop were married. It was a marriage that lasted until Mrs. Brundage's death 44 years later. The Brundages are described in the literature as a very happy couple, with no children. Mrs. Brundage often accompanied her husband on his international trips, although she for the most part preferred to remain at the palatial Brundage estate in Santa Barbara, California.

After Avery Brundage died in 1975, another side of the controversial Olympic leader came to light. It was revealed that he had a second home in California where he conducted an extensive secret life with a Finnish woman. They had two children. It was a surprisingly different side of the man who was renowned for his advocacy of strict rules of behavior.

Olympiad XXI
MONTREAL, 1976

THE SITE ANNOUNCEMENT MIXUP

The selection of the site for the Olympic Games is done via a series of balloting by IOC members until one site has a majority of the votes. If no site has a majority on a particular ballot, the site receiving the fewest votes is eliminated on the next ballot. This allows delegates who voted for the eliminated site to switch their votes to another site. Thus, it is not unusual for one city to have a lead on one or more ballots, only to lose out on a later ballot.

Such was the case in 1970 at the IOC meeting in Amsterdam. The three contenders for the 1976 Games were Los Angeles, Montreal, and Moscow. All three mayors were present as the president of the IOC, Avery Brundage, opened the envelope to announce the results of the first ballot. Brundage said Moscow was ahead, but there was not a majority. Before he could continue, a representative from the Soviet news agency, Tass, left the room and sent the message throughout the world that Moscow would be the site of the 1976 Olympics.

However, on the next ballot, those who had voted for Los Angeles, now eliminated, switched their votes to Montreal, giving the Canadian city a clear majority over Moscow. Mayor Promislov of Moscow, who had been seated in the front row of the auditorium for the announcement, stomped out of the meeting in anger.

A QUESTION OF SECURITY

The newly-elected IOC president, Lord Killanin, decided to hold a press conference in 1973 to provide the press with information about the upcoming Montreal Olympics. After the reporters had asked a number of questions about Montreal's security arrangements that received vague answers, one reporter pressed for a specific answer, asking Killanin if he had discussed the matter of security with the Montreal organizing committee. "Yes," Killanin responded. Not satisfied with the brevity of the answer, the journalist pressed further, asking Killanin, "What have you discussed?" "If I told you that," Killanin shot back, "it would no longer be secure, would it?"

TURMOIL IN MONTREAL

Turmoil was the name of the game in Montreal. It began with construction delays and cost overruns that threatened the very existence of the Games before they began, and ended when an unclad streaker somehow got through the tight security at the stadium and became a conspicuous feature of the closing ceremonies.

In between there were political threats, protests, and boycotts, plus incidents of cheating, doping, and defection. To many who recalled the horrors associated with the 1968 and 1972 Games, the Montreal Olympics were considered successful because there was no violence or loss of life.

SLOW AND COSTLY

After Montreal was selected to host the Olympics, Mayor Jean Drapeau promised the high costs of operating the 1972 Games in Munich would not be repeated in Montreal. Noting that the Munich Olympics had cost the German organizers much more than they had anticipated, he promised the Montreal Games would be smaller and simpler. "It is time to bring back the real truth of the Olympics," he said. "These will be modest, self-financed Games. They will not cost the taxpayers one penny."

A combination of poor planning, extraordinary inflation, and labor delays cost the organizers millions of dollars and eight months of construction time. The Olympic budget of $310 million went to $1.2 billion—almost four times the original estimate. Games that were promised to be self-supporting had become a 25-year tax burden for the citizens of Montreal and the Province of Quebec.

A few weeks before the scheduled opening

ceremonies, the stadium was so far from being finished that there were serious doubts that the Games could be held in Montreal. Amid rumors that the Games would be switched to Mexico or Los Angeles, the Montreal organizers announced: "The Games site will be ready, but not complete."

WHAT'S IN A NAME?

On May 28, only seven weeks before the opening ceremonies, Canada's government announced that the Republic of China (the IOC's official name for the small island nation of Taiwan) would have to compete under the name Taiwan or be barred from the Olympics. Victor Yuen, secretary of the Taiwan delegation, responded, "Either we are the Republic of China or we go home."

The Canadian decision was the result of demands made by the government of mainland (Communist) China. Calling itself the true government of all Chinese people, mainland China said they would cancel their multimillion dollar order for Canadian wheat unless the Republic of China agreed to compete under the name Taiwan.

The conflict was further complicated when the U.S. Olympic Committee backed the Taiwanese, threatening to withdraw all U.S. athletes from the Olympics and taking the $25 million ABC-TV contract with them. Such a move would have ensured financial disaster for the Montreal organizers.

There were discussions among IOC members to cancel the Olympics over the dispute, which would have left the Canadians with no prospect of recovering any of their $1.2 billion debt. Finally, with only three days before the Games were to open, Canada's prime minister, Pierre Trudeau, said the Taiwanese could use their flag and their anthem, "but they can't use a name that isn't theirs." The IOC backed Trudeau's stand and the Taiwanese went home.

THE AFRICAN BOYCOTT

The most serious issue associated with the 1976 Olympics was the angry response of the Supreme Council for Sport in Africa (SCSA) over some rugby games between teams from New Zealand and South Africa. If New Zealand were not barred from the Olympics, the SCSA said, then the black African nations would boycott the Games. (In some books the SCSA is called the Organization of African Unity.)

The IOC responded by explaining it had no authority in the matter since the New Zealand rugby team was on a private tour that was not supported by the New Zealand government. And since rugby was not an Olympic sport, the IOC refused to take any action. It was also noted that at least 20 other countries, including the United States, had competed against South Africa on a regular basis, yet no one called for barring any of those teams in Montreal.

In response, there was a mass withdrawal of African athletes from the Olympic village just before the Games were to begin. The scene in the Olympic village was a sad one as the African athletes packed their bags to return home. For many, they were to miss their only opportunity for success after training for four years for this one chance. Some of the athletes were crying; most were selling their shoes and clothing to try to salvage something from their trip to Montreal.

ALL IN THE ROYAL FAMILY

Queen Elizabeth II of Great Britain arrived at the stadium on the day of the opening ceremonies to declare open the Games of the XXIst Olympiad, first in French, and then in English. She was the fourth member of the British Royal Family to open the Olympics since the Games' revival in 1896. Her grandfather, King Edward VII, had opened the 1908 Games in London; her father, King George VI, opened the 1948 Games in London; and her husband, Prince Philip, opened the 1956 Games in Melbourne.

The Queen, with husband Philip by her side, had an additional interest in the opening ceremonies. Marching among the British athletes was their daughter, Princess Anne, who was a member of Great Britain's equestrian team.

INSTANT FLAME

For the first time, the Olympic flame covered its journey from Greece to the Olympic host country in an instant. The flame was kindled in Olympia, Greece, where it was transferred to a torch and relayed to Athens. (The *Official Olympic Report* says the sacred flame was kindled on Mount Olympia, which appears to be a cross between Mount Olympus in the north of Greece, and ancient Olympia where the fire was actually lit.)

The flame was then transferred from Athens

to Ottawa, Canada, in a fraction of a second. A special electronic device picked up the torch's ionized particles, translated them into electronic impulses, and transmitted them to the satellite. They were then beamed down to Ottawa, where the impulses activated a laser beam which relit the Olympic flame. From Ottawa, 245 runners relayed the flame on to Montreal.

The final torchbearers were 16-year-old Sandra Henderson of Toronto and 15-year-old Stéphane Préfontaine of Montreal, representing the English and French languages. He held the torch and she held his arm as they ran side by side around the track and up to the giant cauldron, where they ignited the flame that would burn for the next two weeks. The two young students stayed in touch after the Montreal Olympics and were married some years later.

THE FLAME GOES OUT

A summer rainstorm proved to be too much for the Olympic flame in Montreal. The sacred fire faced a sudden deluge of water and went out as quickly as it had been lit. A quick-thinking construction worker, Pierre Bouchard, relit the flame with his cigarette lighter. Needless to say, when the Olympic officials heard there was a less-than-sacred flame in the Olympic cauldron, they put out Bouchard's flame and sent for the backup flame from Olympia, which was in storage as a safeguard against such emergencies. A torch lit by the backup flame arrived at the stadium with a full police escort. The fire in the cauldron was then formally relit.

FOOD FOR THOUGHT

The dining halls in the Olympic village, which were open 24 hours a day, served what was described as a super-diet, providing an average of 5,000 calories per athlete per day. This allowed an average of 2,000 calories for female gymnasts and 8,000 calories for weight lifters.

The village dieticians came up with a unique plan to test the food served to the athletes. Besides hiring food tasters to examine the food served before each meal, a small portion of each bit of food was labeled, frozen, and stored. Then, if an athlete were to blame a poor performance on bad food, the dieticians would be able to thaw and test the samples of food that were the same

as those consumed by the athlete.

UKRAINIANS PROTEST

Canadian citizens who had emigrated from the Ukraine staged repeated protests during the Olympics, calling for Ukrainian independence from the Soviet Union. They burned Soviet flags outside the Olympic village, disrupted the soccer matches when the Soviet team was playing, and started rumors of the defections of Ukrainian athletes.

JUSTICE IS BLIND

Tickets to some of the Olympic events were so scarce, illegal scalping became a big business in Montreal. Some $16 tickets were selling for as much as $300. One scalper, who had a supply of almost 1,000 tickets, was arrested and hauled into court, where he had to face the judge. Rendering an unusual verdict, the judge fined the scalper five dollars and told him he did not have to relinquish the tickets. According to newspaper reports, the scalper then sold all of his tickets before leaving the courthouse. His primary customers were judges and lawyers.

A FENCING CHEAT

The Soviets were embarrassed and everyone else was angry when it was discovered that Boris Onischenko, one of the Soviet Union's finest fencers, was caught cheating in the fencing portion of the modern pentathlon. He had wired his épée with an electronic device that would score points on the electronic scoreboard when his sword had not actually touched the opponent.

In a match between Onischenko and Great Britain's Jeremy Fox, Fox lunged forward and then drew back as Onischenko's blade moved forward. Even though it was clear that the épée had missed Fox, the scoreboard showed that Onischenko had scored a hit. Fox protested, Onischenko's épée was inspected and found to be rigged, and he was sent home in disgrace. Not surprising, a comprehensive account of the 1976 Olympics in a Soviet history book does not mention Onischenko or the incident.

There has since been speculation that Onischenko might have used the same illegal implement when he won a silver medal in 1968 and a gold in 1972.

MORE VIREN CONTROVERSIES

Lasse Viren, the Finnish distance runner who was accused of being blood boosted when he won both the 5,000- and 10,000-meter runs in 1972, completed a miraculous "double double" by winning both races again in Montreal. Pointing out that Viren's running during the four years between Olympics had been only mediocre, several athletes said they believed Viren was blood boosted. New Zealand's Dick Quax, who finished second to Viren in the 5,000, referred to him as "a mobile transfusion unit."

Viren added additional controversy to his Olympic achievements when he held his Japanese-made Tiger shoes aloft after the 10,000 meters and took a victory lap in his bare feet. It was what *Newsweek* magazine called "a blatant commercial for the shoe brand that is distributed by his coach."

AN EXTRA LAP

When East Germany's Waldemar Cierpinski won the marathon, he crossed the finish line and continued running, thinking he had one more lap to run. Cierpinski was shocked to reach the finish line and find second place finisher Frank Shorter of the U.S. waiting to congratulate him. Shorter said later it must have been the only time in Olympic history that a silver medalist had finished running before the gold medalist.

THE PERFECT 10

The individual star of the Montreal Games was a sober-faced 14-year-old Romanian gymnast named Nadia Comaneci. She scored the first perfect 10 in Olympic history and went on to score six more 10's before the competition was over. The perfect scores were so unexpected that the sophisticated, state-of-the-art electronic scoreboard, which the experts had said could do anything, could not register a score higher than a 9.99. Comaneci's 10.00 scores appeared as 1.00.

American television viewers saw Comaneci's performances, both live and in repeated videotaped replays, as ABC-TV concentrated on her, often to the exclusion of other outstanding performers. "We figured Comaneci would be big for us," ABC Sports President Roone Arledge said. "We've been working her into *Wide World of Sports* for a year or more."

As Comaneci performed to *Yes Sir, That's My Baby* played on a piano in Montreal, the TV viewers at home heard a completely different song—a haunting melody which they thought was accompanying Comaneci in Montreal. Every time Nadia appeared on the TV screen, the song accompanying her performance was *Nadia's Theme*, which became a hit record. The song, which was composed for the occasion by noted song writer Perry Botkin, originated from the ABC studios in New York, not from Montreal.

A HOT YACHT

The yachting events, which were held at Kingston on Lake Ontario, included a bizarre scene in the Tempest Class race. The two-man crew of a British keelboat named Gift 'Orse, which had fallen far behind in the race, set fire to the boat.

"She went lame on us," said Alan Warren, a yachtsman who was also a funeral director back

Nadia Comaneci

in England, "so we decided the poor old 'Orse should be cremated."

A Canadian destroyer tried to rescue Warren and his partner, David Hunt, from the burning boat, but they refused the help. Finally, when smoke from the boat was obscuring the finish line, the destroyer returned, picked up the two yachtsmen, and rammed the burning boat, sending it to the bottom of the lake.

"It wasn't worth taking her all the way back home," Warren said. "We wanted to give her a proper Viking funeral."

THE NEW TEST FOR STEROIDS

For the first time, the tests for anabolic steroids were sophisticated enough to be effective. Six athletes—five male and one female—were disqualified when they tested positive for anabolic steroids.

The athletes who were caught claimed they were merely the unlucky ones. They said it was virtually impossible to even make it to the Olympic Games without taking steroids. The secret, they said, was to train hard while taking steroids, and to discontinue using them just long enough before the drug testing so the urinalysis would not show traces of the drug. Those who were caught said they were the ones who were being penalized because they had merely misjudged the time between withdrawal and the tests.

In women's swimming, where the Americans had traditionaly done well, the East Germans dominated the competition. Noting the East German women's heavy muscles and deep voices, the U.S. women complained that the women from the East were steroid-trained. An East German coach responded, "They came to swim, not to sing."

THE PHANTOM ATHLETE

An estimated 9,000 armed police officers (of the 16,000 total) were employed to provide security in and around the Olympic village in Montreal. Everyone who entered the village, which was surrounded by a 3-meter (10-foot) fence, had to show credentials and pass through a metal detector. All bags and parcels were searched. Security couldn't have been tighter.

Yet there was an obvious security breakdown when Canadian sprinter Bob Martin managed to sneak a college friend into the village. Martin had credentials prepared for the friend, Paul Wilkinson, who slept in an empty bed in the Canadian quarters and lived the life of an Olympic athlete.

Wilkinson acted like a member of the Canadian team and probably would have been able to keep up the charade for the entire two weeks of the Games except for one mistake. He began giving press interviews.

A reporter who had interviewed Wilkinson did some background checking for his article and discovered that no such Canadian athlete existed. An embarrassed Canadian Olympic Committee banished both Wilkinson and Martin from the Olympics.

LET'S MAKE A DEAL

An embarrassing situation developed in platform diving when the manager of the U.S. team reported to the International Swimming Federation that an official of the Soviet diving team had offered him a deal. The official said the Soviet judges would judge the American divers favorably if the U.S. judges would do the same for the Soviet divers.

When confronted with the charge, the Soviet official denied it vehemently. The matter was finally dropped.

A SOVIET DEFECTION

Shortly after 17-year-old Sergei Nemtsamov, a diver from the Soviet Union, disappeared from the Olympic village, Canadian officials announced that he had defected. The Soviets, claiming Nemtsamov had been abducted (one account says brainwashed), demanded his return or they would withdraw from the Olympics. In response, the IOC said a Soviet withdrawal would seriously jeopardize holding the 1980 Olympic Games in Moscow.

After some haggling, it was agreed that Nemtsamov could remain in Canada for a trial period of six months while he made up his mind whether to stay or not. During the trial period he decided to return to the Soviet Union.

A GOOD TALE

There was a story circulating during the 1976 Games that still is making the rounds. It concerns a dilemma faced by Gonadij Orlov, a sportscaster for the Soviet Union, during a volleyball match between South Korea and mainland China.

The story, which was even reported on National Public Radio, was that Orlov was not allowed to mention Korea on the air because the Soviet Union had severed diplomatic relations with the Koreans, and he was not allowed to mention China on the air because the USSR and China were involved in a border dispute. So, Orlov described the volleyball action over the radio, referring to "the team on the left and the team on the right."

It is a good tale, but it cannot be true, since China did not participate in the 1976 Olympics.

THE CANADIAN STREAKER

The closing ceremonies were typically lavish and joyful, but there was one surprise element—a streaker. The dancers on the field during the closing included a naked young man who was dancing in the center of a circle of women in white dresses. With the tight security in the stadium, it is a mystery how he was able to get onto the field without proper identification, and especially without any place to carry or pin any identification! The man, whose bare image was telecast throughout the world, was ultimately arrested and fined.

Olympiad XXII
MOSCOW, 1980

THE ROAD TO MOSCOW

In 1970, Moscow made a strong bid to host the 1976 Olympic Games, but lost out to Montreal on the second ballot. In 1974, when the IOC met to select a site for the 1980 Games, Moscow decided to try again. The only other candidate was Los Angeles.

The voting wasn't close, according to the new IOC president, Lord Killanin. Moscow was the clear winner in an almost unanimous vote. One reason for Moscow's easy victory might have been a secret part played by U.S. president Richard M. Nixon.

The rumors persist that Nixon made a secret arrangement with General Secretary Leonid Brezhnev, head of the Soviet government, that would ensure that the Games would go to the USSR in 1980.

Nixon went to Moscow in the summer of 1974 to meet with Brezhnev. Detente was uppermost in his mind, as he hoped it would help defuse the Watergate scandal which had been plaguing him for a year-and-a-half.

Brezhnev was anxious to discuss another issue—one of even greater importance to him at the moment. He wanted Nixon to help convince the IOC to select Moscow over Los Angeles as host for the 1980 Olympics. Obviously, Brezhnev was very anxious to have Moscow (and the Soviet system) showcased on the Olympic stage. The premier Communist capital—and certainly one of the foremost Olympic nations in terms of athletic success—had been made to wait long enough for the honor, to Brezhnev's way of thinking. In turn for Nixon's support, the USSR would back Los Angeles' bid in 1984.

Nixon gave his assurances by the conclusion of the meetings, but whether he did exert any influence is not known, since he was forced to resign from office a month later. In comparison to an expensive public relations campaign by Moscow and the millions of rubles spent to construct and upgrade their sports facilities, Los Angeles's bid presentation was fairly lackluster. In the eyes of seasoned observers, Moscow wanted the 1980 Games and Los Angeles was settling for 1984.

Lord Killanin has written, "Suggestions have been made that President Nixon had made a deal that Los Angeles would not make a strong bid to allow the Games to go to Moscow. However, that would have been quite unacceptable to the USOC, the Los Angeles delegation, and, of course, to the IOC." In reality, though, deals in the bidding for the Olympics are fairly common, starting with the Athens-Paris agreement for the 1896 and 1900 Olympics. It is not too farfetched to believe there was a Moscow-Los Angeles agreement and that Nixon played a behind-the-scenes role.

Killanin said later that his greatest qualms at the time were that the Soviets would somehow concoct reasons to keep Israel and other countries with whom they had strong political differences, out of the Olympics. "As it turned out," he said later, "there was little need to worry about that."

SURPASSING POLITICAL BARRIERS?

In 1978, after Sarajevo and Los Angeles were selected to host the 1984 winter and summer Olympics, but before the 1980 Lake Placid and Moscow Games were held, IOC President Lord Killanin wrote of the opposing philosophies of the "foremost communist and capitalist countries."

"The selection of these two countries," he wrote, "combined with the fact that in 1984 Sarajevo and Los Angeles will be hosting the Games, indicates that the Olympics do surpass all political and ideological barriers." The events of the following two years would turn out to be the ultimate test of Killanin's optimistic outlook.

THE INVASION OF AFGHANISTAN

In late December of 1979, the small, mountainous country of Afghanistan was invaded by 80,000 troops from the Soviet Union. The coup, which was condemned by the United Nations, included the execution of the Afghan president, who was replaced by an exiled former deputy minister.

There were immediate protests from around the world as the outnumbered and poorly equipped Afghan tribesmen fought stubbornly against the Soviet invaders. In response to the criticism, the Soviets claimed they had been "invited into Afghanistan to help put down a civil uprising."

THE AMERICAN-LED BOYCOTT

On January 4, 1980, just over six months before the Moscow Olympic Games were to begin, U.S. President Jimmy Carter announced a number of sanctions against the Soviet Union, including the possibility of a boycott of the Olympics.

On January 20, Carter issued a statement, proposing that the Games be moved, postponed, or canceled unless all Soviet troops were out of Afghanistan within one month. At the same time, in what seemed to be a hypocritical stance, the U.S. was preparing to welcome Soviet athletes to the winter Olympic Games in Lake Placid, New York, scheduled to open three weeks later.

On February 9, at the IOC meetings in Lake Placid, held in conjunction with the winter Olympic Games, U.S. Secretary of State Cyrus Vance delivered the opening address on behalf of President Carter. Still pushing to have the Moscow Games moved or canceled, Vance announced that "the United States of America will oppose the participation of a national team in the Moscow Games."

Carter and Vance obviously did not know, first, that the Olympic Games are the exclusive property of the IOC, and second, the IOC had a firm and binding contract with Moscow. The members of the IOC who were present at Lake Placid, including the U.S. representatives, voted 73-0 to continue to support holding the Games in Moscow. A vote of the 26 Olympic federations that govern the various sports agreed unanimously.

In the meantime, the winter Olympics were held in Lake Placid with full participation by athletes from the Soviet Union. While Jimmy Carter was calling for a boycott of the Moscow Olympics, there was no mention of barring Soviet athletes from the winter Games held in the United States.

Carter's next move was to appeal to the world to boycott the Moscow Games and to offer the United States as a site for an "Alternative Olympics." He received support from British Prime Minister Margaret Thatcher and Australian Prime Minister Malcolm Fraser, but even that support eroded when the British and Australian athletes defied their governments' wishes and voted to go to Moscow anyway.

Jimmy Carter's boycott threat, which was originally designed to force the Soviets to withdraw from Afghanistan, didn't work. But since it was too late for the U.S. to back down, the boycott's purpose changed to an attempt to punish the Soviet Union. As it turned out, most historians agree that the U.S. merely punished itself.

Lord Killanin, ending his eight-year term as IOC president, characterized the boycott as "ill-advised, unsuccessful, and only damaging to the athletes and the common interest of sport." He wrote later, "The boycott of the Moscow Games was the most damaging event since the Games were revived in 1896." Had it not been for the support of many countries, including most of the Western European countries and Australia, "the Olympic Games would now be something of the past."

THE AMERICANS VOTE TO BOYCOTT

At President Carter's urging, both the U.S. Senate and House of Representatives voted overwhelmingly to support a boycott of the Olympics. But the final decision appeared to be up to the USOC's House of Delegates.

On April 12, the House of Delegates met in Colorado Springs to vote on the boycott issue. Jimmy Carter sent his vice president, Walter Mondale, to address the delegates before the vote was taken. "If we and our allies and friends fail to use every single peaceful means available to preserve peace," Mondale said, "what hope is there that peace will long be preserved?" The House of Delegates then voted 1,604-797 to support the boycott.

The head coach of the 1980 Olympic track and field team, Jimmy Carnes, reluctantly voted for the boycott. "I didn't really vote to boycott the Olympics," Carnes said later. "I voted to support the U.S. Congress and the President. However, even if we had voted to go, I don't believe we would have been allowed to. I don't think the boycott did a thing to promote world peace."

Lord Killanin was particularly bitter about Carter's decision to block the U.S. athletes from traveling to Moscow. He wrote later: "Politicians had tried to make use of sport and sportsmen for ends they were unable to achieve by political, diplomatic, or economic means."

In the end, the boycott did not affect the Moscow Olympics as adversely as many U.S. politicians had hoped. A total of 81 countries participated in Moscow, with the most notable absences being the United States, Japan, West Germany, New Zealand, and Canada. There were 36 world records set— only two fewer than in Montreal four years earlier.

NO NATIONAL FLAGS OR ANTHEMS

Of the 81 participating nations, there were 16 that decided to display their disapproval of the Soviet intrusion in Afghanistan in another way. They refused to allow their flags or anthems to be used, either during the opening ceremonies or at awards ceremonies. Instead, they chose to participate under the Olympic flag and use the Olympic Hymn.

PERMANENT SITES PROPOSED AGAIN

At the IOC meetings in 1980, partially in response to calls for a neutral Olympic site because of the Afghanistan controversy, a Greek delegate made a surprise proposal. He said Greece would donate land on the Adriatic Sea near Olympia to serve as a permanent site for the Olympic Games and for the IOC's headquarters. As support for this idea spread among political figures and sports associations, Austria joined the debate by offering to become the permanent host for the winter Olympics.

The IOC decided to reject the Greek offer, listing several reasons. First there was the inaccessibility of the area of Greece around Olympia. Second was the question of the funding of the initial construction and the long-term maintenance of the many facilities that would be required. And finally, and most important, the IOC's principle of Olympic universality, which was established at the time of the 1896 Games, did not allow for a permanent Olympic site.

The Greek and Austrian proposals were officially rejected at the IOC meeting in Baden-Baden in 1981. As a consolation, the Greeks believed, as

did many in the Olympic movement, that Athens would be awarded the 1996 Olympics to celebrate the 100th anniversary of the modern Olympic Games. That bitterly controversial decision would be made by the IOC nine years later.

PAYING THE PARTICIPATING NATIONS

Long before the invasion of Afghanistan, Soviet officials began visiting different nations, offering generous subsidies to bolster participation in the Moscow Olympics. Obviously, the USSR feared a limited attendance, even before the boycott was called.

The Soviets were especially anxious to have the African nations send as many competitors as possible to Moscow, even in events they had not participated in before. The USSR paid all their expenses, and even sent planes to transport them to the Games.

The plan backfired for the Soviets in women's field hockey, an event that was certain to be won by the USSR. A team of unheralded women from Zimbabwe beat the Soviet team in a semifinal match and went on to take the gold medals.

PREPARING THE CITY

It was estimated that at least one-third of the residents of Moscow were "evacuated" before the Olympic Games began. Noticeably missing were young children and teenagers, who had been sent to special summer camps for "health reasons." Also rounded up and sent to undisclosed places were drunkards, beggars, the disabled, and anyone who had been known to criticize Soviet life.

Even First Secretary Leonid Brezhnev left Moscow (by his own choice, of course) immediately after the opening ceremonies. He went to his vacation home on the Black Sea and did not return until the Olympics were over.

A DOWNSIZING

Moscow's Lenin Stadium was renovated prior to the 1980 Games. As part of the restoration, the Soviets decided to provide more comfortable seating for the spectators, which reduced the stadium's seating capacity—to 100,000.

THE CLOUDS DISAPPEAR

On the day of the opening ceremonies, it appeared that rain might dampen the festivities. Menacing storm clouds were appearing on the horizon as the day began. But, miraculously, the clouds suddenly disappeared. Later, Soviet officials said that airplanes had seeded the clouds with chemicals that somehow dissolved them. The day turned out to be clear and sunny.

A HUMAN BRIDGE

The opening ceremonies included a colorful "card section" at the center of one side of the stadium, stretching from ground level up to the concrete cauldron in which the Olympic flame would burn for the next 16 days. Holding the cards were 5,000 Red Army gymnasts, who alternated the cards to create a variety of patterns and pictures for the enjoyment of the spectators on the opposite side of the stadium.

As the ceremonies were nearing the end, an image of a lone runner carrying a torch appeared on the huge TV screens at the ends of the stadium. The torch, which had been relayed the 3,000 miles from Greece, through Bulgaria and Romania, was nearing the stadium. All of the 100,000 spectators' eyes were on the runner as he entered the stadium and circled the track carrying the flaming torch.

At that point, some of those watching must have wondered how the runner was going to transfer the flame to the cauldron at the top of the stadium. There were no steps up to the cauldron as there had been at previous Olympics.

When the runner reached the center of the card section at track level, a white line began to form in the card section as a row of the gymnasts began holding white shields over they heads. The white shields formed a human bridge, with each shield appearing just ahead of the runner as he ran to the top of the stadium. When he reached the top, he paused briefly, and then transferred the fire to the cauldron, which burst into flames.

A WAYWARD BIRD

At one point during the impressive opening ceremonies, 22 gymnasts dressed in blue blazers and white slacks marched around the track, in a slow goose-step, to the strains of Beethoven's *Ode to Joy*. The 22 gymnasts, representing the XXIInd Olympiad, each held a white dove aloft in his right hand.

The doves had been trained, when released, to complete one lap in a tight formation inside the stadium, and then turn west, leaving the stadium and heading for home. When the doves were released, 21 of them performed perfectly. The other dove flew around the stadium in the opposite direction, obviously confused, and landed on the stadium roof.

A LONGTIME OLYMPIC FAN

During a press conference conducted by the Russians, a little old man was introduced to the press corps. The Russian spokesman claimed the man, who was a Greek-American named Nick Paul, had attended every Olympic Games from 1896 to 1980.

After Paul stated that the Moscow Olympics were the best he had ever attended, which was obviously the reason the Soviets had called the press conference, the journalists began questioning him. When pressed about dates and events, Paul admitted he was only four years old when he saw the 1896 Athens Olympics, and that he attended all the Games since Athens, but wasn't actually present for all of them. The Russian officials then brought the press conference to a quick close.

THE AFGHAN TEAM

The athletes from Afghanistan managed to get to Moscow to participate in the Olympics, but participants who had sided with the rebel cause were conspicuously absent. Among the missing athletes were most of the members of the field hockey team, who were ambushed and killed a few weeks earlier as punishment "for collaborating with the enemy."

COMPLAINTS OF CHEATING

Throughout the Moscow Olympics there were repeated complaints that the Soviets were cheating whenever it was possible to do so. There were specific charges of favoritism for Soviet athletes in springboard diving, women's gymnastics, pole vaulting, the hammer and discus throws, and the triple jump.

In the hammer, where Soviets swept all three medals, video evidence showed clearly that Yuriy Syedikh had fouled on his winning throw, which was also a world record.

One popular rumor was that the stadium

gates behind the javelin competition were opened each time a Soviet athlete threw, so there would be a following breeze. This is unlikely, however, since a following wind would have been aerodynamically detrimental for the javelin, not helpful.

Perhaps the most blatant examples of favoritism were in the triple jump, where Soviet athletes finished first and second. The world record holder, Joao Oliveira of Brazil, and Australia's Ian Campbell were charged with "sleeping leg" fouls on nine of their 12 jumps, including one of Campbell's jumps that appeared to be good enough for the gold medal.

A sleeping leg foul takes place when the jumper's free foot touches the ground lightly during the step phase of the jump. Such fouls were rarely called and nine in one competition was bizarre. In fact, since it is accepted that the action actually *hampers* the jumper, this type of foul is no longer in the rules.

ANOTHER JUDGING BIAS

Nadia Comaneci of Romania, the darling of the Olympic gymnastics competition in Montreal, was back to defend the titles she had won in 1976. However, she suffered a fall during her uneven parallel bars performance and needed a nearly perfect score of 9.95 on the balance beam to win the gold medal.

She scored only 9.85, but the chief judge, who was also Romanian, argued that the score should have been 9.95 and refused to ratify the lower score. After a 25-minute argument with the other officials, the Romanian judge gave in and Comaneci received the silver medal.

REINSTATED

Two female athletes, Ilona Slupianek of East Germany and Nadezhda Tkachenko of the Soviet Union, had been suspended from competition in 1978 for taking anabolic steroids. However, amid strong protests from Western sports officials, their 18-month suspensions were up in time for them to take part in the Moscow Olympics. Slupianek won the shot put and Tkachenko won the pentathlon, setting a new world record.

AN AGELESS RUNNER

The winner of the 5,000- and 10,000-meter runs was Miruts Yifter of Ethiopia. The date of

Yifter's birth had not been registered when he was born, so even he did not know how old he was. In the Montreal Olympics in 1976, he was listed as 25. Four years later, he was listed as 35. It was estimated by some that he was between 33 and 38 years old when he became a double gold medal winner in Moscow, but there were others who thought he was in his 40's.

Miruts Yifter wins the 10,000m.

ONLY OLYMPIC FLAGS

When the awards ceremony was held for the 4,000-meter individual pursuit cycling event, the three medal winners were all from nations that had chosen to compete under the Olympic flag— Switzerland, France, and Denmark. As the medal winners took the victory stand and the three Olympic flags were raised, the largely Soviet audience responded with jeers and whistles.

COMPARING TIMES

The Olympic swimming events were dominated by the East Germans, who won a total of 34 medals, and the Soviets who won 28. In the women's events, the East Germans won all three medals in six different races.

The U.S. national swimming championships were held in Irvine, California, on the last day of the Moscow Games, obviously for comparison purposes. Journalists who made the comparisons wrote that the Americans would have won ten gold, 12 silver, and five bronze medals if they had been in Moscow.

FOOD FIGHT!

Late one night when the Games were reaching the halfway point, a food fight erupted in the Olympic village cafeteria. The culprits were some 50 athletes from Western nations who had already finished their competitions and were letting off steam. As the athletes were pelting each other with bread rolls and yelling "Free Afghanistan," Soviet police entered the scene and broke up the demonstration. The next day, the revelers were quietly sent home, including a British swimmer named, ironically, Jimmy Carter.

THE GRASS IS ALWAYS GREENER

The president of the International Archery Federation, Ingrid Firth, requested that special grass be installed at the site of the archery events. She wanted "lawns like Wimbledon tennis courts" for the arrows to fly over on their way to the targets. The IOC responded that regular grass, which was already in place, would work just as well.

SEEING DOUBLE

Observers of the rowing events must have thought they were having vision problems during some of the races. Four sets of twins were among the rowers in the Olympic competition.

In the coxless pairs, twin brothers Berndt and Jörg Landvoigt of East Germany won the gold medal, barely finishing ahead of twins Yuriy and Nikolai Pimenov of the USSR. Other twins in the rowing competition were Peter and Roland Stocker of Sweden and Mariusz and Henryk Trzcinski of Poland.

THE PREMIER'S FINAL APPEARANCE

In the absence of First Secretary Leonid Brezhnev, the Soviet Union's premier since 1964, Aleksei Kosygin, sat in the stadium throughout the closing ceremonies. Kosygin and IOC president Lord Killanin stood together as the Olympic athletes marched out. Gravely ill, Kosygin would never appear in public again.

MISCHA SHEDS A TEAR

A giant image of the mascot of the Moscow Olympics, Mischa the bear, appeared on the flash cards in the stadium during the closing ceremonies. Signifying the sadness of the Olympics coming to a close, the cards were manipulated so a series of giant tears appeared in Mischa's left eye and rolled down its cheek. There were many who thought the tear symbolized a sadness created by the unsuccessful political involvement that was designed to destroy these games.

Olympiad XXIII
LOS ANGELES, 1984

A LONG CAMPAIGN

The effort to bring the Olympics to Los Angeles for a second time began in 1939, seven years after the highly successful (and profitable) 1932 Games. At that time, a high-powered committee was formed to begin work to seek approval for hosting the Olympics again. However, the committee's efforts were thwarted, first by the outbreak of World War II, and later by a series of failed bids.

After losing out in bids for the 1976 and 1980 Olympics, the Los Angeles committee decided to make an all-out effort for 1984, with bold plans to finance the Games entirely by private enterprise. When the IOC met to select a host city for 1984, Los Angeles was the only candidate.

The Los Angeles organizers, realizing there was no competition, began to make demands that were beyond the IOC's rules for hosting the Games. The attitude of the Californians was obviously resented by many of the old guard IOC members.

The IOC decided to award the Games to Los Angeles provisionally, subject to the organizers reaching complete agreement with the IOC by August 1, 1978. When that deadline was not met, negotiations continued until March 1, 1979, when the IOC finally gave in on several issues and awarded the Games officially to Los Angeles.

IRAN'S MARATHON PROBLEM

Originally, Tehran, Iran, was a candidate for the 1984 Olympics, but the application was withdrawn early. An interesting facet of the Teheran bid was that they would offer a full Olympic program—except for the marathon. The marathon was associated with the battle of Marathon in 490 B.C. in which the Iranians (then Persians) were soundly defeated by the Greeks on the field of battle. The loss was apparently still a source of embarrassment for the Iranians after more than 2,400 years.

THE SOVIETS RETALIATE

On April 6, just three-and-a-half months before the 1984 Olympic Games were to open, the Soviet press accused the White House of trying to stop Soviet athletes from participating in the Olympics. It was the first inkling that the USSR might attempt to encourage a boycott.

A month later, on May 8, the Soviets issued a formal statement declaring "Participation of Soviet sportsmen in the Games of the XXIII Olympiad in Los Angeles is impossible." Most of the other Communist nations followed the Soviet lead and announced they were also boycotting.

Obviously the Soviet-led boycott was a payback for the U.S.-led boycott of the Moscow Games four years earlier. But the Soviets gave two specific reasons for their decision not to participate. First, they said they feared for the safety of their athletes and officials. Second, they said that the United States government's intervention in the Games was in violation of the Olympic spirit.

In a televised statement, a Russian spokesman was more specific. He said about the American hosts: "Methods have been devised for the abduction of Soviet people, for compelling them not to return to their motherland, and for treating them with special drugs, including psychotropic preparations which destroy the nervous system."

THE SMUGGLED FLAME

A dispute between the organizers of the Los Angeles Olympic Games and the Greek National Olympic Committee almost kept the sacred Olympic flame from being kindled in Olympia for the 1984 Olympics. The Los Angeles plan was to fly the flame from Greece to New York, where it would be relayed in a 9,000-mile zigzag pattern across the United States to Los Angeles.

Each American who volunteered to run one kilometer in the torch relay, or who sponsored someone to run, would pay $3,000, with all of the money to be donated to charities to support local youth programs. The plan was designed to raise $30 million.

The Greeks objected to commercializing the relay and refused to take part. They would allow the flame to be kindled in Olympia, they said, only if the Los Angeles organizers would abandon the plan to charge relay runners for the honor of carrying the torch.

Through weeks of negotiating, including an offer by the Americans to donate some of the money to Greek organizations, there was total impasse. The Americans said they would limit the time for kilometer sales, but would not abandon the idea completely. The Greeks would not kindle the flame unless there was total abandonment of the plan and the return of all money collected to that time.

On May 2, only six days before the torch run was to begin in New York, the L.A. organizers received word that the Olympic flame was in Lausanne, Switzerland, ready to be picked up and flown to New York. It was certainly a surprise announcement. Two Swiss students who were working in Greece had gone to the Temple of Hera at Olympia, and with a small parabolic mirror and a candle, they had kindled the Olympic flame. Then they transferred the fire to an oil lantern and smuggled the flame out of Greece to Switzerland.

As soon as the L.A. organizers knew they had an official Olympic flame, they called the Greeks and requested one last time that they kindle the flame in an official ceremony at Olympia.

When the Greeks learned an Olympic flame was already available to the committee, and that the Los Angeles organizers were also considering having the Greeks march into the stadium in alphabetical order during the opening ceremonies rather than in their traditional first position, the Greeks relented. The "official" flame was kindled with full pageantry at Olympia on May 6 and arrived in New York on May 7, the day before the torch relay was to begin.

AN ETERNAL FLAME

There is now a permanent flame, kindled originally in Olympia, Greece, burning in front of the Olympic Museum in Lausanne, Switzerland. That flame is available to be transferred to any future Olympic site, should there ever be another problem having the flame kindled in Greece.

THE TORCH RELAY

The first two torchbearers, running side-by-side through the streets of New York, were the grandchildren of Olympic legends Jesse Owens and Jim Thorpe. Gina Hemphill and Bill Thorpe Jr. Hemphill was also selected to be the next-to-last torchbearer who would carry the flame into the Olympic stadium 82 days later.

Before the torch had left New York, word came that the USSR would boycott the Games. The next day spectators lined the torch route, some of them holding signs saying "Go America" and "To Hell with the Russians."

When the torch reached Louisville, Kentucky, on its zigzag journey across America, the 1960 Olympic boxing champion, Muhammad Ali, carried it for one kilometer through his hometown before thousands of admiring fans. His run ended at Muhammad Ali Boulevard. "If I fall on my face," the 42-year-old Ali remarked as he took the torch, "I want you to promise not to take my picture."

Another sports celebrity who carried the torch was former University of Southern California and NFL football star, O.J. Simpson, who was to achieve much greater notoriety ten years later when he was charged with murder and was ultimately acquitted in "the crime of the century."

Simpson carried the torch along an uphill stretch of road leading into Santa Monica, California, where he handed the torch to a seven-year-old boy who suffered from cerebral palsy. Simpson walked beside the young boy, encouraging him, as the lad struggled for 15 minutes to advance the torch a short distance.

THE FIRST U.S. PRESIDENT
TO OPEN THE GAMES

In much of the Olympic literature it is stated that the host country's head of state always declares the Olympic Games open. However, the 1984 Games were the fifth Olympic Games hosted by the United States, but the first attended by a sitting U.S. president, Ronald Reagan.

President Theodore Roosevelt did not attend the 1904 Olympics in St. Louis. Presidents Herbert Hoover (1932, Los Angeles), Dwight Eisenhower (1960, Squaw Valley), and Jimmy Carter (1980, Lake Placid) all sent their vice presidents to represent them.

President Reagan was not only the first U.S. president to open the Games, he was the first head of state to rewrite the 17-word statement that the IOC had mandated must always be read verbatim. Reagan rearranged the words, but the total was still only 17.

BOMB THREATS

Just ten minutes before the opening ceremonies were to begin, as President and Mrs. Reagan were being seated, the bomb unit of the Los Angeles police department was called to the peristyle end of the stadium. The overflow stadium crowd was unaware of the tense situation as the bomb squad investigated a report of "suspicious wiring" in an electrical control box. It was a false alarm—one of many during the Los Angeles Olympics. During the two weeks of the Games, the bomb squad was called out an average of twice a day.

The final bomb scare came the day after the closing ceremonies, as the athletes were being transported to the airport. A pipe bomb was discovered in a wheel well of a bus carrying Turkish athletes when it arrived at the airport. A Los Angeles police officer dismantled the bomb by pulling off a wire, and was cited for heroism on the spot by police chief Daryl Gates. It was a huge media event, televised live from the scene. The next day it was learned that the "heroic" police officer had planted the bomb himself.

ROMANIA DEFIES THE BOYCOTT

The only Soviet-bloc nation to travel to Los Angeles in defiance of the USSR's boycott order was tiny Romania, including former Olympic gymnastics star, Nadia Comaneci, who came along as a spectator. The Los Angeles organizers and the IOC paid the Romanians $120,000 toward their travel expenses, and provided a special television feed into Romania so the people back home could watch their countrymen in the Olympics.

The Romanian team received a huge ovation from the overflow crowd in the Coliseum as they marched in during the opening ceremonies.

ED BURKE'S COMEBACK

The flagbearer for the U.S. team was 44-year-old Ed Burke, who had competed in 1964 and 1968, but had been retired through the three

Ed Burke

Olympics since then. He decided to make a comeback while demonstrating the hammer throw for his two daughters, who were curious about the event. When Burke realized he was able to surpass his previous bests during the demonstration, he decided to come out of retirement.

CHINA ENTERS

Mainland China, with a population exceeding one billion, decided to participate in the Los Angeles Olympics. The Chinese, who were entering Olympic competition for the first time since 1932, had never won an Olympic medal. As an incentive to its athletes, the Chinese government offered "scholarships" of $2,000 to everyone winning a medal. As it turned out, there were 32 scholarships awarded, most coming in gymnastics, diving, and women's volleyball.

THE FINAL TORCHBEARER

As soon as it was known that Nadia Comaneci and the Romanian delegation had defied the So-

131

viet boycott, rumors began circulating that Nadia would be selected as the final torchbearer. Then, when it was announced the final runner would be an American citizen, rumors began flying that it would be either former heavyweight champion Muhammad Ali or (believe it or not) singer Michael Jackson.

When the selection was made, it remained a closely-guarded secret until the torch was handed off by Gina Hemphill during the opening ceremonies. Rafer Johnson, who had won the Olympic decathlon silver medal in 1956 and the gold medal in 1960, was the final torchbearer.

There were doubts in the minds of Olympic insiders, and Johnson himself, that at age 47 he would be able to successfully negotiate the steep 96-step run up the stadium stairs. Johnson had been able to complete the run only once during rehearsals and since then had developed a painful case of shin splints. Bruce Jenner, the 1976 Olympic decathlon champion, was standing by to take over if Johnson were to falter.

But Johnson did not falter. The crowd recognized him and roared its approval as he took the torch from Hemphill and ran around the stadium track. Then he climbed the stairs leading from the track, and without hesitation carried the torch up the 96 steps to the top. He turned to the crowd, held the torch high, and then lit the fuse that carried the flame up through the huge Olympic rings to the cauldron at the top of the Coliseum peristyle.

It was a dramatic and fitting end to the torch journey which was witnessed by millions of people across America and netted nearly $11 million for youth sports programs.

Fittingly, when the torch relay started in Los Angeles for the 1996 Olympics, Rafer Johnson ran the first leg.

POLICE PROTECTION

Security for the Los Angeles Olympic Games was extremely thorough. There were 20,000 security officers from local police departments, the FBI, and the Department of Defense. The cost was $100 million.

As an example of the strict safety measures, when the Israeli team and officials arrived at the Los Angeles airport, their movements were monitored by air and ground police units until they reached the Olympic village. The FBI also formed a

50-member hostage rescue team, in case there was an attempt to repeat the 1972 hostage debacle.

There were some incidents of security gaffes, including the case of the track coach who was working with athletes at the University of Southern California track. When the coach took a starter's pistol out of his pocket, he was jumped and wrestled to the ground by a security officer.

THE ZOLA BUDD-MARY DECKER INCIDENT

Probably the most memorable controversy associated with the 1984 Olympics involved two of the best female distance runners of the day—Zola Budd of South Africa and Mary Decker of the United States.

Budd was a shy 18-year-old who ran her races barefoot. Because South Africa was barred from Olympic competition, Budd, one of whose parents had English citizenship by birth, moved to England just five months before the Games and was granted immediate British citizenship so she could compete in the Olympics. This did not sit well with every British citizen and Budd was subjected to various acts of harassment before the Games.

Decker, at the age of 25 and with 11 years of international running experience, was confident and outspoken. She was the reigning world champion in both the 1500- and 3000-meter runs.

The 3,000-meter Olympic final was touted by the press as the race of the Games, to the dismay of track fans who knew Budd was not in Decker's class at that distance, and to the two runners, who did not relish the rash of prerace publicity.

The race began with Decker leading the tightly bunched pack at a very fast pace, but after the one-mile mark, the pace had slowed and it was a four-woman race. Budd and Decker were leading Wendy Sly of Great Britain and Maricica Puica of Romania. Coming out of the turn, Decker bumped into Budd's leg, causing her to stumble slightly. A few strides later, they bumped again, but this time Decker stumbled, her spikes slicing into Budd's bare foot, and then Decker fell hard onto the infield. She tried to get up, but couldn't. She lay there sobbing.

The partisan crowd booed Budd as she ran the final three laps of the race. With her foot bleeding and her spirit gone, Budd slowed to a

**Mary Decker watches the field continue without her as she
lies stunned in the infield. Budd is No. 151, Puica 316.**

jog and finished seventh. Puica was the eventual winner.

At first Budd was blamed for the incident and was disqualified, but reviews of the videotape showed that neither runner was at fault. However, the controversy raged on for months after the Games were over.

BENOIT WINS THE FIRST WOMEN'S MARATHON

When the women's 800-meter run was added to the Olympic program in 1928, the race's unfortunate finish (with some unconditioned competitors collapsing on the track) convinced the IOC to drop the event. Not until 1960, when the 800 meters returned to the program, were women again allowed to participate in an Olympic race longer than 200 meters.

It took another 12 years before the women's 1500-meter run was added, and another 12 years to acknowledge the burgeoning popularity of women's distance running by including the 3000 meters and the marathon. The 26-mile, 385-yard marathon race was more than 50 times longer than the "physically dangerous" 800-meter run of 1928.

America's Joan Benoit, who had won two Boston Marathons and had posted the world's fastest time, was a favorite to win the first Olympic marathon for women, but she suffered a disabling knee injury in the spring of 1984. The severe pain allowed her to hobble only a couple of miles on her daily training runs. Just 17 days before the U.S. women's marathon trials, Benoit, in desperation, had arthroscopic knee surgery. The knee felt better but was still not right and

Benoit tried various therapies, including electrical stimulation—especially for a hamstring pull which developed in her other leg. In serious doubt at the starting line, Benoit started off with the field of 238 hopefuls. Miraculously, she held together and outdistanced the pack to win the race and make the team.

When the women's marathon was run in the Olympics three months later, the participants made history as soon as they passed the 1500-meter mark. Never before had women run so far in an Olympic race.

At three miles, Benoit pulled away and was never challenged after that. She maintained her steady pace and triumphed by more than 400 meters over Norway's Grete Waitz. Doffing her white painter's cap during a victory lap before an adoring crowd, Benoit was obviously relishing her place in Olympic history.

AN UNREMOVABLE FLAG

Canada's first-ever gold medal in swimming was won by Alex Baumann in the 400-meter individual medley. Baumann, who was born in Czechoslovakia and emigrated to Canada by way of New Zealand, was easily identified as a Canadian, even when he was not wearing his shirt. He had a red maple leaf tattooed on his chest.

MORE BLOOD BOOSTING

Blood boosting, which first became a controversial issue in the 1972 Olympic Games, became a headline event in 1984. Several members of the U.S. cycling team, including surprise gold medal winner Steve Hegg, were blood-boosted before their races.

Blood boosting is the procedure which requires drawing and freezing about one liter of an athlete's blood, and then reinfusing it later after the athlete's red blood cell count has returned to normal. The result is a dramatic increase in endurance. But the American cyclists, who had not had their own blood drawn previously, used other people's blood, causing some to question the difference between boosting and doping.

One of the cyclists said later, "If anybody did do any blood boosting, it's their own business." Another said, "I didn't think it was wrong at the time because you can't detect it."

Allan J. Ryan, M.D., editor of *The Physician*

and Sports Medicine, wrote later: "Whether the procedure was ethically, morally, or medically correct didn't seem to matter. The key question they apparently asked themselves was 'Can we get away with it?'"

Blood boosting in the Olympic Games was banned the following year.

A DELAYED DRUG REACTION

The final of the 10,000-meter run was a two-man race at the finish, with Italy's Alberto Cova pulling away from Finland's Martti Vainio to win easily. After the race, when the mandatory drug tests were given to all the medal winners, Vainio's test showed traces of an anabolic steroid. He was disqualified immediately.

Vainio protested, even appearing on television to proclaim his innocence. Vainio knew the tests could not detect steroids unless they had been taken in recent weeks, and he knew he had not taken any banned substances during that time period. He did admit, however, that he had participated in blood boosting, which was not yet against the rules.

Then it was realized that the blood that had been taken from his body and reinfused before the Olympic race was taken from him six months earlier, during a period when he was taking anabolic steroids. The reinfused blood contained the banned steroids, causing the disqualification and the loss of the silver medal.

FROM YOUNGEST TO OLDEST

In the 1972 Olympic Games in Munich, the women's high jump winner was 16-year-old Ulrike Meyfarth of West Germany, the youngest individual-event Olympic track and field champion in history. In the 1984 Olympics in Los Angeles, at the age of 28, Meyfarth won the high jump again, this time becoming the oldest winner of an Olympic high jump competition.

PROUD MOROCCANS

The winner of the 400-meter hurdles for women was Nawal El Moutawakel, the first gold medal winner in Morocco's history. King Hassan II of Morocco was so pleased with the victory, he decreed that all female babies born in Morocco during the next month would be named Nawal.

DUPLICATE GOLDS

Two gold medals were awarded in an Olympic swimming event for the first time when the first two finishers in the women's 100-meter freestyle clocked identical times. America's Nancy Hogshead and Carrie Steinseifer, who were roommates in the Olympic village, finished in a dead heat in 55.92, with each winning a gold medal.

PRO TENNIS PLAYERS

Although tennis was an Olympic event for the first time since 1924, it was an exhibition sport in 1984, not one of the official sports. Entry was open to both amateur and professional players, opening the door for further relaxing of the long-protected amateur code. The two individual gold medal winners, well-known teenagers Steffi Graf of West Germany and Stefan Edberg of Sweden, were among several of the competitors who were making "a comfortable living" on the pro tour.

A JUBILANT VICTOR

Freestyle wrestler Bobby Weaver was so elated when he pinned Japan's Takashi Irie to win the light flyweight gold medal, he did a back somersault on the mat. Then he ran into the crowd, grabbed his infant son, ran back onto the mat, and raised his son's tiny right hand in a victory salute.

A HAPPY CLOSING

One hundred thousand people jammed into the Coliseum for the closing ceremonies, bringing the total attendance for the Los Angeles Games to nearly six million. With athletes singing and dancing, and a variety of speeches, songs, and fireworks, the 1984 Games came to a close. The first "private enterprise" Olympic Games ended with a handsome surplus of $215 million.

Olympiad XXIV
SEOUL, 1988

SEOUL IS SELECTED

In 1981, the IOC selected Seoul to host the 1988 Olympic Games. The decision to conduct the Games in Korea, rather than in Nagoya, Japan, was a controversial one, not because of concern about Seoul's ability to host the Games, but because of the proximity of the hostile and unpredictable North Koreans, whose military forces were only 30 miles north of Seoul.

Although the Korean War ended in 1953, there was technically still a state of war between the two nations. With North Korea described as "one of the most repressive and heavily armed countries in the world," there were fears that anything might happen, even an armed conflict, in an effort to disrupt the Seoul Olympics. During the time of the Games, a fleet of U.S. ships, including two aircraft carriers, were stationed in the waters near Korea to discourage the North Koreans from initiating any military action.

There were also concerns that North Korea might merely try to engineer a massive boycott to undermine the Seoul Olympics. There had been significant boycotts at the three previous Olympics, so the prospect was not out of the question. However, 160 nations made the trip to Seoul—the most ever to attend an Olympic celebration.

THE EFFORT TO CO-HOST

As soon as Seoul was awarded the 1988 Olympic Games, the North Koreans called the decision "a criminal act against the Korean people." Then they began making demands of the Olympic organizers, insisting on co-hosting the Games, with half the events held in the North.

Some concessions were made by the South, including an offer to move three of the Olympic events to Pyongyang, North Korea, but the North Koreans kept demanding more, finally insisting on splitting the television revenues. Three days before the opening ceremonies in Seoul, the North Koreans were still making demands that they co-host the Olympics.

TIGHT SECURITY

There was an armed military presence in Seoul from the time the first athletes arrived until the last athletes left. A total of 120,000 police officers kept the order. They checked people's identity, searched handbags and packages, and used metal detectors at all of the venues. The security even included the use of mirrors to check under cars for possible bombs.

THE FLAME ARRIVES

Among the demands made by the North Koreans was to have a portion of the Olympic torch relay pass through North Korea. Originally the plan was approved, but as the Games approached and the North Korean demands increased, the negotiations fell apart completely. On August 27, the flame arrived at Seoul's Cheju Airport to begin its three-week relay throughout South Korea.

COMFORT FOR SOME

The opening ceremonies were typically exciting and entertaining for the crowd in the stadium and for millions of TV viewers, but they were, as always, a cause of discomfort for the athletes who had to stand in the middle of the infield throughout the three-hour spectacle.

One of the teams, however, managed to remain comfortable throughout the opening ceremonies. The team from The Netherlands marched into the stadium carrying and waving orange umbrellas. When the team reached the infield, the umbrellas were converted into "shooting sticks," with the handles unfolding into seats. They were the only team that was able to sit through the long ceremonies.

A JOYFUL TORCH BEARER

When the Olympic flame arrived in Seoul after its long journey from Greece, it was carried into the stadium by 76-year-old Sohn Kee-chung, who had won the Olympic marathon as a reluctant Japanese subject in 1936. After rounding the track and completing several jumps for joy, Sohn passed the flame to Lim Chun-ae, winner of three gold medals at the 1986 Asian Games. Lim then transferred the flame to torches held by a teacher, a high school student, and a university student.

The three final torchbearers stood on a large metal ring that circled the base of "the World Tree," a 95-foot column with the Olympic cauldron at its top. The ring began to rise slowly until it reached the top, where the three torches were all dipped into the cauldron at the same time, lighting the flame that would burn throughout the Seoul Olympics.

Earlier in the opening ceremonies, 2,400 white pigeons had been released, but it soon became clear they were not homing pigeons. Most of them stayed around the stadium throughout the Games. Even as the three torchbearers ignited the flame in the giant cauldron, 11 of the pigeons were sitting on the cauldron's rim. Needless to say, those pigeons moved on quickly.

BIONDI STARS IN SWIMMING

Before the Olympics, there had been speculation that U.S. swimmer Matt Biondi might win seven gold medals at Seoul, equalling the number won by Mark Spitz in 1972. However, Biondi himself dismissed the idea, saying, "I'm convinced that will never happen again."

Biondi did turn out to be the star of the Olympic swimming events, winning five gold medals, one silver, and one bronze. Biondi was very close to winning his sixth gold in the 100-meter butterfly, but he lost it to Anthony Nesty of Surinam by the smallest of margins.

Nesty, the only Olympic entry from the tiny South American nation thus became the first black athlete to win a swimming gold medal, the first South American Olympic swimming champion, and the first medalist from the country of Surinam.

Biondi, whose time was 53.01 to Nesty's 53.00, said later, "I guess I shouldn't have cut my fingernails. That might make up for one-hundredth of a second."

SAMMY LEE RETURNS

The Olympic diving events began with a brief, but moving ceremony featuring Korean-American Dr. Sammy Lee, who had won gold medals for the United States in platform diving in 1948 and

1952. Now 62 years old, Lee was dressed in a traditional Korean folk costume as he opened the competition by hitting a large gong. He received a standing ovation from the fans in the packed swimming hall.

BLOOD IN THE POOL

Favored in 3-meter springboard diving was 28-year-old Greg Louganis of the U.S., who had won the gold medal in 1984. To complete the preliminary round, Louganis was performing a series of ten qualifying dives. His ninth dive was one of his most difficult—a reverse two-and-a-half somersault in the pike position.

As Louganis was turning in the air, disaster struck. He hit his head on the board and fell flat in the water, with blood spurting out of the wound on the top of his head. Gamely, he climbed out of the pool, received emergency medical treatment including four temporary stitches and a waterproof patch, and went back for his tenth and final preliminary dive.

After the preliminaries, Louganis was taken

Greg Louganis on the victory stand.

to a hospital to have the wound restitched and covered. He returned to the pool the next day, where he won the gold medal in a dramatic showdown with Tan Liangde of China. Lauded for his skill and courage, Louganis was later presented the coveted "Spirit Award" by his Olympic teammates.

Seven years later, Greg Louganis made a startling announcement. He said he was HIV positive and had known he was carrying the deadly infection that causes AIDS since March of 1988, a full six months before he went to Seoul. There certainly would have been panic at the time if it had been known that the blood in the Olympic swimming pool was HIV positive blood.

In his autobiography, *Breaking the Surface*, Louganis wrote that he was unable to sleep the following night, worrying about whether or not he had "put anyone in danger."

MORE BOXING INCIDENTS

In a bantamweight boxing match, Alexander Hristov of Bulgaria decisioned Korean Byun Jong-il, 4-1. Five angry Korean officials, including the head coach, Lee Hong-soo, climbed into the ring and began jostling the referee. The Korean fighter refused to leave the ring. Finally, order was restored and the ring was cleared. The five Korean officials were all suspended from amateur boxing indefinitely.

In the final match in the lightweight division, America's Roy Jones dominated the fight over Korean Park Shi-hun. However, in a startling decision, Park was declared the winner over Jones, 3-2. Jones stood in disbelief when the decision was announced. Even the winner Park said Jones had won. The controversy was heightened later when Jones was named the best boxer at the Games.

STEROIDS GO PUBLIC—IN A BIG WAY

The widespread use of anabolic steroids by Olympic athletes was finally brought to the fore in an abrupt and startling way in Seoul. Ben Johnson of Canada, the winner of the Olympic 100 meters race and thus billed as "the world's fastest human," was disqualified after testing positive for anabolic steroids. He would have to surrender his gold medal to his arch-rival, Carl Lewis of the United States.

Johnson's coach, Charlie Francis, admitted that Johnson had been taking various anabolic steroids for seven years prior to the 1988 Games, but he was certain Johnson had only used steroids that could not be detected or had discontinued using the detectable steroids well ahead of the accepted "clearance time."

Francis was shocked to learn that Johnson had tested positive for stanozolol, a drug that everyone knew would show up on a test. When Johnson's "endocrine profile" showed that he had been using steroids for some time prior to the Seoul drug tests, the IOC executive committee upheld the disqualification.

The coach was quick to respond. He reported that ten other athletes failed drug tests in Seoul, 20 others tested positive but were cleared of any wrongdoing because of politics, and 80 percent of the male track and field athletes had endocrine profiles showing previous steroid use. He also cited a statement by a leading sports medical

Ben Johnson takes the 100 (temporarily).

138

officer that "a majority of Olympic athletes used steroids in training." Johnson's case was special, the coach said, "because he got caught."

The following year, Francis appeared as a witness at a Canadian government hearing on drug abuse in Olympic sports. He testified that steroids were widely used in the U.S., Canada, the Soviet Union, Great Britain, East and West Germany, New Zealand, and Cuba. He even used performance graphs to show that recent sports improvements could be linked directly to drug use.

Francis gave examples of officials condoning drug use and implicated several Olympic champions and world record holders who, he said, had admitted to him they used steroids. "It became clear," he said, "we had no reason to believe anyone at the highest levels was not using performance-enhancing drugs."

Four-time U.S. Olympian Hal Connolly agreed with Francis about the widespread use of steroids. "I know people who have tested positive but have been passed through in the Olympic Games for political reasons," Connolly said, "and I know people who have tested positive and have been the scapegoats."

The information provided by Francis and Connolly was supported by Prince Alexandre de Merode of Belgium, chairman of the IOC's Medical Commission, who said that 50 track and field athletes "showed evidence of steroid use but tested negative at the Seoul Olympics."

OTHER DRUG DISQUALIFICATIONS

There were ten athletes disqualified for drug use in Seoul besides Ben Johnson, including two Bulgarian weight lifters who won gold medals. When the Bulgarians tested positive for Furosemide, a drug which is used as a masking agent for anabolic steroids, the remainder of the Bulgarian weight lifters withdrew from competition.

TENNIS PROS IN THE GAMES

Tennis had been an exhibition event in Los Angeles in 1984, and was open to both amateurs and professionals. Several well-known professional players took part, even though their performances were not "official."

In 1988, tennis became an official Olympic sport for the first time since 1924, and for the first time fully-paid professionals were eligible to participate in Olympic events. It was the first step in allowing professionals to take part in other Olympic sports in the future.

FLOJO

The darling of the 1988 Olympics was sprinter Florence Griffith Joyner, known to all as FloJo, whose unusual and sometimes garish uniforms and fingernails endeared her to millions of fans. She was also the fastest woman in the world, winning three gold medals and one silver.

Griffith Joyner won the 100 meters so handily that second-place finisher, Evelyn Ashford, who had held the Olympic and world records, commented, "Only a man can run faster." As it turned out, even some men were not faster. Griffith Joyner's time was faster than 12 of the men in the second round of the men's 100 meters and faster than all of the men running the 100 meters in the decathlon.

Flojo

139

In the 200m final, run four days later, she set a world record that has still not been approached by any other woman. Flojo won a third gold on the U.S. 4x100 team and a silver medal in the 4x400 relay, certainly one of the most remarkable Olympics for any female track athlete.

GROWTH HORMONE

In the early 1980s, a completely new "drug" of choice appeared on the sports scene—growth hormone (GH). This hormone, which was originally taken from the pituitary glands of human cadavers or from primate animals and then injected into athletes, reportedly works as an anabolic agent in developing lean muscle mass. GH is especially popular among athletes because it cannot be detected by any known drug testing procedures.

In 1986, the use of GH among athletes increased greatly with the development of a synthetic form, which is manufactured and distributed by two major drug companies. The introduction of these synthetic products made GH more available and much less expensive for use in the 1988 Games.

There have been many Olympic athletes suspected (or even accused in some cases) of having used GH, but only one athlete has stepped forward and admitted it. Sprinter Diane Williams said in 1979 that she had used GH and anabolic steroids prior to the 1984 Olympic Games, but she passed all drug tests without a problem.

THE BASKETBALLERS ACCEPT DEFEAT

The U.S. basketball team, which had an 85-1 record since basketball was introduced as an Olympic sport in 1936, lost in the semifinals in Seoul. (The previous loss had been the controversial final game against the Soviet Union in 1972.) There were no arguments this time as the Soviets beat the Americans, 82-76.

Although the U.S. basketball fans agreed their team had been outplayed and had lost fairly, they said they would not have lost if America's professional basketball players had been allowed to participate. Why not just open up the Olympics to everyone, they asked. Four years later, in Barcelona, that's exactly what happened.

AN UNPARALLELED PHOTO-FINISH

Perhaps the most bizarre finish ever in a cycling race took place at the end of the women's 82-kilometer (51-mile) road race. No less than 45 cyclists pedaled madly along the final stretch to the finish line, where photos had to be studied to determine the medalists. Monique Knol of The Netherlands was determined the winner in 2 hours, 00.52 seconds—the exact same time as the second and third place finishers.

SUCCESSFUL GAMES

When the Seoul Olympic Games came to an end, it was said that the Koreans had demonstrated the courtesy typical of Asia, the organizational skills of the Germans, and the financial savvy of the Americans. It was the perfect combination for hosting the very successful Games of the XXIVth Olympiad.

During the closing ceremonies, IOC president Juan Antonio Samaranch said the Seoul Olympics had been "the best and most united Games in history. No terrorism. No boycotts.* But 160 countries and nearly 10,000 competitors assembled in the world's most visible demonstration of friendship."

Samaranch must have meant no massive boycotts. The 1988 Olympics were boycotted by North Korea, Cuba, Ethiopia, Albania, Nicaragua, Madagascar, and The Seychelles.

Olympiad XXV
BARCELONA, 1992

BARCELONA WINS OUT OVER PARIS

In October of 1986, the IOC met in Lausanne, Switzerland, to select the site for the 1992 Olympic Games. Paris was a strong candidate, but the influence of the newly elected IOC president, Juan Antonio Samaranch, obviously swayed the delegates to select his hometown, Barcelona. As it turned out, the Barcelona Olympics were the first that were "fully-attended" in 40 years. There were no boycotting nations; a record 172 nations participated.

GROWING TV COVERAGE

In 1936, a new era in communications was launched when a few thousand Germans were able to watch live telecasts of the Olympic track and field and swimming events in theaters around Berlin. In 1992, 3.5 billion people worldwide watched the Barcelona Olympic Games.

In 1960, the first year the Olympic Games were telecast to the U.S., CBS-TV paid $394,000 for the rights to bring the Rome Olympics into American homes. In 1992, NBC-TV paid $401 million for the Barcelona TV rights. In 32 years, the tab had increased by more than 100,000 percent.

MANY CHANGES

The parade of athletes during the opening ceremonies showed the world that the Olympic Games had undergone several significant changes in just four years.

First and foremost, there were wealthy professional athletes marching into the stadium along with their amateur countrymen. Basketball and tennis players, millionaires because of their sports skills, were in Barcelona simply to compete for Olympic medals.

The South African team marched in for the first time in 32 years. The flagbearer was Jan Tau, a black marathon runner who was born in 1960, the last year South Africa was allowed to participate in the Olympics.

The former Soviet Union was split into several different nations as they marched into the stadium. However, Russia and 11 of the other former Soviet states participated as the Commonwealth of Independent States (CIS). It was the first and last appearance for the CIS. They would compete as separate nations in 1996.

The team from the reunited Germany marched in, the first time that Germans from East and West had competed under the same flag since they were forced to do so in 1956.

Even teams from Cuba and North Korea took part, after staying away from the Olympics for 12 years because of boycotts.

A LONG SHOT

At the close of the opening ceremonies, the sun had already set before the final torchbearer jogged into the stadium, ran onto a circular stage at one end of the stadium, and came to a halt beside an archer, with bow and arrow in hand. The archer was Antonio Rebollo from Madrid.

The torchbearer transferred the flame from his torch to the arrow, Rebollo took aim, and the flaming arrow was shot in a long arching trajectory, up into a cauldron high above the spectators. As the arrow entered the cauldron, the Olympic flame was ignited. It was one of the most dramatic and impressive endings for an Olympic torch relay.

A FAMILY TRAGEDY

When Ron Karnaugh qualified for the U.S. swimming team in the 200-meter individual medley, the hometown fans in Maplewood, New Jersey, raised funds to send Ron's parents, Jane and Peter Karnaugh, to Barcelona.

Shortly after Ron Karnaugh marched into the Olympic stadium with the American team during the opening ceremonies, 60-year-old Peter Karnaugh suffered a heart attack and was taken to a hospital. A short time later he died.

In the individual medley final a few days later, Ron Karnaugh finished sixth as his obviously grieving mother sat in the stands. "The thought of not swimming never crossed my mind," Karnaugh said. "My father would have wanted me to swim, no matter what happened."

WHAT A DIFFERENCE A CENTURY MAKES

Baron Pierre de Coubertin, the founder of the modern Olympic Games, would probably have been shocked had he witnessed the first awards ceremony of the 1992 Olympics. In 1892, when the Baron was first making plans for the Olympics, he made it clear that women would be strictly forbidden from participating in the Games. He also said the awards would be silver and bronze, but never gold. And he insisted that shooting events would never be part of the Olympic program because shooting is not sport. The first Olympic champion of 1992 was a woman who won a gold medal in the air rifle competition.

A HIGH PRICE FOR GOLD

Baron de Coubertin, an advocate for a strict amateur code, would have been shocked further had he heard of the deal the Spanish government offered its athletes. Each Spanish athlete who won a gold medal would receive a $1 million annuity, with the payments beginning as soon as the gold medalists reach the age of 50. There were 13 Spanish athletes who took advantage of this generous offer.

KING CARL

The most enduring athlete of the Barcelona Olympics was America's Carl Lewis, who added two more gold medals to his collection.

In 1984, Lewis had duplicated Jesse Owens' feat of winning four track and field gold medals in one Olympics. He won the 100 meters, 200 meters, long jump, and ran a leg of the winning 400-meter relay, the same four events as Owens.

In 1988, Lewis repeated as the 100-meter winner (overshadowed somewhat by the disqualification of Canada's Ben Johnson), finished second in the 200, and won the long jump. He was denied a further medal by the disqualification of the favored U.S. 4x100 team in the heats.

In the 1992 Olympic trials, Lewis, at age 31, qualified to compete in Barcelona in the long

Carl's sweetest victory—the Barcelona 4x100.

jump, but he did not qualify in the sprint events or the relay. On his first attempt in the Olympic long jump competition, he jumped 28 feet, 5½ inches for the gold medal. Then, when sprinter Mark Witherspoon pulled up lame in the semifinal round of the 100 meters and was unable to compete in the 400-meter relay, Lewis took his place. The team won the gold medal and set a new world record.

King Carl, with eight gold medals, had left his mark on Olympic history.

BEN JOHNSON'S COMEBACK

Ben Johnson had lost his gold medal in Seoul for testing positive for anabolic steroids, but his story was not over. After suffering through two years of hearings, recriminations, and a series of apologies, Johnson was reinstated to the Canadian national team, making him eligible to compete in the 1992 Olympics. Johnson's coach, Charlie Francis, predicted a big-money showdown with Johnson's longtime rival, Carl Lewis, but it never happened.

In the semifinals of the 100 meters in Barcelona, the "new" Ben Johnson stumbled coming out of the blocks and failed to qualify for the final. The next year he tested positive for drugs again and was banned from competition for life.

FIRSTS FOR SOUTH AFRICANS

Olympic history was made early in the Barcelona Games when Trevor Strydon, participating in the modern pentathlon, became the first South African to participate in the Olympics in 32 years. A few hours later, boxer Fana Thwala became the first *black* South African ever to compete in the Olympic Games. Thwala's coach said, "For our boxer, for our sport, for our country, this is a start."

A GALLANT FINISH

One of the most dramatic scenes at the Barcelona Olympics took place in the first semifinal of the 400 meters. Among the eight starters was Derek Redmond of Great Britain, who had suffered an achilles injury in 1988, forcing him to withdraw from the Seoul Olympics. Now, four years later, Redmond was running better than ever.

When the race began, Redmond appeared to be a certain qualifier, running strong and relaxed. But at the halfway point he heard what he described later as a "pop." It was a severe hamstring pull in his right leg.

Hobbling along in pain and watching the rest of the field race to the finish line, Redmond refused to leave the track. Suddenly, Jim Redmond, Derek's father, leaped out of the stands and ran to his son. When young Redmond told his father he had to finish the race, his father said, "We'll finish it together."

Arm in arm, father and son slowly proceeded down the final straightaway to the finish line while the sympathetic crowd cheered Redmond's courage. It was a most touching moment.

THE DREAM TEAM

The opening of the basketball competition to professional players in 1992 completely changed the complexion of Olympic basketball. Not only did the United States select the best players from the NBA and field the greatest basketball team ever assembled, but they also fielded a team that was so popular that the players had to be protected constantly from the adulation of hundreds of thousands of admirers. According to Dream Team Coach, Chuck Daly: "It was like traveling with 12 rock stars."

The team was truly a "galaxy of superstars." With such famous names as Michael Jordan, Magic Johnson, Larry Bird, Charles Barkley, Scottie Pippin, and Patrick Ewing, it was not surprising that the U.S. players were mobbed and photographed wherever they went.

The favorite among the fans was Magic Johnson, who had announced only ten months earlier that he was retiring from basketball because he had tested positive for HIV. "Whenever the team left the hotel to play a game," Johnson

ALLSPORT/MIKE POWELL

Dream Team action—Magic Johnson does his thing.

said later, "three or four thousand people were lined up outside *just to see us get on the bus.*"

During the opening ceremonies, athletes from other countries broke ranks to run over to Johnson, to shake his hand, ask for his autograph, or take his picture. Even during the Dream Team's games, all of the opposing teams wanted their pictures taken with the Americans. During timeouts, opposing players were handing their cameras to teammates to take pictures of them with some of the U.S. players.

The Dream Team won all eight of its games on the way to the championship by an average margin of 43.8 points. The closest score was a 32-point win over Croatia in the final game.

Magic Johnson reminisced later, "It's more meaningful for me than for the other guys. I've won every major championship there is to win. You can throw all of them in a hat and they can't compare with this."

A GAME COMEBACK

Pablo Morales had won the silver medal for the U.S. in the 100-meter butterfly in 1984, but even though he was the world record holder four years later, he failed to make the team for the Seoul Olympics. Morales decided then to quit swimming and enroll in law school at Cornell University.

In his second year at school, Morales changed his mind and decided to try for a comeback. "My mom was very sick with cancer," he said later. "She was alive when I decided to make the comeback and she was in complete support of it. She always shared my victories and my disappointments." However, she died soon after that without seeing her son swim again.

In Barcelona, Morales swam the race of his life, winning the gold medal by a mere two-hundredths of a second. After the race he said, "It really adds to my fulfillment to know that she is watching now and is happy."

FULL CIRCLE

In the 1904 and 1908 Olympic Games, the "drug of choice" was strychnine. There were no rules against doping in those days, and coaches and trainers who advocated drug use were open about the amounts and frequency of doses they provided their athletes. After 1908, the use of strychnine as a performance-enhancing drug faded into obscurity.

In Barcelona, strychnine made a surprise reappearance. During the women's volleyball competition, one of the players from China, Wu Dan, tested positive for strychnine and was disqualified from further competition. She claimed she had taken a popular Chinese "folk medicine" before the competition and did not know it contained any banned substances.

A RASH OF ASTHMATICS

In the ongoing game that some athletes play to stay a step ahead of the testing procedures, a new drug surfaced in the early 1990s, leading to the oddest drug story of the century. The drug is albuterol, which is manufactured in the United States and in other countries under several different product names and is available by prescription in tablet or inhaler form.

Albuterol is a "miracle drug" for asthma sufferers. It treats and prevents the symptoms of asthma, bringing quick relief for a variety of breathing difficulties.

Albuterol is also described by some as the most powerful performance-enhancing drug ever developed. It has some of the same stimulant properties as amphetamines, the same muscle-building properties as anabolic steroids, and is much safer than either. It also supposedly reduces fat while building lean muscle mass. The athlete who takes it is able to train harder and recover faster.

The drug tests used at the Games can detect and identify albuterol easily, and one athlete was accordingly disqualified in Barcelona, but athletes whose physicians register them as asthmatics can use the albuterol inhaler for "health" reasons without fear of disqualification.

At the 1994 winter Olympics, an inordinate number of participants were registered asthmatics—more than half the competitors on one of the teams, in fact.

The test can't distinguish tablet from inhaler form, so some athletes take large doses of the oral medicine and are not disqualified. It is currently one of the major problems being addressed by the IOC and other bodies striving to keep the playing field as level as possible.

THE FIRST OLYMPIC
CENTURY COMES TO A QUIET END

As the Games of the XXVth Olympiad came to a close in Barcelona, the first century of the modern Olympic Games was also coming to a close. Although the Olympiad would not officially end until the end of 1995, the highly successful Games of the XXVth Olympiad had been completed.

The close of the Barcelona Games was the perfect time to reflect on the first century's Olympic successes and failures, a time to look forward to 1996, the official beginning of the second century of Olympic history, and especially a time to begin anticipating the celebration of the Games of the XXVIth Olympiad in Atlanta.

THE SELECTION OF THE
CENTENNIAL CITY

Two years before the Barcelona Olympics were held, the IOC met in Lausanne, Switzerland, to select the city to host the 1996 Olympics, the Games that would celebrate the 100th birthday of the modern Olympic movement. The candidates were Athens, Atlanta, Belgrade, Manchester, Melbourne, and Toronto.

The Greeks were so certain Athens would be selected that they had already begun construction of sports facilities, including a new "Olympic" stadium. They also began selling countless Olympic souvenirs that read "Athens, 1996, The Golden Olympics." There were no doubts in Greece that Athens would be selected on the first ballot.

The balloting was as dramatic as any ever held. Athens led on the first ballot, but did not have a majority; Belgrade was eliminated. Athens led again on the second ballot; Manchester was eliminated. Atlanta took the lead over Athens on the third ballot; Melbourne was eliminated. Atlanta led again on the fourth ballot, but still did not have a majority over Athens and Toronto; Toronto was eliminated. On the fifth and final ballot, Atlanta won out over Athens.

The response from the Greeks was outrage. Signs began to appear in Athens showing a dove of peace carrying a Greek flag and an olive branch next to an eagle carrying an American flag and a bottle of Coca-Cola. But as happened a century earlier when the Greeks thought they were being robbed of their heritage because Athens was not selected as a permanent Olympic site, outrage turned to indifference. The Greeks seemed to become more interested in their border disputes with Turkey than with the Olympic Games.

WINTER OLYMPIC HIGHLIGHTS

THE BIRTH OF THE WINTER OLYMPICS

The winter Olympic Games were an outgrowth of the Nordic Games, which were first organized in Sweden in 1899 by Professor Johan Widmark, with the strong support of Professor Viktor G. Balck. Balck was head of Stockholm's Central Physical Education Institute at the time and was also a founding member of the International Olympic Committee.

The Nordic Games featured the usual winter sports events, but also included competitions in fencing, swimming, gymnastics, hunting on horseback, skiing behind reindeer, car racing, and ballooning. There were also national, cultural, and social displays, excursions, banquets, and artistic performances.

The Nordic Games were held every four years—the year following the Olympic Games—and were always open to all the Nordic countries, and occasionally to other countries for certain world championships.

The first Nordic Games were held in 1901 in Stockholm and the Games continued—with occasional cancellations or site changes, usually because of a lack of snow—until the birth of the winter Olympics in 1924.

In the meantime, figure skating was included in the Olympic program for the 1908 Games in London. Actually, figure skating had been included as an official Olympic event at the first IOC conference in 1894, but since there were no suitable ice rinks in Athens, Paris, or St. Louis, the first Olympic figure skating competition had to wait to become an Olympic event until 1908.

At the 1909 IOC meeting in Berlin, a special commission, which included Professor Balck, presented a proposal for standardizing the events in the Olympic Games. The commission decided not to include winter sports in the Olympics, not even figure skating.

When the IOC met again in 1910 in Luxembourg, Balck was asked whether winter sports were planned for the 1912 Games in Stockholm. Balck responded that there was no need, since the Nordic Games were scheduled for the next year. Following spirited protests from the British, Balck agreed to prepare a program of winter sports for the 1912 Games, if the IOC insisted, and present it at their next session.

At the 1911 meeting in Budapest, Balck was reminded of his promise to present a program of winter sports for 1912, but he again insisted it would be impossible, since the Nordic Games were scheduled for 1913. Count Brunetta of Italy then suggested that the Olympic schedule be extended—from June 1912, through May 1913—and the Nordic Games could then become part of the Olympics. However, that would have violated an important Olympic rule: The Olympic Games must be completed during the first year of the Olympiad.

After much discussion, described in the literature as "animated," voting was delayed until May 27, just over one year prior to the opening of the 1912 Games. At that time, the IOC voted to exclude winter events from the Olympics.

The Nordic Games continued to be held every four years, usually in the Stockholm area. After World War I it was decided the Nordic Games would be held in the even-numbered years that fell between Olympic years, beginning in 1922.

THE FIRST WINTER GAMES— AN AFTERTHOUGHT

A strange turn of events in 1924 signaled the death of the Nordic Games and the establishment of the winter Olympics. Early that year, a ten-day International Winter Sports Week was held in Chamonix, France. It was a huge success, with the competitions dominated by participants from the Nordic countries, who won nine of the 14 gold medals.

At the IOC meetings held in Prague in 1925, there was so much discussion about the successful competitions at Chamonix that the IOC delegates decided to recognize the 1924 International Winter Sports Week, retroactively, as the first Winter Olympic Games. It was a perfect way to ensure a successful beginning for the new winter Games.

The IOC then decided to number the winter Olympics Ist, IInd, IIIrd, etc., beginning with 1924, and not to associate the word Olympiad with the winter Games.

THE OLYMPIC STEPCHILD

When the winter Olympic Games were born in 1924, it was obvious they were not going to be treated the same as the summer Games. From the beginning they were considered little more than an afterthought. True, the winter Games had their own advocates, mostly among IOC delegates from the northern nations, but there were also many detractors. There were even persistent calls over the years to do away with the winter Olympics completely.

The greatest advocate for abolishing the winter Olympics was Avery Brundage, who began his campaign against the winter Games when he was elected to the IOC in 1936 and carried it on until his retirement in 1972. Brundage, who was the unbending champion of Olympic amateurism, was incensed that winter athletes, skiers in particular, were in blatant violation of the Olympic amateur code. They were taking money for advertising products on their clothing and equipment and didn't seem to care who knew it. "Professionals," Brundage argued, "do not belong in the Olympic Games."

Brundage and other Olympic purists also argued that winter sports are available only to a few countries, disqualifying from competition the majority of the nonwhite people in the world, especially those from emerging nations. And, they said, the winter sports require the competitors to have a certain affluence, even to get started, which discriminates against most of the poor people of the world.

Brundage's best opportunity to do away with the winter Olympics was in 1970 when Denver was selected to host the 1976 winter Olympics and the citizens of Colorado, for environmental reasons, voted not to accept the bid. Brundage urged the IOC to cancel the Games rather than reschedule them. Calling the winter Olympics limited in scope, scandal-ridden, and sick, he said, "May they receive a decent burial at Denver." Brundage lost the campaign and the winter Olympics survived.

SCHEDULING THE WINTER GAMES

Although the IOC has always managed to find a time and a place to conduct the winter Olympics (except for cancellations because of World War II), there have been times when the scheduling of the winter Games has perpetuated the Olympic stepchild image.

From the beginning, the winter Olympic Games were to be scheduled in the first year of each Olympiad, the same as the summer Games, and were originally to be held in the same country as the summer Games. The plan to conduct the Games in the same country had to be abandoned immediately, since the 1928 summer Games were to be held in Amsterdam. Because there was no way the flat Dutch countryside could be used for some of the winter events, the IOC was forced to select St. Moritz, in mountainous Switzerland, instead. Since then, the same country has hosted both Olympics in the same year only twice—the United States in 1932 and Germany in 1936.

In 1994, another move affecting the scheduling of the winter Olympics was introduced. The winter Games were moved to the even-numbered years falling between the summer Olympics, creating a different quadrennial cycle. It was necessary to separate the summer and winter Games to ease their administration and for marketing purposes, but it created some Olympic "heroes" who might not have been repeat Olympic champions had they had to wait the usual four years between Olympics. A total of 12 gold medal winners from the 1992 winter Olympics repeated in 1994.

A MATHEMATICAL ERROR IS CORRECTED

When the ski jumping distances were totaled during the 1924 Olympic Games, the judges made a mathematical error, giving the bronze medal to Thorleif Haug of Norway by mistake. Fifty years later the error was corrected, and Norwegian-American Anders Haugen was moved from fourth to third place. In a special ceremony in 1974 in Oslo, Haugen was presented a bronze medal. At the age of 86, Haugen received the only ski jump medal ever won by an American citizen.

THE FIRST "GOLDEN GIRL" OF SKATING

An 11-year-old figure skating champion from Norway, Sonja Henie, participated in her first Olympic Games in 1924. Although she finished only eighth, she later adapted ballerina movements to figure skating and became the world's most famous skater, winning the Olympic gold medals with ease in 1928, 1932, and 1936.

When her amateur skating career was over, at the age of 23, Henie moved to Hollywood and became a film star. She was immensely popular and became the number three box office attraction (behind Shirley Temple and Clark Gable), earning $1 million a year long before such salaries were common in the entertainment business.

PAWNED AND GONE

Irving Jaffe of the United States felt he was the fastest skater at the 1928 winter Olympics in St. Moritz, but he was not given the opportunity to prove it. Although he had the fastest qualifying time in the 10,000 meters, the weather began to warm before the final, the ice was melting, and the race was called off.

Jaffe made up for his 1928 disappointment in 1932 in Lake Placid when he won both the 5,000- and the 10,000-meter races. He treasured his two gold medals, but when times became hard during the depression, he was forced to pawn them so he could eat. When he returned for them later, the pawn shop was out of business. More than 40 years later he was still looking for his two gold medals.

THE FEARLESS BOBSLEDDER

The flagbearer for the U.S. team in the 1932 winter Olympic Games in Lake Placid was Billy Fiske, the daredevil bobsled driver who had steered his team to a gold medal in St. Moritz four years earlier at the age of 16. In 1932, he was the driver again and the team won another gold medal with ease.

Fiske went on to become another of history's "firsts." In 1939, he was among the Americans who joined Great Britain's Royal Air Force to help repel the continuing air attacks by the Germans during the Battle of Britain. On August 16, 1940, Fiske's plane was shot down; he died of his injuries the next day. Fiske became the first American pilot killed in World War II.

Sonja Henie

SUMMER AND WINTER GOLD MEDALS

Riding behind daredevil driver Billy Fiske in the 1932 bobsled race was Eddie Eagan, the only person to win gold medals in both the summer and winter Olympics. Twelve years before the bobsled team took the gold, Eagan had won the light heavyweight boxing title in the 1920 Olympics in Antwerp.

A DISPUTE OVER NATIONALITY

The 1936 winter Olympics in Garmisch-Partenkirchen were marred by a major dispute during the ice hockey competitions. Officials from Canada filed a protest, complaining that 11 of the 13 members of the British team were Canadians and should have been representing Canada.

Under the rules of the International Hockey Federation, however, members of the "British Empire" living in England could participate for Great Britain. The protest was rejected and Great Britain went on to win the Olympic title. Canada finished second.

AN ENDURING PERFORMER

Birger Ruud of Norway was a consistent winner in Olympic ski jumping. He won the gold medal in the 1932 Games in Lake Placid when he was only 20. In 1936 at Garmisch-Partenkirchen he won again, becoming the first to win successive gold medals in ski jumping.

It appeared then that Ruud's ski jumping days were over. World War II broke out, the 1940 and 1944 Olympic Games were canceled, Norway was occupied by Germany, and Ruud was imprisoned for refusing to cooperate with the Nazis.

When the Olympics were revived in 1948 at St. Moritz, Ruud was an assistant coach for the Norwegian team. The day of the ski jumping, with the weather conditions marginal and potentially dangerous, he was asked if he would replace one of the young, less experienced jumpers. Ruud jumped and finished a close second to his Norwegian teammate, Petter Hugsted, to win the silver medal—at the age of 36.

Birger Ruud

CANCELED GAMES

As was the case with the summer Olympic Games, the winter Games of 1940 and 1944 had to be canceled because of World War II. Ironically, the sites selected for both Olympics were in "Axis nations"—Japan and Italy. The 1940 Games were originally scheduled for Sapporo, Japan, and then rescheduled, first to St. Moritz, Switzerland, and then Garmisch-Partenkirchen, Germany. The 1944 Games were scheduled for Cortina d'Ampezzo, Italy.

REFUSING THE CAR—TEMPORARILY

Canada's Barbara Ann Scott was the top figure skater in the world in 1948 and was favored to win the Olympic gold medal in St. Moritz. But the year before, after she had won the world figure skating title, Scott was presented a special gift from the city of Ottawa—a bright yellow convertible.

When word of the gift got to the IOC's Avery Brundage, who was already known as "the watch-

149

dog of amateurism," he told Scott that acceptance of the automobile would deem her a professional and make her ineligible for the Olympics. Scott gave up the car, won the figure skating gold medal in the 1948 winter Olympics, and then gave up her amateur status and reaccepted the car.

THE FIRST WINTER FLAME

The organizers of the 1952 winter Olympics in Oslo decided to include an Olympic torch relay for the first time, but they also decided the flame ceremony would be different from the summer Games ceremony. Rather than have the fire kindled at Olympia, Greece, as had been done for all of the summer Olympics since 1936, they had it kindled in the fireplace of Sondre Nordheim in Morgedal, Norway.

Nordheim, known to Norwegians as "the God of Skiing," had gained his fame by jumping 18 meters (59 feet) in 1868 without the aid of ski poles. From Nordheim's fireplace the flame was transferred to a torch and relayed by skiers the 138 miles to Oslo.

Today, the flame for the winter Olympics is kindled in Greece and transported by various modes of transportation to the site of the winter Games, the same as for the summer Olympics.

A LACK OF SNOW

Several of the winter Olympics have been marred by weather problems, but never has warm weather been a bigger problem for the Games than in Oslo in 1952. There was no snow on the downhill and slalom courses.

Norwegian soldiers dug and carried tons of snow from nearby ravines to the courses, and then packed it in place on the slopes. The snow was melting at such a rapid rate, it was decided to conduct one of the bobsled events and the women's giant slalom the day before the Games were scheduled to begin.

A similar problem faced the organizers of the winter Games in Squaw Valley eight years later. But rather than trying to transport snow to the various courses, the officials hired a tribe of Paiute Indians to perform a "snow dance." The result: It poured rain, making the slopes even worse. At the last moment, with hope almost gone, there was a miraculous plunge in temperature and the rain turned to snow. The Games were saved.

A FALL WITH THE TORCH

The final torchbearer for the 1956 winter Olympics in Cortina d'Ampezzo was one of Italy's speed skating heroes, Guido Caroli. Caroli was skating toward the officials' box, with torch in hand, when he tripped on a television cable and fell. He regained his composure and continued the ceremony as though nothing had happened. The flame did not go out.

A BARRAGE OF FRUIT

The Italian fans at the 1956 winter Games were surprisingly unruly during the pairs skating event. Whenever the fans were unhappy with the judging, which was often, they would hurl oranges at the officials. On three occasions the competition had to be halted so crews could clear the oranges from the ice.

DEATH AT THE GAMES

Fatal accidents plagued the 1964 winter Games in Innsbruck. Prior to the opening ceremonies, two competitors were killed in practice runs. Downhill skier Ross Milne of Austria died after crashing into a tree. British competitor Kazimierz Kay-Skrzypeski, who had emigrated to Britain from Poland during the war, died in a luge crash. A black ribbon was hung from the Olympic rings during the Games.

After the Innsbruck Games closed, two skiers, Bud Werner of the United States and Barbi Henneberger of Germany, died in a Swiss avalanche during the filming of a movie.

SPORTSMANSHIP

When the two-man bobsled team from Great Britain had a serious equipment problem in Innsbruck, an Italian competitor saved the day for them. A bolt on the British sled had broken, which normally would have knocked them out of the competition. But Eugenio Monti, who had just finished the bobsled run, pulled a bolt out of his own sled and gave it to the Englishmen. With the new bolt in place, the British team won the gold medal. Monti and his partner finished third.

Monti received his reward four years later in the Grenoble Olympics when he and his partners won gold medals in both the two-man and four-man bobsledding. "Now I can retire a happy man," he said later. It completed two sets of medals for Monti. He had won two silvers in 1956, two bronzes in 1964, and two golds in 1968.

EXPENSIVE OPENING CEREMONIES

The French government, under the authority of president Charles de Gaulle, spared no cost in staging the 1968 winter Olympics in Grenoble. An unprecedented $240 million was spent, including the cost of constructing a 60,000-seat stadium that was used only once—for the opening ceremonies. The day after the Grenoble Games were opened, workmen began tearing the stadium down.

AMATEURISM QUESTIONED AGAIN

The success of the 1968 winter Games in Grenoble was seriously threatened when IOC president Avery Brundage, always uncompromising in matters of amateurism, decided that the skiing events should be canceled because the competitors were all displaying the manufacturers' names on their skis. This form of advertising was against the IOC's code of amateurism, he said. He finally backed down, insisting only that no photographs be taken of the athletes with their skis.

Four years later, what Brundage called "shamateurism" reared its ugly head again, at the winter Games in Sapporo. Brundage named 40 skiers who he said had violated the rules of amateurism. However, only one skier, Austria's Karl Schranz, was barred from the Games, and that was because he was not as subtle as the others. He had been earning some $60,000 a year advertising ski products, with his name and photograph appearing in the ads.

WINTER BLOOD BOOSTING

The topic of blood boosting became the subject of numerous rumors at the 1976 winter Olympics at Innsbruck. "We have no means of detecting this or proving that it has been done," said Prince Alexandre de Merode, president of the IOC's medical commission. Still the rumors continued circulating.

Medical sources at the Games all agreed that at least one rumor was absurd—that East German skiers had been seen with bandages on their ears, indicating that blood had been drawn from the lobes. Merode responded that removing enough blood for blood boosting—up to a liter—"would require that it be taken from the arm."

THE OLYMPIC PRISON

When Lake Placid, a village with only 3,500 residents, was selected to host the 1980 winter Olympics, they were not able to provide lavish facilities equal to those of the two previous winter hosts. One particular problem facing the Lake Placid organizers was the financing of an adequate Olympic village.

To help out, the U.S. government agreed to build a federal prison near the Olympic venues that could serve as an Olympic village until after the Games. The rooms were small, of course, but generally it was considered an excellent choice. Unfortunately, however, the athletes referred to it as the Olympic prison.

THE JAMAICAN BOBSLEDDERS

Despite coming from a snow-free country, Jamaica sent a two-man bobsled team—a reggae singer and a helicopter pilot—to the 1988 Olympics in Calgary. Paying their way by selling reggae records and tee-shirts, the two men had practiced in Jamaica by riding in a pushcart in the snowless Blue Mountains.

The Jamaicans, who had gained worldwide attention, did not fare well in Calgary, but they decided to try again in 1992 in Albertville. There they became so popular that a fictionalized version of their experiences became the motion picture, *Cool Runnings*, which was released in 1993.

In the 1994 Games in Lillehammer, the Jamaican four-man bobsled team finished 14th, which was better than the finish of the U.S. team.

THE CENTURY'S MOST BIZARRE
OLYMPIC STORY

It is fitting that a century of facts and fables would close with a series of events that might be better characterized as Olympic facts and foibles. The 1994 winter Games in Lillehammer were overshadowed by an incident that developed into an American melodrama, complete with a heroine and villains, that was played out in the world's media for six weeks prior to the Games.

It began on January 6, 1994, at the U.S. National Figure Skating Championships in Detroit. A 1994 Olympic skating favorite, Nancy Kerrigan, who had won the Olympic silver medal in 1992, was leaving the ice after a practice session when a "six-foot man dressed in black jacket and cap" approached her. Suddenly, the man whacked Kerrigan across the knee with a metal rod and then ran toward an exit. The assailant, who soon learned his planned escape route was through a locked plexiglass door, smashed through the glass with his head and made his escape.

Kerrigan's injury wasn't disabling, but she did sit out the national championships and watched her arch-rival, Tonya Harding, take the title.

Then the bizarre chapters in this story began unfolding. Investigators soon determined that the attempt to injure Nancy Kerrigan was an ill-conceived plot put together by Tonya Harding's ex-husband, Jeff Gillooley, along with three "bodyguards," Shawn Eckhardt, Derrick Smith, and the assailant, Shane Stant.

From the beginning Harding denied any knowledge of the plot and insisted she would skate in Lillehammer. But she was implicated by Gillooley in a plea bargain with prosecutors, causing Olympic officials to begin exploring ways to bar Harding from participating in the Games.

In the meantime, Kerrigan, completely recovered, had captured the hearts of fans throughout the world and was aiming for the gold medal in Lillehammer. The incident in Detroit had transformed her into one of the world's best-known and most-admired sports personalities.

After most of the Olympic teams had arrived in Norway, the U.S. Olympic Committee announced they would hold an inquiry into Harding's involvement in the incident. But they backed down when Harding filed a lawsuit, charging the USOC with violating her rights and asking for $25 million in damages. The USOC agreed she could skate if she dropped the suit, which she did.

So the stage was set for the fight for the gold medal between Nancy Kerrigan and Tonya Harding. When the two finally skated in the Olympic competition, nearly half the television sets in America were tuned in to see the conclusion to the six-week drama.

The melodrama had developed into a media circus, with both skaters' every move covered by

Tonya Harding

the press. And most were surprised at what they saw. While Kerrigan and Harding had captured the attention of the media, a teenager from the Ukraine, Oksana Baiul, outclassed them both and captured the gold medal. Skating with a bruised tailbone and stitches in her right leg, the result of a fall in practice, Baiul performed flawlessly to take the gold. Kerrigan again took silver. Harding finished eighth.

And what about the awards for the "villains" in this melodrama? Harding pleaded guilty to conspiring to hinder the prosecution and was given three years' probation, a $160,000 fine, and was ordered to do 500 hours of community service. Gillooley received a two-year jail sentence and was fined $100,000. Eckhardt, Smith, and Stant were each sentenced to 18 months in jail.

SELECTED READINGS

Albertson, Lisa, ed. *Athens to Atlanta—100 Years of Glory.* Salt Lake City: Commemorative Publications, 1993.

Ali, Muhammad. *The Greatest.* New York: Random House, 1975.

Barrett, Norman. *Great Moments in Sport.* Paulton, England: Purnell Books, 1982.

Booker, Christopher. *The Games War.* London: Faber & Faber, 1981.

Cayleff, Susan E. *Babe.* Urbana, IL: University of Illinois Press, 1995.

Coffey, Wayne. *Jesse Owens.* Woodbridge, CT: Blackbirch Press, 1992.

Connolly, Olga. *The Rings of Destiny.* New York: David McKay Company, 1968.

Coote, James. *A Picture History of the Olympics.* New York: The MacMillan Company, 1972.

Cosell, Howard. *Cosell.* New York: Simon & Schuster, 1974.

Donald, Keith, and Don Selth. *Olympic Saga.* Sydney: Futurian Press, 1957.

Durant, John. *Highlights of the Olympics.* New York: Hastings House Publishers, 1961.

Edey, Maitland A., ed. *The Olympic Games.* New York: Time-Life Books, 1967.

Edey, Maitland A., ed. *Yesterday in Sport.* New York: Time-Life Books, 1968.

Espy, Richard. *The Politics of the Olympic Games.* Berkeley, CA: University of California Press, 1979.

Francis, Charlie, and Jeff Copion. *The Speed Trap.* New York: St. Martin's Press, 1990.

Greenspan, Bud. *100 Greatest Moments in Olympic History.* Los Angeles: General Publishing Group, Inc., 1995.

Guiney, David. *The Olympic Games.* Lavenham, England: Eastland Press, 1989.

Guttmann, Allen. *The Olympics.* Urbana, IL: University of Illinois Press, 1994.

Henry, Bill. *An Approved History of the Olympic Games.* Sherman Oaks, CA: Alfred Publishing Co., 1984.

Holmes, Burton. *The Olympian Games in Athens.* New York: Grove Press, 1984.

Holmes, Judith. *Olympiad 1936.* New York: Ballantine Books, 1971.

Johnson, William O. *All That Glitters Is Not Gold.* New York: G.P. Putnam's Sons, 1972.

Johnson, William O. *The Olympics.* New York: Bishop Books, 1992.

Kiernan, John, Arthur Daley, and Pat Jordan. *The Story of the Olympic Games.* Philadelphia: J.B. Lippincott Company, 1977.

Killanin, Lord. *My Olympic Years.* New York: William Morrow & Co., 1983.

Lucas, John A. *Future of the Olympic Games.* Champaign, IL: Human Kinetics Books, 1992.

Lucas, John A. *The Modern Olympic Games.* New York: A.S. Barnes & Co., 1980.

MacAloon, John J. *The Great Symbol.* Chicago: The University of Chicago Press, 1981.

Mandell, Richard D. *The Nazi Olympics.* New York: The MacMillan Company, 1971.

Nelson, Cordner. *Track's Greatest Champions*. Los Altos, CA: Tafnews Press, 1986.

O'Neill, Terry. *The Game Behind the Game*. New York: Harper & Row, 1989.

Palenski, Ron, and Terry Maddaford. *The Games*. Auckland, NZ: MOA Publications, 1983.

Rice, Grantland. *The Tumult and the Shouting*. New York: A.S. Barnes, 1954.

Rodda, John, and Lord Killanin. *The Olympic Games*. London: Barrie and Jenkins, Ltd., 1976.

Pound, Richard W. *Five Rings Over Korea*. Boston: Little, Borwn & Co., 1994.

Schaap, Richard. *An Illustrated History of the Olympics*. New York: Alfred A. Knopf, 1963.

Schoor, Gene. *The Jim Thorpe Story*. New York: Julian Messner, Inc., 1961.

Scott, Jim. *Bob Mathias*. New York: Prentice-Hall, Inc., 1952.

Shteinbakh, V. *From Athens to Moscow*. Moscow: Fizkultura i Sport Publishers, 1979.Toomey, Bill, and Barry King. *The Olympic Challenge*. Costa Mesa, CA: HDL Publishing, 1988.

Tyler, Martin, and Phil Soar. *The History of the Olympics*. London: Marshall Cavendish Books, 1980.

Ueberroth, Peter. *Made in America*. New York: William Morrow & Co., 1985.

Voy, Robert. *Drugs, Sports, and Politics*. Champaign, IL: Leisure Press, 1991.

Wallechinsky, David. *The Complete Book of the Olympics*. Boston: Little, Brown & Co., 1991.

Wels, Susan. *The Olympic Spirit*. San Francisco: Collins Publishers, 1995.

Wright, James E. *Anabolic Steroids and Sports*. Natick, MA: Sports Science Consultants, 1978.